Psychoanalysis

Psychoanalysis:

Philosophy, Art and Clinic

Edited by

David Henderson

Cambridge Scholars Publishing

Psychoanalysis: Philosophy, Art and Clinic

Edited by David Henderson

This book first published 2015

Cambridge Scholars Publishing

Lady Stephenson Library, Newcastle upon Tyne, NE6 2PA, UK

British Library Cataloguing in Publication Data
A catalogue record for this book is available from the British Library

ISBN (10): 1-4438-8046-9
ISBN (13): 978-1-4438-8046-6

CONTENTS

List of Figures

INTRODUCTION

DAVID HENDERSON

This volume grew out of 'Psychoanalysis, Culture and Society,' a conference for postgraduate students and research fellows organised by the Centre for Psychoanalysis, Middlesex University, London in June 2014. The range of themes addressed at the conference demonstrates the interdisciplinary character of psychoanalytic studies. Few of the contributors are affiliated with established psychoanalytic research centres and subsequently can feel isolated within their respective departments. They were pleased to have the opportunity to meet with others who are pursuing related questions.

Giacomo Croci offers a Lacanian analysis of a psychoanalytic theory of time, in his chapter entitled, 'Philosophy of Time and Psychoanalysis: The Temporality of the Unconscious.' He argues that Lacan provides "another conception of time… which focuses on the faculty of memory as linguistically mediated." Lacan's concept of *future anterieur* has the potential to bind together "the three temporal dimensions in a knot which exceeds both a linear and a circular representation of time."

In 'Attributive Judgment and a Source of Freud's *Project*,' Ben Hooson explores among other things, Freud's reliance on John Stuart Mill in *Aphasia* and *Project for a Scientific Psychology*. He asks, "Can it make sense that Freud found a prototype of the signifier system (Saussurean language) in a mid-19th century work by J.S. Mill?"

Raphael Montague's chapter, 'Philosophy at the *Bar* with Freud and Lacan; the *Subject*: Being, Always in the Wrong Place at the Wrong Time…', considers the work of Freud, Lacan, Derrida, Laruelle and Meillasoux. Among the questions he entertains are, "What is the relationship between the work and the thing?" and "What is the relationship between psychoanalysis and ontology?"

João Gabriel Lima da Silva's 'Peace Beyond Reason: Psychoanalytical Remarks on *The Better Angels of Our Nature*' is not simply a critique of Steven Pinker's book. Beyond this da Silva discusses Freud's work on violence and the death instinct, and "the problem of the weakness of reason in psychoanalysis."

In '"Will It Not Be Better": Recognising the Indian Psychoanalytical

Society,' Akshi Singh draws out a number of themes at play in the relationship between psychoanalysis in India and the West. These range from Freud's statues of Indian gods to Girindrasekhar Bose's correspondence with Freud and Ernest Jones. She discusses some of the institutional, cultural and theoretical complexities that accompanied the emergence of psychoanalysis in India.

Chenyang Wang questions Judith Butler's reading of Freud in his chapter entitled, 'Anti-Melancholia: The Failure of Melancholy Gender and Its Alternative.' He suggests that Butler's "theory of melancholy gender… not only misreads Freud's theory of melancholia, but becomes a melancholic fantasy itself." Wang argues that a Lacanian understanding of lack offers a solution to this impasse.

In 'Victorian Visions of Youth: The Child in Art and Psychoanalysis' Melissa L. Greenberg examines "the diverse ways in which children were viewed during the second half of the 19th century – in the public eye, in medical literature, and in the arts." This provides an understanding of the complex context within which Freud introduced his theory on child sexuality.

Carla Ambrósio Garcia's chapter, 'Dimensionality and Adhesiveness in Jonathan Glazer's *Under the Skin*,' calls on the work of Esther Bick and Donald Meltzer. She demonstrates that their theories can help us to understand the central concern of the film – how the "primal anxieties of falling apart, dispersing or liquefying… need to be passively contained by another, before a capacity for emotionality can emerge."

'"Suffering From Reminiscences": Memory and Trauma in Elizabeth Bowen's Short Fiction' by Olena Lytovka explores the role of domestic space as a container for traumatic experience. She maintains that for Bowen the house, far from being an image of comfort or security, is portrayed as "antagonistic to its inhabitants… [who] feel threatened and uncertain of their identity."

In 'Extracting the Extract: From Clinical Practice to Literature and Back, Utilizing a Signifier' Amir Klugman introduces a new concept 'the extract of jouissance.' He advocates the "movement of one signifier between a number of language games." He draws on Lacanian theory, a story by David Grossman and a number of clinical vignettes to understand "**ex-tract**ive listening."

Mauricio Rugels Schoonewolff in 'On Money and Psychoanalysis: From the Freudian Anal Object to Lacan's Surplus-Enjoyment' explores how psychoanalysis has thought and theorized money. He describes the character of anal eroticism in Freud's work, especially in the Rat Man. Lacan borrow's Marx's concept of surplus-value to develop the idea of

surplus-*jouissance*. Schoonewolff insists that "money plays a unique role for each subject in his singularity."

Naftally Israeli's 'Representing the Inner World' asks whether we use language "as a means of communication which transmits a message… or as a means of expression that establishes an experience." He develops the concept of 'paradoxical representation' using the thought of D.W. Winnicott, Melanie Klein and Hannah Segal, and demonstrates how this concept can help us to understand aspects of A.A. Milne's *Winnie the Pooh*.

Thomas Harding describes autism as "a distinct subjective position which, as such, cannot be straightforwardly reduced to any set of linear causes, biological or otherwise, in his chapter, 'Biological Complexity and Subjective Singularity in the Clinic of Autism.' Because "psychoanalysis is more interested in the contingent encounter between language and the body which functions as an exception to any causal chain," it can provide "a reflective approach to clinical work."

The authors of these chapters offer the reader a rich tapestry of psychoanalytic thought. They demonstrate bold creativity in their use of psychoanalytic concepts to think about a wide range of problems in philosophy, art and the clinic.

CHAPTER ONE

PHILOSOPHY OF TIME AND PSYCHOANALYSIS: THE TEMPORALITY OF THE UNCONSCIOUS

GIACOMO CROCI

1. Time, Subjectivity and Consciousness

This paper aims at delineating a fruitful interaction between philosophy and psychoanalysis from the standpoint of the interrogation about the notion of time. First of all, an introductory difference needs to be posited to delimit the spectrum of the analysis: time can be conceived either as a feature of things as they are or as something that appears once the condition of subjectivity is assumed. Two general categories of time-theories are therefore defined.

An example for the second category of time-theories, which constitutes the object of this inquiry, is Aristotle's definition of time as "number of motion in respect of before and after": motion is numbered and this requires a perceiving and numbering soul[1]. Thus, time appears when something that changes is perceived and numbered by someone. In a more modern conceptuality, time appears as the result of the activity of a time-constituting subject[2]. Subjectivity constitutes an intrinsically atemporal reality as something that is temporally organised and is therefore a condition of time, which is fundamentally related to subjectivity. My question is then: once the hypothesis of a time-constituting subjectivity is assumed, does our notion of subject determine our notion of time?

In fact, it can be argued that many, if not most of the time-theories that think of time as subject-related reduce subjectivity to, or understand subjectivity mainly as consciousness. Subjectivity, considered as centred on the faculty of conscious perception of a given reality, constitutes time and its shape. Time is hence understood, broadly speaking, as the result of the activity of our conscious perception.

2. Time and the Unconscious: Freud and Lacan

Once Freud's teaching is taken into account, especially in regard of its theoretical results, it is clear that for him subjectivity cannot be conceived exclusively as consciousness, since unconscious processes relate structurally to it. More specifically, it can be argued that Freud's theories drastically challenge the philosophical inquiry, since they don't recognise the faculty of conscious perception as the main theoretical path of approach to the notion of subject. On the contrary, Freud's researches look more like an investigation about memory[3]: how and why we remember, what's the meaning of an occasional inability of remembering and how our past effectively acts upon our present life and habits, eventually appearing through symptomatic phenomena – such are the questions that we find at the heart of Freud's works (let's think at Freud's early and most renown formula, according to which hysterics mainly suffer from reminiscences). Does this radical modification in the way we look at ourselves affect our comprehension of temporality?

Even though at first sight the question seems legitimate and promising, Freud's words sound peremptory: in his text *Das Unbewußte* it's stated that the unconscious is timeless and that time relations are limited to the activity of the "consciousness system"[4]. More or less five years later, in *Jenseits des Lustprinzips*, Freud repeats again that our abstract representation of time seems to relate to the way in which the perception-consciousness system works and corresponds to a sort of self-perception of that system itself[5]. A challenging interrogation seems to be frustrated at its roots and Freud's claims are transparent: psychoanalytical experience deals with the past not as past, but as a present, powerful force that directs an individual's habits and choices[6]. According to this, 'being past' is a feature that has a meaning only in the context of our conscious experience, since it doesn't apply to unconscious processes. Time is still conceived as time for a subject and that subject is considered from the perspective of its conscious life: a dead-end agreement between philosophy and psychoanalytical theory[7].

I feel that this conclusion isn't necessary. In fact, my aim is to show how Lacan's rereading of Freud allows a more specific understanding of the topic – a notion of time that could apply to the psychoanalytical unconscious –, which will in the end result in a very peculiar theoretical configuration, manifesting a primary philosophical relevance.

Before the exposition begins, it seems reasonable to remember some facts, related to a general attitude towards the philosophical corpus (and especially to the subject matter of this paper) that is to be found in Lacan's

works. In fact, if Freud was quite sceptical about philosophy, showing only a superficial interest, Lacan never shared such a stance[8]. In his works a strong anti-philosophical critique coexists with the baroque usage of a mostly philosophical conceptuality[9]. Among the many names of Lacan's flourishing intellectual background, at least two must be brought to attention: Kojève, the most famous interpreter of Hegel, and Heidegger; it would be redundant to repeat how cardinal for them the questioning about time and temporality is. Secondly, the problem of time maintains a central position throughout Lacan's intellectual adventure and dates back at least to 1935, when he wrote a review about Minkowski's *Le temps vécu*[10]. Time always remained a fundamental focus of Lacan's theoretical efforts during his whole life, as Choi points out[11].

Finally, it's of fundamental importance to underline the central role that the discipline of structural linguistics had for Lacan's arguments and constructs. It's actually from Lacan's ruminations about language and speaking, that I'll try to isolate and define his contribution to the inquiry about the notion of time.

3. Lacan and the Concept of Language

It would be hard to overestimate the role that the fact of speech plays for Lacan: psychoanalysis is first of all a "talking cure", as the renowned analysand Anna O. put it.

How multifaceted, complex and stratified Lacan's legacy might be, it would be an error to misjudge the varying focuses and periodic changes in Lacan's interests to the point of concluding that, at the beginning of his career, Lacan gave no importance to the dimension of speech, while developing only later a sort of linguistic turn. In fact, as Lacan tried to give in 1936 a "phenomenological description of the psychoanalytical experience", he clearly stated that psychoanalytical experience is a fact of language[12]. Roughly speaking, language always stayed in the middle of Lacan's interests, even if in different shapes and modulations[13].

In a somehow arbitrary, though not unjustified way, I'd like to focus in the next paragraphs on a Lacanian formula, in order to cast a little light on the key position held by language in Lacan's theories and to show how the indissoluble entanglement that occurs in Lacan's theoretical constructions, and binds together language, subjectivity and the psychoanalytical unconscious, works. Lacan's theories of language, of subjectivity and of the unconscious mutually imply one another.

In a very summarising way, I'd fix this theoretical constellation as follows: language implies a speaking being and to be a speaking being

means to be a subject; but a subject is a living being, too, and once a living being enters in the dimension of language, it must face the necessity of speaking speak and living in a symbolic environment. The organic dimension of his needs is therefore necessarily mediated by the symbolic dimension. This implies, in the end, the unconscious in a Lacanian sense.

Lacan firmed this theoretical junction by defining the signifier as something that represents a subject for another signifier[14]. From this definition I'll try to infer some other notions that will ultimately cooperate in determining Lacan's original contribution to the problem of temporality.

4. Language, Subjectivity, Individual History

Lacan's understanding of language is centred on the concept of signifier ("*signifiant*"). Borrowed from Saussure's linguistics[15], the term relates, in Lacan's theory at least, to a necessary logical moment implied by the fact of speaking, which a phenomenological analysis of speech acts isolates and shows, as Juranville puts it[16].

Once the previously mentioned definition of signifier is considered, it implies the following conclusion: if there is a signifier, then there is a subject[17]. To bind indissolubly through a definition the notions of subject and signifier means in first place to refuse the hypothesis of an ideal language spoken by an ideal speaker in an ideal situation: that would be an abstraction. If there is language, then there are speakers, concrete speaking beings. No subject is to be thought outside of the dimension of speech, as well as no language is thinkable if not given in concrete signifiers. Lacan's language theory remains throughout a theory of the speaking being: subject and linguistic phenomena, even in the minimal structure of signifying chain, cannot be thought independently[18].

No language is, if it's not spoken, and implies necessarily what Lacan calls a subject. Once the other side of the definition is taken into account, it must be remembered that not only language, but also subjectivity gains a specific determination: the subject is defined through his structural relation to language, understood through the notion of signifier. What does this imply? In particular, that every individual is born in a specific and already articulated socio-symbolic system: languages are already given before the actual birth of the individual. They pre-exist and precede the individual, who is born into historically determined social institutions (e.g. the family, specific social environments, etc.), and who is raised speaking historically determined languages[19]. The individual enters the pre-given socio-symbolic dimension.

Lacan's paradigmatic description of such an entrance fulfils the function of a general model for the understanding of the relationship between individual and language, as Haas accurately recognises[20], and bases on a particular interpretation of Freud's *Jenseits des Lustprinzips*. I won't summarise here Freud's description and explanation of the famous "*Fort-Da Spiel*"[21]. Anyway, Lacan's theoretical trick consists in relating Freud's observations to his own idea of a subject whose central focus is the fact of language: the situation described by Freud becomes therefore nothing more than the "point of insemination" of a symbolic order that pre-exists the infantile subject[22] and represents therefore the moment of entrance into the symbolic order.

There's a specific feature of this moment, as Lacan determines it, that I'd like to stress. Lacan posits a logical equivalence between the entrance into the symbolic dimension and the entrance into the dimension of history, up to the point that he talks of a "primary historization"[23]. I'd summarise as follows: a living being enters into the dimension of language and, at the same time and necessarily, has to be determined as an historical being. Mere life is mediated through language, society and culture and, consequently, among the names that belong to Lacan's subject of the signifier is "historical being" to be found.

Lacan recognises his debt towards Heidegger's idea of the historicity ("*Geschichtlichkeit*") of the *Dasein*[24], while keeping a specific theoretical originality in the fact that the notion of historicity bases on the necessity of the entrance into the symbolic dimension. An individual enters into the dimension of language and is therefore to be determined as historical. This moment could also be understood as the emergence of a primary, most general narrative dimension, that makes it possible for a life to undergo narration[25].

Once it has been considered that language, for Lacan, is always an incarnated, spoken language, given in concrete speech acts and linguistic manifestations, and that the fact of language implies at the same time the fact of history, it can be easily understood why Lacan, in 1966, states that the unconscious is history, while repeating that experience is marked by a "primary historization"[26]. The first result of a closer commentary of Lacan's definition of signifier terminates therefore in positing the necessity of the relation between language, subjectivity and history, as just presented.

5. The Signifiers' Synchronicity

Lacan's definition of signifier doesn't determine its object only in respect of its necessary bound with subjectivity. Stating that a signifier represents

a subject for another signifier means to imply that every time that there is a signifier, there is another signifier, too. No signifier is given alone, there must be at least more than one signifier: more than just an affinity with the Saussurean linguistics is here at stake.

A signifier is defined through the structural opposition to another signifier. A signifier alone is not a signifier, since a signifier is defined by its mutual relations to other signifiers. In other words, this is the classical structuralist claim according to which language consists in nothing but differences[27]: the notion of pure difference regards necessarily the fact of language, as understood by structural linguistics[28].

Language, considered as "*langue*" in Saussurean terms, appears in Lacan's writings as the synchronic system of differential oppositions that define the involved signifiers and thus deserves the designation of structure[29]. The set of a structure's defining relations is considered as synchronic: a time-related notion makes here its appearance, although only negatively. All signifiers, their structural and defining relations, are given at the same time, i.e. the structure is given as synchronic; in other words: there's no before and after in it.

The idea that we obtain from this second step of interpretation of Lacan's definition of signifier is that language, understood as "*langue*" in Saussurean terms, appears as a structure, whose elements consist in nothing more than the place they occupy in the defining system of reference and every system of signifiers must be understood as characterised by synchronicity.

I'll try now to show how this idea relates to Lacan's conception of the unconscious, as well as with his understanding of psychoanalysis itself.

6. Repetition and the Timelessness of the Unconscious

Let's consider now Lacan's following formulation: "[t]he unconscious is that chapter of my history that is marked by a blank or occupied by a falsehood: it is the censored chapter"[30]. It could be clarifying to also take into account some statements Lacan made during his 1958-1959 seminar, nowadays to be found in the sixth book of the official transcription:

> Essentially, the unconscious presents itself as an indefinitely repeated articulation. [...] [T]he subject is in the end the one who bears the mark, the stigmata of a repetition, which remains for him not only ambivalent, but properly speaking inaccessible, too, until the analytic experience […] allows him to nominate, situate, designate himself for being the support of that sanction.[31]

The unconscious presents itself in the form of a repetition. What is repeated? An articulation is repeated. The unconscious, since it is structured like a language, has to be thought[32] as an articulation, as a structure, a synchronically given system of oppositions and differences, and it presents itself as the constant repetition[33] of the multiple structures that determine the life of the subject, its habits and speech acts. Freud's hypothesis of the timeless of the unconscious gains at this point a particular facet: Lacan's notion of the synchronicity of the signifiers, borrowed from Saussurean linguistics, allows a more precise understanding of the absence of time regarding the Freudian unconscious.

Once Lacan's allegorical[34] reading of Poe's *Purloined Letter* is considered, these arguments become even clearer: Lacan distinctly argues that articulations repeat themselves because of their being structured like a language[35] and, as already underlined, the synchronic, structural relations between signifiers are not liable to be said 'past', 'present' or 'future', since they're simply synchronic, given at the same time.

The Freudian link between timelessness of the unconscious and repetition compulsion is therefore vehemently stressed by Lacan[36] and understood through the lens of his already presented idea of the symbolic constitution of subjectivity. Lacan explains Freud's point of view by analysing it from a specific standpoint.

This is the reason why it isn't completely false, in a Lacanian sense, to state that the unconscious is timeless. This is indeed, in a specific sense, true: a socio-symbolic structure, that unconsciously determines the life of the subject, repeats itself indefinitely, continuously, even if it occurred in what our conscious experience would make us call the past. But conscious experience isn't directly, as already remarked, the centre of Freud's inquiry about subjectivity. An unconscious articulation is not to be considered as an event of the past, but as a “present-day force”, as Freud writes in *Erinnern, Wiederholen und Durcharbeiten*[37].

The difference between Lacan and Freud lies, in this respect, in Lacan's explanation of the Freudian timelessness, which isn't immediately a primary feature of the unconscious, but rather bases on the symbolic constitution of subjectivity: it is consequently understood as the synchronicity of the fundamental signifiers, unconsciously articulated, that effectively determine the life of the individual.

7. The Necessity of Diachronic Realisation in Speech

The baroque convolutions of Lacan's arguments do often appear as arbitrary exhibitionism, if not as theoretical sophistries: such a rereading

of some basic Freudian notions risks to come out as an outstanding example of Lacan's tendency to conceptual tortuousness. But, as a matter of fact, his linguistic (if we ought to call it so) model for the understanding of phenomena linked to the unconscious happens to enhance psychoanalytical theory, as it offers the chance to think positively some necessary features of the psychoanalytical praxis. I'll try now to explain in which sense and why.

Let's consider some aspects of Saussure's linguistic theory: the dimension of "*langue*", characterised by the feature of synchronicity, does not cover alone the whole dimension of linguistic phenomena, since the concrete speech act, the "*parole*", shows for Saussure some specific properties that do not apply to the field of "*langue*". But – and here's the point – the dimension of the synchronic system of signifiers implies necessarily its concrete realisation in speech acts. We always face concrete speech acts, we do not experience a "*langue*" as such[38].

One of the distinctive features of the "*parole*" is its diachronic unfolding: diachronicity is a structural property of every speech act, i.e. every speech act is organised following a diachronic sequence. Its elements are organised as a series. In order to be meaningful, every speech act must present itself as a diachronically organised succession.

If we now translate these arguments into the Lacanian field of research, i.e. psychoanalytical theory, something more interesting than a mere analogy appears: the timelessness of the unconscious, that was previously understood as the synchronicity of the articulation of the fundamental signifiers, begs for its realisation, must be spoken out, realised every time. And each realisation of a synchronically given system of signifiers has to be understood as a diachronic unfolding of a series of elements. Thus, the so-called formations of the unconscious are to be considered as diachronic unfoldings, as speech acts are, once their structural relation to the unconscious, understood as the articulation of signifiers, is assumed.

I'll try now to explain why this way of understanding the phenomena that pertain to the field of psychoanalysis not only brings psychoanalytical theory a little further, but also offers a most original approach to the problem of time, which can be indeed of particular philosophical relevance.

8. The Notion of Afterwardness

From the inquiry about language Lacan obtains once again the theoretical devices that allow him to reinterpret some notions which relate originally to Freud's psychoanalytical theory. Lacan actually invests of new meaning,

partially thanks to linguistics, Freud's ideas, so that they end up presenting specific features which are absent in Freud's formulas. Exactly the same happens concerning Saussure's observations.

Once Saussure's idea of the necessary diachronicity of speech acts is taken into account, the figure of a line emerges: an element, as already mentioned, follows the other, building up a linearly organised sequence. For example, the sentence 'I am in this room' is meaningful because every constituting element follows the one or the ones preceding it, being the whole ruled by a given system of conventions.

For Lacan, things get a little more complex. If we consider the following different sentences: 'I am', 'I am in this', 'I am in this room', it's evident that they do not have the same meaning. Lacan states therefore that diachronicity in speech can't be understood as a mere linear unfolding, but as a repeated and retroactive rearticulation of the relationships between the elements of the speech act, i.e. between signifiers.

Every signifier that comes after the others does effectively change the mutual relations that define the elements of the sentence. But once we assume that a signifier is nothing more than the defining structural relations that situate it in a system, as mentioned before, it is by necessity that the following conclusion is then formulated: the signifier coming after the others actually changes the preceding signifiers.

This is a smaller picture of the Lacanian way of reading the originally Freudian notion of "*Nachträglichkeit*", or afterwardness[39]. The relevance of Lacan's theoretical effort lies not only in putting the accent on a concept too often forgotten or left aside, which gains again under the name of "*après-coup*" its proper centrality, but also in formulating or at least outlining a specific form of temporality which could include the notion of "*Nachträglichkeit*" as constituting.

Such specific form of temporality is indicated by Lacan with the name of "*futur antérieur*", future anterior, and relates essentially to a way of comprehending time that is able to include the reference to subjectivity as structurally marked with the psychoanalytical unconscious.

Lacan writes:

> What is realised in my history is not the past definite of what was, since it is no more, or even the present perfect of what has been in what I am, but the future anterior of what I shall have been for what I am in the process of becoming.[40]

The realisation of individual history that is at stake in psychoanalytical experience has to face the fact that the past, or what our conscious experience would make us call the past, constantly acts upon us, as

understood through the notion of a synchronically articulated structure of fundamental signifiers. The past dooms the individual in the form of an indefinitely always-recurrent repetition.

But psychoanalytical experience should be able to actively change the frame of such a repetition, or better, put the individual in a position that enables him to do so: the past would otherwise, as an unchanging constellation of petrified signifiers, unavoidably shape the life of the subject, without escape. It is in this sense that Žižek claims that the repressed comes from the future[41].

From this perspective, "*Nachträglichkeit*" is the fundamental aspect of the act of rewriting the subject's history, which should be understood as a way of 'changing the past'[42] – or rather the way in which the past acts upon our lives. The form of temporality which includes it and is defined by it is indicated by Lacan with the term of "*future antérieur*". The aim of this notion is to conceive a dimension of time which doesn't reduce temporality to a linear succession of experienced moments, neither dooms the individual to a predetermined and unchangeable repetition of the past.

A time theory[43] that is based on the psychoanalytical way of understanding subjectivity has to be able to conceive time so, that time itself becomes the condition of possibility for a praxis that, through the individual's rewriting, remembering, making history of the past[44], actively changes the life of the subject, its concrete "process of becoming". In this sense, the Lacanian "*future antérieur*" identifies a specific form of temporality which conceives time as structurally related to a subjectivity characterised by the psychoanalytical unconscious.

9. Some Conclusions

A brief summary of the conclusions should now be outlined, in regard of some of the results that appear as the most relevant gains of the preceding arguments.

First of all, a change of views can be derived from the Lacanian 'return to Freud', since the traditional statement of the timelessness of the unconscious happens to face a revision: the unconscious is sure timeless, if a specific form of temporality is considered, which is linked with a comprehension of subjectivity that posits its fundamental point of theoretical access in the faculty of conscious perception. But it's also possible to look for another conception of time, as indeed Lacan does, which focuses on the faculty of memory as linguistically mediated and involves the psychoanalytical unconscious.

The second relevant conclusion consists consequently in the fact that, among the time theories that conceive time as structurally related to subjectivity, a specific construct can be found, which not only relates temporality to subjectivity, but also conceives the considered subjectivity as characterised by the psychoanalytical unconscious. Its central theoretical device is the Lacanian "*future antérieur*", which emerges as an intricate figure that binds together the three temporal dimensions in a knot which exceeds both a linear and a circular representation of time.

Thirdly then, and more radically, it must be underlined that Lacan's conception of time does not think time as something that can be reduced to the fact of perception. If time also depends on language, on the symbolic constitution of subjectivity, and language and the symbolic dimension as such implicate the dimension of history, it has to be therefore stated that the dimension of history cooperates in giving to temporality its own position and meaning.

It's not history that is conceived as based on a previous comprehension of time, but it's time that is thought as strictly based on the dimension of history. As Lang writes, time is historised, linguistically mediated[45].

A specific comprehension of history has to shape our conception of time. Such a point of view is expressed in an exemplary way by Walter Benjamin, in particular in the "*Passagen-Werk*" and in the theses on the concept of history, which I'd like to quote, at the end of this short contribution:

> Historicism contents itself with establishing a causal nexus of various moments of history. But no state of affairs is, as a cause, already a historical one. It becomes this, posthumously, through eventualities which may be separated from it by millennia. The historian who starts from this, ceases to permit the consequences of eventualities to run through the fingers like the beads of a rosary.[46]

I feel that this structural similarity could open an interesting and potentially fertile field of research.

Notes

---

[1] Aristotle, *Physics*, *Books III and IV*, Translated with Introduction and Notes by Edward Hussey, Oxford University Press, Oxford 1983, 219b, 223a.

[2] For this general categorisation, cf. also: G. Böhme, *Zeit als Medium von Darstellungen und Zeit als Form lebendiger Existenz*, p. 235, in: K. Münch, E. Löchel (Ed.), *Zeit und Raum im psychoanalytischen Denken. Arbeitstagung der Deutschen Psychoanalytischen Vereinigung in Bremen, 27. bis 30. April 2005*, Geber+Reusch, Frankfurt a. M. 2005, pp. 234-241.

[3] Cf.: P. Hutton, *The Art of Memory Reconceived: From Rhetoric to Psychoanalysis*, in: "*Journal of the History of Ideas*", Vol. 48, No. 3, 1987, pp. 371-392; N. Langlitz, *Die Zeit der Psychoanalyse. Lacan und das Problem der Sitzungsdauer*, Suhrkamp, Frankfurt a. M. 2005, pp. 18-54.
[4] S. Freud, *Das Unbewußte*, in: S. Freud, *Gesammelte Werke, Band X. Werken aus den Jahren 1913-1917*, Fischer, Frankfurt a. M. 1969, p. 286.
[5] S. Freud, *Jenseits des Lustprinzips*, in: S. Freud, *Gesammelte Werke, Band XIII. Jenseits des Lustprinzips / Massenpsychologie und Ich-Analyse / Das Ich und das Es*, Fischer, Frankfurt a. M. 1969, p. 28.
[6] S. Freud, *Erinnern, Wiederholen und Durcharbeiten*, in: S. Freud, *Gesammelte Werke, Band X, op. cit.*, p. 131.
[7] Cf.: J. Derrida, *Freud et la scène de l'écriture*, in: J. Derrida, *L'écriture et la différence*, Seuil, Paris 1967, pp. 317-318.
[8] Even a quick reading of Lacan's biography by Roudinesco gives a clear picture of Lacan's involvement with more or less traditional philosophers, as well as with the intellectual debate of his time. Cf.: E. Roudinesco, *Jacques Lacan. Esquisse d'une vie, histoire d'un système de pensée*, Fayard, Paris 1993.
[9] How misleading Lacan's readings for a traditional philosophy scholar may be, it must be remembered that Lacan always pointed out quite clearly that he worked in the field of psychoanalysis, not of philosophy. Cf.: J. Lacan, *Autres écrits*, Seuil, Paris 2001, p. 204.
[10] J. Lacan, *Psychologie et esthétique*, in: "*Recherches philosophiques*", 5, 1935/36, http://www.ecolelacanienne.net/documents/1935-00-00a.doc (consulted on 13.03.2014).
[11] Y.-H. Choi, *Saussure et Lacan: autour du problème du temps*, in: M. Arrivé, C. Normand (Ed.), *Linguistique et psychanalyse*, Hermann, Paris 2013, p. 268.
[12] J. Lacan, *Écrits*, Seuil, Paris 1966, p. 82.
[13] Notable and nowadays become almost scholastic is Žižek's identification of three moments in Lacan's conception of the Symbolic dimension. Cf.: S. Žižek, *Lacan – at What Point is he Hegelian?*, in: S. Žižek, *Interrogating the Real*, Continuum, London 2005, pp. 26-37.
[14] J. Lacan, *Écrits*, *op. cit.*, p. 819.
[15] It must not be forgotten that, although Lacan uses a pseudo-Saussurian terminology, he doesn't immediately apply Saussurian notions; he forces them instead to fit into a partially different theoretical field, in order to fulfil specific functions. From another point of view, it can't be argued that many notions, e.g. "signifier" and "signified", are not, in Lacan's theory, related to Saussure's linguistics at all. Lacan's use of Saussure is a complex topic and needs a specific treatment. I'd like to mention here Michel Arrivé, whose systematic research focuses often on Lacan's legitimate (or not) commitment with linguistics. Arrivé point out how Lacan's "signifier" does not correspond entirely to Saussure's, being rather the case of a homonymy, and not a synonymy; Lacan's usage of the term is not, however, strictly illegitimate (cf. particularly on this point: M. Arrivé, *Linguistique et psychanalyse. Freud, Saussure, Hjelmslev, Lacan et les autres*,

Méridiens/Klincksieck, Paris 1986, p. 123; M. Arrivé, *Langage et psychanalyse, linguistique et inconscient. Freud, Saussure, Pichon, Lacan*, PUF, Paris 1994, p. 82).

[16] A. Juranville, *Lacan et la philosophie*, PUF, Paris 1984, p. 120.

[17] Cf. Lang's interpretation of Lacan's definition of signifier: H. Lang, *Die Sprache und das Unbewusste. Jacques Lacans Grundlegung der Psychoanalyse*, Suhrkamp, Frankfurt a. M. 1986, pp. 257-258.

[18] Cf.: M. Hatzfeld, *« Le signifiant est ce qui représente le sujet pour un autre signifiant »*, in: M. Arrivé, C. Normand (Ed.), *Linguistique et psychanalyse*, *op. cit.*, p. 343; J.-C. Milner, *L'Œuvre claire. Lacan, la science, la philosophie*, Seuil, Paris 1995, p. 105.

[19] J. Lacan, *Le Séminaire. Livre II. Le moi dans la théorie de Freud et dans la technique de la psychanalyse*, Seuil, Paris 1978, pp. 30-31.

[20] N. Haas, *Fort/da als Modell*, in: D. Hombach (Ed.), *ZETA 02/Mit Lacan*, Rotation, Berlin 1982, p. 29.

[21] S. Freud, *Jenseits des Lustprinzips*, *op. cit.*, pp. 12-13.

[22] J. Lacan, *Écrits*, *op. cit.*, p. 594; J. Lacan, *Le Séminaire. Livre VI. Le désir et son interprétation*, Martinière, Paris 2013, p. 490. It's not of real relevance here to find out whether Lacan's reading is proper or not. What is important to me, is to show how the inner structure of some of Lacan's notions and their developed consequences actually allow to give a specific understanding of time that involves the psychoanalytical unconscious.

[23] J. Lacan, *Écrits*, *op. cit.*, p. 261; J. Lacan, *Le Séminaire. Livre V. Les formations de l'inconscient*, Seuil, Paris 1998, p. 493.

[24] E.g.: M. Heidegger, *Sein und Zeit*, in: M. Heidegger, *Gesamtausgabe, I. Abteilung: Veröffentlichte Schriften 1914-1970, Band 2. Sein und Zeit*, Klostermann, Frankfurt a. M. 1977, pp. 503-525. Hock underlines this aspect of Lacan's thought, too: U. Hock, *Das Unbewusste Denken. Wiederholung und Todestrieb*, Psychosozial-Verlag, Gießen 2012, p. 237.

[25] R. Hofmann, *Beschreibungen des Abwesenden. Lektüren nach Lacan*, Peter Lang, Frankfurt a. M. 1996, p. 27.

[26] J. Lacan, *Interview au Figaro Littéraire (relue par Lacan) par Gilles Lapouge*, in: "*Figaro Littéraire*", 1966, http://www.ecole-lacanienne.net/documents/1966-12-29.doc (05.03.2014).

[27] F. de Saussure, *Cours de linguistique générale*, Payot, Paris 1972, pp. 166-169.

[28] A. Juranville, *Lacan et la philosophie*, *op. cit.*, p. 45; J.-C. Milner, *L'Œuvre claire*, *op. cit.*, p. 101.

[29] J. Lacan, *Écrits*, *op. cit.*, p. 501.

[30] J. Lacan, *Écrits. A selection*, translated by A. Sheridan, Routledge, London 1989, p. 55.

[31] J. Lacan, *Le Séminaire. Livre VI. Le désir et son interprétation*, *op. cit.*, pp. 466-467. Translation is mine.

[32] I'd like here to suggest to read Lacan's statement, "the unconscious is structured like a language", underlining the word "like", "*comme*". Properly speaking, to say that something is structured, for Lacan, is to say that it presents itself in the form of a language (cf.: *Interview au Figaro Littéraire*, *op. cit.*: "pour moi, le mot structure

désigne exactement l'incidence du langage comme tel dans ce champ phénoménal qui peut être groupé sous la rubrique de ce qui est analysable au sens analytique. Je précise: dans le champ de ma recherche, dire 'structuré comme un langage', c'est un pléonasme"); anyway, the exact meaning of the formula remains open in regard to a realist or constructivist interpretation. On this topic: H.-D. Gondek, *„La séance continue". Jacques Derrida und die Psychoanalyse*, postface to: J. Derrida, *Vergessen wir nicht – die Psychoanalyse!*, transl. H.-D. Gondek, Suhrkamp, Frankfurt a. M. 1998, p. 203. A more precise inquiry is nevertheless needed and begs for discussion.

[33] The mutual implication of difference and repetition is one of the points made by Deleuze: G. Deleuze, *Différence et répétition*, PUF, Paris 1968, p. 96ff.

[34] S. Felman, *Jacques Lacan and the Adventure of Insight. Psychoanalysis in Contemporary culture*, Harvard University Press, Cambridge, Massachussets 1987, p. 32ff.

[35] J. Lacan, *Écrits*, *op. cit.*, p. 11.

[36] Green also describes the repetion compulsion as "murder of time". A. Green, *Freuds Konzept der Zeitlichkeit im Unterschied zu heutigen Auffassungen*, in: *Zeit und Raum im psychoanalytischen Denken*, *op. cit.*, p. 84.

[37] See footnote 6.

[38] Saussure didn't strictly, if I'm not wrong, put it this way; what can be found, anyway, in his *Cours* is the historical precedence of the "*parole*" in respect to the "*langue*" and the reciprocal necessity of the two fields of language. F. de Saussure, *Cours de linguistique générale*, *op. cit.*, p. 37.

[39] I can't develop here in details a complete discussion about the concept. For a summary of the word's occurrences in Freud's work and some observations about its translation and reception in the psychoanalytical tradition, cf.: F.-W., Eickhoff, *On Nachträglichkeit: The modernity of an old concept*, in: "*International Journal of Psychoanalysis*", 87, 2006; for further observations about the notion of "*Nachträglichkeit*": J. Bernat, *„Psyché n'est qu'après-coup" (les temporalités psychiques)*, in: "*Cahiers d'Études Germaniques*", 57, 2009; G. Dahl, *Nachträglichkeit, Wiederholungszwang, Symbolisierung. Zur psychoanalytischen Deutung von primärprozesshaften Szenen*, in: "*PSYCHE*", Heft 5, 2010; U. Hock, *Die Zeit des Erinnerns*, in: "*PSYCHE*", Heft 9, 2003; G. Botta, *Nachträglichkeit, la risignificazione del passato tra tempo lineare e circolare*, in: "*Psichiatria e Psicoterapia*", 31, 2, 2012; C. Kirchhoff, *Das psychoanalytische Konzept der »Nachträglichkeit«. Zeit, Bedeutung und die Anfänge des Psychischen*, Psychosozial-Verlag, Gießen 2009; J. Laplanche, *Problématiques VI. L'après-coup*, PUF, Paris 2006.

[40] J. Lacan, *The Language of the Self: The Function of Language in Psychoanalysis*, translated by A. Wildern, John Hopkins University Press, Baltimore, Maryland 1981, p. 63.

[41] S. Žižek, *The Truth Arises from Misrecognition*, in: E. Ragland-Sullivan, M. Bracher (Ed.), *Lacan and the Subject of Language*, Routledge, New York 1991, pp. 188-189.

[42] Cf. also: H.-D. Gondek, *Subjekt, Sprache und Erkenntnis. Philosophische Zugänge zur Lacanschen Psychoanalyse*, in: H.-D. Gondek, R. Hofmann, H.-M. Lohmann (Ed.), *Jacques Lacan – Wege zu seinem Werk*, Klett-Cotta, Stuttgart 2001, pp. 154-156.

[43] In this sense, a more specific research that focuses on the hereby mentioned notions of "*Nachträglichkeit*" and "*après-coup*", as well as on the "*future antérieur*", is needed, i.e. a precise inquiry about the relations that bind together the three dimensions of time, understood as past, present and future, in such a conceptual constellation and in its relationship to other time theories. This kind of research cannot obviously be developed here: I simply tried to outline its background and to underline its relevance, both in the psychoanalytical and in the philosophical field of interests.

[44] Kettner points out that the centre of the notion of history is, for psychoanalysis, not the "*Veridikalität*" (veridicality) but the "*Kausalität*" (causality) of memories. M. Kettner, *Nachträglichkeit. Freuds brisante Erinnerungstheorie*, in: J. Rüsen, J. Straub (Ed.), *Die dunkle Spur der Vergangenheit. Psychoanalytische Zugänge zum Geschichtsbewußtsein. Erinnerung, Geschichte, Identität, 2*, Suhrkamp, Frankfurt a. M. 1998, p. 43.

[45] H. Lang, *Die Sprache und das Unbewusste*, *op. cit.*, pp. 146-147.

[46] W. Benjamin, *Gesammelte Schriften*, *I*, Suhrkamp, Frankfurt a. M. 1972, p. 704, translated by D. Redmond (http://members.efn.org/~dredmond/ThesesonHistory.html, consulted on 31.07.2014). For a more or less systematic research on the affinities between Lacanian theory and Walter Benjamin's thought, cf. among others: U. Hock, *Das Unbewusste Denken*, op. cit.; G. Schwering, *Benjamin – Lacan. Vom Diskurs des Anderen*, Turia+Kant, Wien 1998.

References

Aristotle, *Physics*, *Books III and IV*, Translated with Introduction and Notes by Edward Hussey, Oxford University Press, Oxford 1983.

Arrivé, M., *Linguistique et psychanalyse. Freud, Saussure, Hjelmslev, Lacan et les autres*, Méridiens/Klincksieck, Paris 1986.

—. *Langage et psychanalyse, linguistique et inconscient. Freud, Saussure, Pichon, Lacan*, PUF, Paris 1994.

Arrivé, M., Normand, C. (Ed.), *Linguistique et psychanalyse*, Hermann, Paris 2013.

Benjamin, W., *Gesammelte Schriften*, *7 Bände*, Suhrkamp, Frankfurt a. M. 1972ff.

Bernat, J., *"Psyché n'est qu'après-coup" (les temporalités psychiques)*, in: "*Cahiers d'Études Germaniques*", 57, 2009.

Botta, G., *Nachträglichkeit, la risignificazione del passato tra tempo lineare e circolare*, in: "*Psichiatria e Psicoterapia*", 31, 2, 2012.

Dahl, G., *Nachträglichkeit, Wiederholungszwang, Symbolisierung. Zur psychoanalytischen Deutung von primärprozesshaften Szenen*, in: "*PSYCHE*", Heft 5, 2010.

Deleuze, G., *Différence et répétition*, PUF, Paris 1968.

Derrida, J., *L'écriture et la différence*, Seuil, Paris 1967.

Eickhoff, F.-W., *On Nachträglichkeit: The modernity of an old concept*, in: "*International Journal of Psychoanalysis*", 87, 2006.

Felman, S., *Jacques Lacan and the Adventure of Insight. Psychoanalysis in Contemporary culture*, Harvard University Press, Cambridge, Massachussets 1987.

Freud, S., *Gesammelte Werke*, *18 Bände und ein Nachtragsband*, Fischer, Frankfurt a. M. 1940-1952.

Gondek, H.-D., *„La séance continue". Jacques Derrida und die Psychoanalyse*, postface to: J. Derrida, *Vergessen wir nicht – die Psychoanalyse!,* transl. H.-D. Gondek, Suhrkamp, Frankfurt a. M. 1998.

Gondek, H.-D., Hofmann, R., Lohmann, H.-M. (Ed.), *Jacques Lacan – Wege zu seinem Werk*, Klett-Cotta, Stuttgart 2001.

Heidegger, M., *Gesamtausgabe*, Vittorio Klostermann, Frankfurt a. M. 1975ff.

Hock, U., Udo, *Die Zeit des Erinnerns*, in: "*PSYCHE*", Heft 9, 2003.

Hock, U., *Das Unbewusste Denken. Wiederholung und Todestrieb*, Psychosozial-Verlag, Gießen 2012.

Hofmann, R., *Beschreibungen des Abwesenden. Lektüren nach Lacan*, Peter Lang, Frankfurt a. M. 1996.

Hombach, D. (Ed.), *ZETA 02/Mit Lacan*, Rotation, Berlin 1982.

Hutton, P., *The Art of Memory Reconceived: From Rhetoric to Psychoanalysis*, in: "*Journal of the History of Ideas*", Vol. 48, No. 3, 1987.

Juranville, A., *Lacan et la philosophie*, PUF, Paris 1984.

Kirchhoff, C., *Das psychoanalytische Konzept der »Nachträglichkeit«. Zeit, Bedeutung und die Anfänge des Psychischen*, Psychosozial-Verlag, Gießen 2009.

Lacan, J., *Psychologie et esthétique*, in: "*Recherches philosophiques*", 5, 1935/36.

—. *Écrits*, Seuil, Paris 1966.

—. *Interview au Figaro Littéraire (relue par Lacan) par Gilles Lapouge*, in: "*Figaro Littéraire*", 1966.

—. *Le Séminaire. Livre II. Le moi dans la théorie de Freud et dans la technique de la psychanalyse*, Seuil, Paris 1978.

—. *The Language of the Self: The Function of Language in Psychoanalysis*, translated by A. Wildern, John Hopkins University Press, Baltimore, Maryland 1981.

—. *Écrits. A selection*, translated by A. Sheridan, Routledge, London 1989.

—. *Le Séminaire. Livre V. Les formations de l'inconscient*, Seuil, Paris 1998.

—. *Autres écrits*, Seuil, Paris 2001.

—. *Le Séminaire. Livre VI. Le désir et son interprétation*, Martinière, Paris 2013.

Lang, H., *Die Sprache und das Unbewusste. Jacques Lacans Grundlegung der Psychoanalyse*, Suhrkamp, Frankfurt a. M. 1986.

Langlitz, N., *Die Zeit der Psychoanalyse. Lacan und das Problem der Sitzungsdauer*, Suhrkamp, Frankfurt a. M. 2005.

Laplanche, J., *Problématiques VI. L'après-coup*, PUF, Paris 2006.

Milner, J.-C., *L'Œuvre claire. Lacan, la science, la philosophie*, Seuil, Paris: 1995.

Münch, K., Löchel, E. (Ed.), *Zeit und Raum im psychoanalytischen Denken. Arbeitstagung der Deutschen Psychoanalytischen Vereinigung in Bremen, 27. bis 30. April 2005*, Geber+Reusch, Frankfurt a. M. 2005.

Ragland-Sullivan, Bracher, E., M. (Ed.), *Lacan and the Subject of Language*, Routledge, New York 1991.

Roudinesco, E., *Jacques Lacan. Esquisse d'une vie, histoire d'un système de pensée*, Fayard, Paris 1993.

Rüsen J., Straub, J. (Ed.), *Die dunkle Spur der Vergangenheit. Psychoanalytische Zugänge zum Geschichtsbewußtsein. Erinnerung, Geschichte, Identität, 2*, Suhrkamp, Frankfurt a. M. 1998.

de Saussure, F., *Cours de linguistique générale*, Payot, Paris 1972.

Schwering, G., *Benjamin – Lacan. Vom Diskurs des Anderen*, Turia+Kant, Wien 1998.

Žižek, S., *Lacan – at What Point is he Hegelian?*, in: S. Žižek, *Interrogating the Real*, Continuum, London 2005.

CHAPTER TWO

ATTRIBUTIVE JUDGMENT AND A SOURCE OF FREUD'S *PROJECT*

BEN HOOSON

The notion that our experience of the world can be described in terms of impressions, sense data, memory images and suchlike is as old as Western philosophy. If it has gone out of fashion in recent years, the credit or blame rests largely with Ludwig Wittgenstein in his later work, most famously in the *Philosophical Investigations*. Let me start with a quote from that work:

> "When I imagine something, or even actually see objects, I have got something which my neighbour has not."—I understand you. You want to look about you and say: "At any rate only I have got THIS."—What are these words for? They serve no purpose.—Can one not add: "There is no question of a "seeing"—and therefore none of a "having"—nor of a subject, nor therefore of "I" either.[1]

The extent of what is called into question is apparent. It is not just our phenomenal experience, but also the conscious subject. At various places in the *Philosophical Investigations*, Wittgenstein produces paradoxes to challenge our understanding of what it means to have bodily sensations, sense experience, memories, etc.

One target, perhaps the main target, of Wittgenstein's challenge appears to be *self*-consciousness: the idea that we don't merely have experiences but are aware of ourselves having them. Consider this passage:

> (The temptation to say "I see it like this", pointing to the same thing for "it" and "this".) Always get rid of the idea of the private object in this way: assume that it constantly changes, but that you do not notice the change because your memory constantly deceives you.[2]

In a situation where self-consciousness failed, this deception could indeed happen: if the experiencing subject is not split between brute experiences, on the one hand, and the observance of himself having these experiences, on the other hand, he will have no means of judging when one experience stops and another starts.

But Wittgenstein does not make his point merely as a critique of self-consciousness. I think we can see more deeply into the problem if we stop and consider the word, which I just used: "judging". Wittgenstein says that we are tempted to make a judgment, "I see it like *this*", and that the problem with this supposed judgment is that we make it while pointing to the same thing for "it" and "this".

The idea, I think, is that the manner in which the "private object" (sensation, memory, sense experience, etc.) is felt, remembered, seen, etc., by the person who experiences it is part and parcel of its identity, so the pretended judgment is really no more than "x = x". Indeed, Wittgenstein says elsewhere that such a judgment "reminds us of a tautology".[3]

One might then say: if such a judgment is a problem, then don't make it. It is, after all, not evident that we accompany our conscious states by a running commentary, "I see/feel/imagine it like this". But there is something very convincing in the idea that such judgments are at least implicit in self-conscious experience, and anyone who reads the many lively examples that fill the *Philosophical Investigations* will probably be persuaded of this.

I would note here that the kind of judgment in question is attributive, i.e. it is a judgment that ascribes some quality (attribute) to an item. What the experiencer wants to assert is not merely that an experience occurs, but that it feels a certain way to him ("I see it like this"), and that "certain way" is the attribute that is ascribed to the experience.

If we then ask what exactly the attribute can be, which would be ascribed to phenomenal experience by the person who has it, we see that the challenges to self-consciousness and to the possibility of judgment in such a case are really two sides of one and the same coin. Consider Wittgenstein's remark:

> When it makes sense to say "I see this", or "this is seen", pointing to what I see, it also makes sense to say "I see this", pointing to something I don't see.[4]

A good interpretation of what he means, I think, is that the attributive judgment implicit in any experience would really be a matter of drawing a line around that experience, a line that defines it as mine: its attribute is precisely that of being mine. So self-consciousness and attributive

judgment are one and the same here, and (Wittgenstein thinks) they cannot work because it cannot possibly make sense to point to something I don't see, as would be necessary in order to draw the line between "mine" and "not mine".

Wittgenstein leaves us to conclude that phenomenal experience occurs, but it is like a slide show with nobody to watch it. Or, as he responds to someone who would accuse him of reducing sensation to nothing:

> It is not a something but not a nothing either. The conclusion was only that a nothing would serve just as well as a something about which nothing could be said.[5]

The conclusion is bewildering and I would ask: what if there *is* some mechanism, which renders self-consciousness experience and the attributive judgment implicit in it workable, and which Wittgenstein fails to appreciate? Perhaps it does, after all, make sense "to point to something I don't see"?

It is evident, even from the few passages cited, that Wittgenstein treats the phenomenal realm as dividing neatly into units (sensations, mental images, etc.). This idea is a commonplace of the philosophical tradition from antiquity through the British empiricists – Locke, Berkeley, Hume, Mill (of whom more below) – to Brentano and Russell. It may also occur to us that the division of experience into separate bits is a necessary consequence of putting it into the "picture frames" of an individual perspective: Wittgenstein's "I see it like this" and "this is seen". Which brings us back to the issue of attributive judgment.

Jacques Lacan, like any sensible non-philosopher, did not accept the fragmentation of human experience into discrete units as a primitive phenomenon – one that "goes without saying", – but he had an explanation of why it is more than a philosophical prejudice. He believed that the very fabric of human experience (not just the language we speak) is woven by the differential system of the signifier – the set of essential phonemic oppositions, which characterises any natural language and which was Lacan's borrowing from Ferdinand de Saussure:

> We know of no other basis by which the One may have been introduced into the world if not by the signifier.[6]

Specifically, and of special interest for our purposes, Lacan held that the predisposition to psychotic illness consists in the failure to adopt a certain stance towards the signifier system, for which the French psychoanalyst took the German term "Bejahung" ("affirmation") from Freud's 1925 paper, *Negation.*[7] In that paper Freud makes such affirmation synonymous

with a form of attributive judgment,[8] carried out by the human infant, a judgment that characterises a thing (Freud's German word is "Ding") as "good or bad, useful or harmful"[9] and which, at the same time, has the force of proclaiming "'it shall be inside me' or 'it shall be outside me'".[10] Lacan's contention is that what Freud really means to describe in *Negation* when he writes of affirmation and attributive judgment is a "primitive symbolization", which creates:

> [...] an original within, which is not a bodily within but that of an initial body of signifiers.
>
> It's inside this primordial body that Freud posits the creation of the world of reality, which is already punctuated, already structured in terms of signifiers.[11]

Let it be said: nothing in the text of *Negation* would suggest to the unsuspecting reader that Freud had in mind anything remotely connected with a symbolization, primitive or otherwise. But *Negation*, like all Freud's theoretical papers, has a superficial consistency that leaves any careful reader puzzled, not unlike a dream report marked by secondary revision.[12] Lack of visible evidence for a certain reading of Freud is not a ground for dismissing it if a strong connection can be traced between the text and thoughts elsewhere in his work, which support the reading (again there is a curious parallel with Freud's own technique of dream interpretation).

What I will therefore do in the rest of this chapter is to take a quick trip around Freud's most extensive treatment of attributive judgment and the concept of the "thing" ("das Ding"), which is found in his early, large-scale theoretical work: the posthumously published *Project for a Scientific Psychology* of 1895.[13] On the way I will visit what I believe to be a key source of his thought in that work, a source that helps us to see how these concepts were indeed tied to a mechanism of "primitive symbolization" for Freud in 1895. We will then see Lacan's justification for supposing that, when Freud used the same concepts in a very similar context 30 years, such a symbolization was his real theme. Justifying the start-point in Wittgenstein, I will make a brief application of Freud's understanding of attributive judgment to show why, contrary to what the philosopher thinks, "When it makes sense to say 'I see this', or 'this is seen', pointing to what I see," it does make sense, perhaps not to point to but (in a special manner to be defined) to *believe in* "something I don't see", and how the disbelief in this possibility could be a symptom of psychosis.[14]

The building blocks of the *Project* are quantity (often abbreviated by Freud to "*Q*" or "*Qη*") and neurones, which together furnish "the principle

of neuronal inertia: that neurones tend to divest themselves of *Q*". Quantity is the impact of the outside world on the nervous system, but it is also our physiological needs – Freud lists "hunger, respiration, sexuality" – which impact the nervous system from inside the body. The principle of neuronal inertia leads the system to discharge quantity that enters from the outside world by reflex movement, whether random or purposeful (ending the stimulus by putting distance between the body and the stimulus source), while the ending of a physiological stimulus requires what Freud calls a "specific action".[15] Freud's paradigm of the latter is the infant sucking on the mother's breast, and he states that the "experience of satisfaction" resulting from the specific action leaves a memory of the object, which gave satisfaction. The idea is that the infant keeps a memory of the satisfying object, which he/she can use to find further instances of that object in perception so that the experience of satisfaction can be repeated.

What is found in perception, Freud says, might coincide with the memory only in part, for:

> the time has come to remember that perceptual cathexes are never cathexes of single neurones but always of complexes. So far we have neglected this feature; it is time to take it into account.[16]

Partial coincidence, Freud continues, is far more common than complete coincidence and therefore deserves closer study. He offers this puzzling passage:

> The perceptual complex [...] can be dissected into a component portion, neurone *a*, which on the whole remains the same, and a second component portion, neurone *b*, which for the most part varies. Language will later apply the term *judgement* to this dissection, and will discover the resemblance which in fact exists between the nucleus of the ego and the constant perceptual component (on the one hand) and between the changing cathexes in the pallium and the inconstant component (on the other); it (language) will call neurone *a* the *thing* and neurone *b* its activity or attribute - in short, its *predicate*.[17]

The mechanical idea, which Freud then develops, is that the memory of the satisfying object may, for example, consist of $a + b$, while a later perception contains $a + c$ and the infant finds a way (by making certain movements) of getting from c to b in order to have the original satisfying object before him/her. Freud's simple example is a situation where the infant sees the mother's breast with a side view of the nipple $(a + c)$ and

then manoeuvres to a front view of the same ($a + b$) where he/she can obtain satisfaction by sucking.[18]

But what is most interesting in the last passage are not the mechanics, but the references to attributive judgment, to the duplex nature of every perception ("perceptual cathexis") as consisting of thing and attribute, and to a supposed resemblance between this duplex nature and that of the ego. The ego ("das Ich") in the *Project* is just the entirety of quantity in the nervous system (Freud calls it the "ψ system"):

> Thus the ego is to be defined as the totality of the ψ cathexes, at the given time, in which a permanent component is distinguished from a changing one.[19]

The "permanent component" is situated in the nuclear neurones of ψ (the "nucleus the ego" in the passage above), which receive quantity from inside the body, while the "changing" component (the "changing cathexes in the pallium" above) consists of neurones that are only occasionally cathected.[20]

We can begin to understand the logic of Freud's linkage between attributive judgment, the perception (or memory) of a satisfying object and the ego by investigating what, I believe, is the principal source of these *Project* concepts. The source is to be found by following up Freud's own footnote to the following passage in his monograph *On Aphasia*, which was published four years before the *Project* was written:

> According to philosophical teaching [...] the appearance of a "thing", the "properties" of which are conveyed to us by our senses, originates only from the fact that in enumerating the sensory impressions perceived from an object, we allow for the possibility of a large series of new impressions being added to the chain of associations (J.S. Mill*). This is why the idea of the object does not appear to us as closed, and indeed hardly as closable.[21]

In the footnote (marked by an asterisk) Freud writes: "Cf. J.S. Mill, *A System of Logic* (1843), 1, Book 1, Chapter III, also *An Examination of Sir William Hamilton's Philosophy* (1865)." John Stuart Mill, in his philosophy of mind, was an idealist in the spirit of Bishop Berkeley. Roughly put, his position, as set out in the part of the *System of Logic* that Freud refers to, is that the supposition of an external reality independent of the mind is unjustified because all we know are our sensations.

The precise argument, to which Freud refers in the *On Aphasia* passage, is not found in the *System*, but in Freud's second reference. In Chapter XI of the *Examination of Sir William Hamilton's Philosophy*,

entitled "The Psychological Theory of the Belief in an External World",[22] Mill sets out to explain, in what he calls "psychological" terms, why we believe in the existence of a world independent of our mind – an "external world" – despite the (as Mill thinks) evident fact that all we know are our sensations. He bases his "psychological theory" on several points. The first is "that the human mind is capable of Expectation". The second is "the laws of the Association of Ideas", including a principle whereby :

> Facts which have been experienced or thought of simultaneously, recall the thought of one another.[23]

Expectation along with association of ideas accounts, according to Mill, for our belief that we with are faced with a rich slice of the external world at any given moment:

> What we see is a very minute fragment of what we think we see. We see artificially that one thing is hard and another soft. We see artificially that one thing is hot, another cold. We see artificially that what we see is a book, or a stone, each of these things being not merely an inference, but a heap of inferences from the signs which we see, to things not visible.[24]

We expect to see a host of what Mill calls "possible sensations" along with our (minimal) current perceptual data because such sensations have been experienced simultaneously with the current data on other occasions. The expectation is so strong that we deceive ourselves and it seems to us that we see these possibilities realised: our actual sensory experience at any given moment is thus enriched by a phantom legion of possible sensations.

Mill then develops this idea into his "Psychological Theory of the Belief in an External World" in the following passage:

> There is another important peculiarity of these certified or guaranteed possibilities of sensation; namely, that they have reference, not to single sensations, but to sensations joined together in groups. When we think of anything as a material substance, or body, we either have had, or think that on some given supposition we should have, not some one sensation, but a great and even an indefinite number and variety of sensations [...] so linked together that the presence of one announces the possible presence at the very same instant of any or all of the rest. In our mind, therefore, not only is this particular Possibility of sensation invested with the quality of permanence when we are not actually feeling any of the sensations at all; but when we are feeling some of them, the remaining sensations of the group are conceived by us in the form of Present Possibilities, which might be realized at the very moment. And as this happens in turn to all of them, the group as a whole presents itself to the mind as [...] as a kind of

> permanent substratum, under a set of passing experiences or manifestations: which is another leading character of our idea of substance or matter, as distinguished from sensation.[25]

Through the rest of the Chapter, Mill uses the term "Permanent Possibilities" to emphasise how these possibilities of sensation acquire the aura of permanence that generates our belief in "substance or matter, as distinguished from sensation".

The argument in this passage is surely that cited by Freud in the two sentences from On Aphasia. When Freud says that "the idea of the object does not appear to us as closed, and indeed hardly as closable", the idea and (to some extent) the sentence structure echo Mill's comment that our belief in material substance is really a belief in the possibility of our having "a great and even an indefinite number and variety of sensations".

Returning to the passage that interests us in the *Project*, we can note a similar correspondence of both content and syntax between Mill's statement that his possibilities of sensation "have reference not to single sensations, but to sensations joined together in groups" and Freud's comment, cited above, that "perceptual cathexes are never cathexes of single neurones but always of complexes".[26]

This offers a possible interpretation of the different status that Freud accords in the *Project* passage to the two parts of a perceptual cathexis – respectively "thing" and "attribute".[27] Might he be thinking of Mill's analysis of "sensations joined together in groups", which contain, on the one hand, present sensations and, on the other hand, possibilities of sensation, and where the latter are what generate the belief in an external world, taking the role of what Freud calls "das Ding" ("the thing")? It might be objected: although Freud's "das Ding" chimes well with Mill's "external world", "substance" or "matter", it is hard to see how Freud's "attribute" can be made to match Mill's "present sensation". But it can. Mill, for a specific "history of philosophy" reason, used "sensation" and "attribute" interchangeably in the *System of Logic* (Freud's other reference in *On Aphasia*).[28]

In order to see why it is probable that the *Project* borrows from Mill and why Mill's argument in the *Examination* could be so valuable to Freud's thinking in the *Project*, we need to take the parallel between the two works one step further. In the *Project* passage, which I already quoted, Freud tells us that:

> Language [...] will discover the resemblance which in fact exists between the nucleus of the ego and the constant perceptual component (on the one hand) and between the changing cathexes in the pallium and the inconstant

> component (on the other); it (language) will call neurone *a* the *thing* and neurone *b* its activity or attribute - in short, its *predicate*.[29]

Can reference to Mill help us to understand the "resemblance" that Freud talks about here? The chapter of the *Examination* where Mill presents his "Psychological Theory of the Belief in an External World" is immediately followed by a chapter entitled "The Psychological Theory of the Belief in Matter, How Far Applicable to Mind".[30] Mill begins by saying that he has now disproved one half of "the doctrine [...] that Mind and Matter, an ego and a non-ego, are original data of consciousness".[31] What Mill thinks he has done, by means of his "psychological theory" is to show how our belief in matter (the "external world") could perfectly well be what he calls an "acquired" belief, i.e. an extrapolation from the nature of our sensory experience, which is psychologically explicable but has no more solid foundation than that. The belief is, so to speak, an unwitting leap of faith that we all make. In the next chapter, Mill promises to show how "the conception of Self as a permanent existence" could also be "acquired".[32] The argument is succinct, occupying barely a page. It starts like this:

> We have no conception of Mind itself, as distinguished from its conscious manifestations. We neither know nor can imagine it, except as represented by the succession of manifold feelings which metaphysicians call by the name of States or Modifications of Mind.[33]

Nonetheless, as with matter so with mind, we have "the notion of a permanent something, contrasted with the perpetual flux of the sensations and other feelings or mental states which we refer to it".[34] This notion is to be explained along the same lines as our belief in matter:

> The belief I entertain that my mind exists when it is not feeling, nor thinking, nor conscious of its own existence, resolves itself into the belief of a Permanent Possibility of these states.[35]

Note the term "Permanent Possibility" – the very same term used in the previous chapter of the *Examination* to explain our belief in the external world. Mill continues:

> Thus far, there seems no hindrance to our regarding Mind as nothing but the series of our sensations (to which must now be added our internal feelings), as they actually occur, with the addition of infinite possibilities of feeling requiring for their actual realization conditions which may or may not take place, but which as possibilities are always in existence, and many of them present.[36]

This argument is really just a less detailed version of the argument for our belief in an external world beyond our sensations (it is, as Mill makes clear by the chapter title, his "theory of the belief in matter" applied to mind). In both cases, the issue hinges on our belief in "permanent possibilities" of sensation or feeling and on these possibilities being a background to any actual mental content. It is almost as if, for Mill, matter, on the one hand, and mind (ego/self), on the other hand, are really one and the same construct. And this, I think, is where Freud took his "resemblance... between the nucleus of the ego and the constant perceptual component (on the one hand) and between the changing cathexes in the pallium and the inconstant component (on the other)".[37]

Let me spell out the pairings: Freud's nucleus of the ego and constant perceptual component are both on the side of Mill's permanent possibilities, while Freud's changing cathexes in the pallium (the other part of the duplex ego) and inconstant perceptual component are both on the side of Mill's "sensations ((...) internal feelings) as they actually occur" (his expression in the last passage above).

I have now mapped what I take to be the borrowing from Mill. The next task is to see what exactly in Mill's argument could have served Freud.

Mill's theory purports to explain how we come to believe in the existence of an external world and of our own self, and, curiously, seems to conflate these two beliefs. Both beliefs, for Mill, involve an implicit attributive judgment: when I instinctively take perception to be of an external world and when I take perception or any mental presentation to be *my* perception or presentation, I am (Mill thinks) judging these items to be attributes of material substance or of the self (ego). In actual fact, however, the attributive judgment is, for Mill, illusory: what I am *really* doing in these instances is manifesting my propensity, driven by expectation and association of ideas, to conceive all of the absent presentations as "Present Possibilities, which might be realized at the very moment".

A little way into the third part of the *Project*, Freud resolves to address what he calls:

> the most obscure problem: the origin of the "ego" - that is, of a complex of neurones which hold fast to their cathexis.[38]

What is obscure for Freud is how there can possibly be such a thing as "a complex of neurones which hold fast to their cathexis". Why is this obscure and why should such a complex be the ego? Freud had introduced the ego (in the *Project*'s first part) in order to fulfil a specific function,

which he calls "inhibition" and which is intimately related to the experience of satisfaction. As described above, that experience leaves behind a memory of the object, which brought satisfaction (the breast), but it also leaves a memory of the movement, which the infant made in order to obtain the satisfaction (sucking on the breast). Freud immediately produces "a basic law of association by simultaneity",[39] by which neurones that have once been simultaneously cathected will thereafter allow quantity to pass between them without hindrance (this is surely Mill's association by simultaneity, described above). The problem then, Freud says, is that as soon as the memory of the satisfying object is cathected (i.e. remembered), the memory of the movement will also be cathected and the child will start to suck, which is highly inexpedient since the breast is not really there. The mechanism of inhibition is brought in to prevent this. Specifically, when the memory of the object is cathected:

> If an adjoining neurone is simultaneously cathected, this acts like a temporary facilitation of the contact barrier lying between the two, and modifies the course [of the current], which would otherwise have been directed towards the one facilitated contact-barrier. A *side-cathexis* thus acts as *an inhibition of the course of* $Q\eta$,[40]

The ego deploys such an inhibiting "side-cathexis" to draw quantity ($Q\eta$) away from the neurone that is a memory of the satisfying object, thus preventing a flow of quantity from that memory to the associated movement memory and the inexpedient action that would ensue.

The "most obscure problem", the origin of the ego, is the outcome of this Heath-Robinson arrangement. Freud considers the state, in which quantity is pinned down ("bound") in neurones by the mechanism of inhibition, i.e. by the judicious, mutually compensating distribution of quantity. He writes:

> If the (bound) state consists in only small Qs being left for displacement (...), how can it draw fresh neurones into it - that is, cause large Qs to travel into fresh neurones? And, carrying the same difficulty further back, how can an ego compounded in this way have been able to develop at all? Thus we find ourselves quite unexpectedly before the most obscure problem: the origin of the "ego" - that is, of a complex of neurones which hold fast to their cathexis.[41]

Freud is saying that it would seem impossible to deploy a quantity for the purpose of inhibition if the only source for the inhibiting quantity is precisely that which is to be inhibited. You can make a bucket of water balance another bucket of water on opposite ends of a see-saw, but the

water won't separate into two buckets of its own accord. Freud's definition of the ego, as we already saw, is "the totality of the ψ cathexes, at the given time".[42] But in order to do the job, for which it is intended – that of inhibiting the flow of quantity – the ego must be *outside* this totality, controlling it by inhibition. How can it possibly get outside of itself?

Freud tackles the "most obscure problem" head on in this passage:

> The ego consists originally of the nuclear neurones, which receive endogenous $Q\eta$ [...]. The experience of satisfaction has brought about an association between this nucleus and a perceptual image (the wishful image) and information of a movement [...]. The education and development of this original ego takes place in a repetitive state of craving, in *expectation.* It [the ego] learns first that it must not cathect the motor images, so that discharge results, until certain conditions have been fulfilled from the direction of the perception. It learns further that it must not cathect the wishful idea beyond a certain amount since otherwise it would deceive itself in a hallucinatory manner.[43]

Most of this, I hope, makes rough sense based on the accounts I have given above (the "information of a movement" and the "motor images" both refer to the memory of the movement made to obtain satisfaction). The concept of hallucinatory self-deception requires comment. The *Project* has a (highly implausible) theory of the nature of consciousness, by which a special set of neurones, dubbed "ω neurones" are supposed sensitive to a certain "period" in quantities coming from the outside world, such that stimulation of the ω neurones by this period produces consciousness.[44] Freud adds that "the ω excitation leads to ω discharge and information of this as of every discharge, reaches ψ" and he concludes that "*The information of the discharge from ω is thus the indication of quality or of reality for ψ*".[45] It can serve as an "indication of reality" because, Freud says, only a perception (not a memory) has the special "period" that can stimulate ω. However, Freud allows an exception to this rule: if the memory of an object "is abundantly cathected, so that it is activated in a hallucinatory manner, the same indication of discharge or of reality follows too as in the case of external perception. In this case the criterion fails".[46]

This hallucinatory self-deception is a good place to start unpicking the last passage. If the ego has learnt that it must not over-cathect the "wishful idea", or else risk self-deception, then it *already knows* that this idea is just an idea, and not a here-and-now perception. So how could it possibly "deceive itself" on this point? Freud here seems to express, in a form so blatant that it seems incredible he did not notice it, the paradox, which inspired Sartre's famous critique of psychoanalysis.[47]

There is also an objection to be addressed to the German and English editors of the *Project* text. Strachey inserts a footnote after the word "education" in the sentence "the education and development of this original ego...", where he writes: "The MS. reads quite clearly "Entzieh(un)g" ("withdrawal')".[48]

Strachey says that he accepted the amendment of this word by the German editors to "Erziehung" ("education") because it is "very plausible". I disagree. Surely, "withdrawal" is just the sort of concept we are looking for in order to explain the "origin of the ego", to explain how the ego can, as I have put it, "get outside of itself".

But, if we put back the word "withdrawal", the effect (in conjunction with the previous sentence) is not to express any partition of the ego. Rather, the withdrawal is clearly that of the ego nucleus from association with two other items, "a perceptual image (the wishful image) and information of a movement".

I think we now have to take seriously my suggestion earlier that questioning of a superficial consistency in Freud's theoretical texts is sometimes necessary in order to follow a deeper logic, just as it is necessary to look beyond secondary revision in a dream text.

I have called attention to Freud's assertion of a "resemblance which in fact exists between the nucleus of the ego and the constant perceptual component" (i.e., one part of the duplex perception of the satisfying object) and have tried to show how this idea comes from Mill, whose explanation of our belief in mind and matter place both of the latter in a structurally identical place. I think that the point Freud is circling around is not mere resemblance, but *identity* between the object perception and the ego. And (here I make the Lacanian jump) Mill's set of sensations / presentations linked by association are what mediate this identity, because Freud intuits in them the system of the signifier. The duplex nature of the object perception is Freud's expression of how the essence of the signifier system, as articulated, goes proxy for the object and thereby generates the ego, which is just the Lacanian subject

That may sound like a metaphysical incantation, but let me try to show how it works in Freud's text. We would naturally assume that the last two sentences of his response to "the most obscure problem", where Freud expresses the paradox of self-deception with apparent naivety, are based on the mechanism, described above, by which over-cathexis of a memory in ψ produces consciousness in the ω-neurones, causing ω-discharge, information of which comes back to ψ.[49] But when Freud describes the experience of satisfaction earlier in the *Project*, shortly after a detailed account of consciousness as dependent on the ω-neurones, he writes:

> there is a basic law of association by simultaneity [...] which is the foundation of all links between the ψ neurones. We find that consciousness—that is the quantitative cathexis of a ψ neurone, α,—passes over to another, β, if α and β have at some time been simultaneously cathected.[50]

It is clear from the context that α and β here refer to the object memory and the memory of a movement from the experience of satisfaction and, as Strachey writes in a note, "it is surprising to find consciousness thus defined, apparently without reference to ω".[51] Indeed, coming just a few pages after an extensive explanation of consciousness in terms of the ω neurones, it is an aberration no less surprising than the absurdity in our "origin of the ego" passage, whereby the ego supposedly does not cathect a memory image in order to avoid taking it for a perceptual image (if it knows enough to withhold cathexis, it must already know that the image is not perceptual)

I think that these two aberrations are to be explained together. In the "origin" passage (contrary to Freud's own words) there is not really any learning by the ego, and it is not the ego that has to learn not to "cathect the wishful idea beyond a certain amount", because the ego only comes into existence *by means of this withholding of cathexis*. What Freud is really describing is how, first, the whole of the signifier system with its mutually defining elements goes proxy for a "Vorstellung", the image of the satisfying object (this proxying is what Freud is referring to when he equates consciousness with free passage of quantity between two neurones, earlier in the *Project*,[52] and the neurones are to be taken as signifiers) and then, second, how this free passage is curtailed by primal repression (this is what is described in the last two sentences of the "origin" passage),[53] when association from one particular signifier is prevented. That signifier is thereafter the core of the repressed, but, mysteriously, it is also Lacan's subject (Freud's and Mill's ego), which is thereby brought into being, or, perhaps better to say, placed in a certain position – that of an exteriority to the signifier system, a position which enables the whole system, including the repressed signifier itself, to be encompassed simultaneously. This is Lacan's primordial symbolization, the creation of "an original within, which is not a bodily within but that of an initial body of signifiers."[54]

Freud's intuition is that conscious experience, as containing an implicit self-awareness, is somehow dependent on a gap where, contrary to what Wittgenstein thinks, there *is* "something I don't see",[55] but something that (sidestepping Wittgenstein's impossible demand) I don't point at, but *believe in*. The fact that the philosopher disallows the possibility of such a

place could be symptomatic of the "Unglauben" (lack of belief) that Freud and Lacan take as definitive of psychosis.[56] [refs].

What drew Freud to the *Examination* chapters and made him build their arguments into the *Project* at a very deep level is Mill's manoeuvre, which makes belief in the ego and in the object (the two beliefs are really the same) into a belief in absent sensations, those "sensations" being, in fact, signifiers. This arrangement gives Freud the structure of repression, which I have just described.

This raises the obvious question, which I will briefly address in conclusion. Can it make sense to suppose that Freud found a prototype of the signifier system (Saussurean langue) in a mid-19th century work by J.S. Mill? I think it can. Consider a passage such as this in the first of the two *Examination* chapters that have interested us:

> The differences which our consciousness recognises between one sensation and another, give us the general notions of difference, and inseparably associate with every sensation we have, the feeling of its being different from other things: and when once this association has been formed, we can no longer conceive anything, without being able, and even compelled, to form also the conception of something different from it.[57]

What other field is defined by constituents, each of which is inconceivable without the conception of "something different from it"? And in the passage cited earlier[58] what are we reminded of when Mill tells us that sensations are "so linked together that the presence of one announces the possible presence at the very same instant of any or all of the rest"? I find these passages highly evocative of Saussure's system of "langue", and a direct influence of Mill's work on the invention of structural linguistics was traced by no less a figure than Roman Jakobson.[59]

Notes

[1] Wittgenstein, *Philosophical Investigations*, 120.
[2] Ibid., 207.
[3] Wittgenstein, *The Blue and Brown Books*, 71.
[4] Ibid., 71.
[5] Wittgenstein, *Philosophical Investigations*, 102.
[6] Lacan, *Seminar XX*, 50.
[7] Freud, *Standard Edition,* Vol. XIX, 233-240.
[8] Ibid., 238.
[9] Ibid., 236.
[10] Ibid., 236.
[11] Lacan, *Seminar III*, 150.

---

[12] Freud, *Standard Edition,* Vol. V, 488-509.
[13] Freud, *Standard Edition,* Vol.I, 281-391.
[14] Lacan suggested such a diagnosis based on consideration of the philosopher's work (*Seminar XVII*, pp. 59-62) and William Bartley III's affectionate and unsanctimonious biography (*Wittgenstein)* gives a strong sense of how genius and mental instability were combined in the philosopher.
[15] Freud, *Standard Edition.* Vol.I, 296-297 (all preceding references in this paragraph).
[16] Ibid., 327.
[17] Ibid., 328.
[18] Ibid., 328-329.
[19] Ibid., 323.
[20] Ibid., 328, 369.
[21] Freud, *On Aphasia*, 77.
[22] Mill, *An Examination of Sir William Hamilton's Philosophy,* 177-187.
[23] Ibid., 177.
[24] Ibid., 178.
[25] Ibid., 180.
[26] Freud, *Standard Edition*, Vol.I, 327.
[27] Ibid., 328.
[28] The reason, in brief, is that Berkeley, Mill's idealist forefather, treated the substance/attribute contrast as equivalent to the contrast between the real world and our sense experience.
[29] Ibid., 328.
[30] Mill, *An Examination of Sir William Hamilton's Philosophy,* 188-195.
[31] Ibid., 188.
[32] Ibid., 188.
[33] Ibid., 189.
[34] Ibid., 189.
[35] Ibid., 189.
[36] Ibid., 189.
[37] Freud, *Standard Edition*, Vol.I, 328.
[38] Freud, *Standard Edition*, Vol.I, 369.
[39] Ibid., 319.
[40] Ibid., 323.
[41] Ibid., 369.
[42] Ibid., 323.
[43] Ibid., 369.
[44] Ibid., 310.
[45] Ibid., 325.
[46] Ibid., 325.
[47] Sartre, *Being and Nothingness*, 88-117.
[48] Freud, *Standard Edition*, Vol.I, 369
[49] Ibid., 325.
[50] Ibid., 319.

[51] Ibid., 319.
[52] Ibid., 319.
[53] Ibid., 369.
[54] Lacan, *Seminar III*, 150
[55] Wittgenstein, *The Blue and Brown Books*, 71
[56] Freud, *Freud-Fliess*, 168; Lacan *The Four Fundamental Concepts*, 238.
[57] Mill, *An Examinaton of Sir William Hamilton's Philosophy*, 185
[58] Ibid., 180.
[59] Jakobson, *Roman Jakobson. Selected Writings*, Vol. 2, 429-449.

References

Bartley, W.W. III. *Wittgenstein*. La Salle, IL: Open Court, 1979.

Freud, S. "Negation". *The Standard Edition of the Complete Psychological Works of Sigmund Freud*, Volume XIX. London: The Hogarth Press and the Institute of Psychoanalysis, 1953-74.

—. "The Interpretation of Dreams". *The Standard Edition of the Complete Psychological Works of Sigmund Freud*, Volume V. London: The Hogarth Press and the Institute of Psychoanalysis, 1953-74.

—. "Project for a Scientific Psychology". *The Standard Edition of the Complete Psychological Works of Sigmund Freud*, Volume I. London: The Hogarth Press and the Institute of Psychoanalysis, 1953-74.

—. *On Aphasia*. Translated by E. Stengel. London: Imago Publishing, 1953.

—. *The Complete Letters of Sigmund Freud to Wilhelm Fliess, 1887-1904.* Translated by Jeffrey Moussaieff Masson. Cambridge, Massachusetts: Belknap Press, 1985.

Jakobson. R. "Znachenye Krushevskogo v razvitii nauki o yazyke" ["Kruszewski's part in the development of linguistic science"] in *Roman Jakobson. Selected Writings,* Vol. 2. The Hague: Mouton, 1971.

Lacan, J. *The Psychoses. The Seminar of Jacques Lacan, Book III.* Translated by Russell Grigg. London: Routledge, 1993.

—. *The Four Fundamental Concepts of Psychoanalysis*. Translated by Alan Sheridan. London: Penguin Books, 1979.

—. *The Other Side of Psychoanalysis*, *The Seminar of Jacques Lacan, Book XVII.* Translated by Russell Grigg. New York: Norton, 2007.

—. *Encore, The Seminar of Jacques Lacan, Book XX.* Translated by Bruce Fink. New York: W.W. Norton, 1999.

Mill, J.S. *An Examination of Sir William Hamilton's Philosophy*. Toronto: University of Toronto Press, 1979.

—. *A System of Logic*. Toronto: University of Toronto Press, 1979.

Sartre, J.P. *Being and Nothingness*. New York: Washington Square Press, 1992.

Wittgenstein, L. *Preliminary Studies for the "Philosophical Investigations", generally known as The Blue and The Brown Books.* Oxford: Basil Blackwell, 1958.

—. *Philosophical Investigations*. Oxford: Basil Blackwell, 1958.

CHAPTER THREE

PHILOSOPHY AT THE *BAR* WITH FREUD AND LACAN; THE *SUBJECT*: BEING, ALWAYS IN THE WRONG PLACE AT THE WRONG TIME...

RAPHAEL MONTAGUE

1. Introduction: *Ontos/Logos*

> […] there exists a problem in semantics which is finally insoluble […] [1]

The following essay in terms of method is, broadly speaking, operating at the interface of philosophy and psychoanalytic theory; with regard to the ontology of the subject and the implicit relation therein to the question of language. The initial aim is to situate generally the emergence of psychoanalytic theory against a background of traditional, as well as continental, metaphysics and epistemology. The work does not however represent a philosophical study, in the sense of an assessment, with regard to the various strengths and weaknesses of the arguments and themes presented. Such a study may be of future merit, in order to provide support for say, a *weak* materialism *versus* a *strong* idealism, or other such typical philosophical correlations. This essay with regard to method is rather a contextualisation which aims to establish a Lacanian theorisation of the subject as emerging through discourse, in a relatedness to general philosophical thematics. The findings, as they emerge over the course of the study, do however have distinct relevance for both ontology and epistemology, with perhaps correlative implications for both philosophy and science.

In Section Two will we examine something of the philosophical origins of psychoanalytic theory in the work of Freud, in particular with regard to the themes *Eros*, the primordial lost-object and lack. We will engage in a discussion of epistemology and symbolic systems, science and

psychoanalytic theory, in relation to concepts of displacement and lack as well as those of the signifier and the temporal facticity of language. This discussion engenders the formulation and re-formulation of one of the key questions of the essay: "What is the relationship between the word and the thing?" Also presented is an engagement regarding the binary oppositions of metaphysics, in the work of Derrida, Laruelle and Meillasoux, which will serve to facilitate a general positioning of Lacanian theory in terms of various strands of thinking about ontology.

Section Three involves a reading of Lacanian theory from *Seminar XI* regarding the ontological status of lack and the gap of the unconscious. This is connected to an examination of the origins of Freud's *Trieb* in traditional Greek philosophical thought, as well a contemporary psychoanalytical discussion of the function of lack and the death drive. Here we ultimately arrive at the point that perhaps fundamental ontology, in the traditional sense, at least from the point of view of Aristotle, is insufficient to account for the Freudian death drive and the Lacanian concept of *jouissance*. Particular reference is made to Freud's discoveries in his study of the neurotic's symptom and therefore the theorised conflict between *Ich Trieb* and the pleasure principle.

In Section Four we return to the question of the relationship between the word and the thing, giving attention to the structural interface between *Trieb*, language and *das Ding*. In this section, in an effort to disclose something of the correlations between the unconscious, language, subjectivity and the drive, we will further examine the causality of the subject in the context of Lacan's Structuralism. This discussion is to allow us to situate a contextualisation of the "logic of the signifier", in relation to the emergence of the subject as divided by language and to Freud's theory of *Trieb*. Section Five represents a discussion of the "logic of the signifier" as that which establishes a connection between displacement and lack, as well as providing us with a representation of the emergence of the subject within a logical rather than phenomenological framework. The function of metaphor and metonymy in the Lacanian *oeuvre* are here discussed in relation to subjectivity and causality.

In the essay's Conclusion we will return to a number of key questions and themes which have emerged during the course of reading and writing. What is the relationship between the word and the thing? Is there a constitutive relationship, with structural underpinnings, between the subject and the thing-in-itself? And if so what are the roles of the symbolic order, language and lack in that structure? Does language effect a disturbance in the real of the body? If the subject is an effect then what is its cause? What is the relationship between psychoanalysis and ontology?

These questions are again considered in terms of constitutive, theoretical links (by way of findings) in relation to the subject and the Other with regard to the main concepts of the text: the drive, the signifier, the unconscious, *das Ding* and lack. The broad conclusion is that, essentially the Lacanian divided subject has no essence or ontological substance and in fact is no more than a pre-ontological, indeterminate non-being, where identity is a retrospective *ego*.

2. The Lack_The Void_The Break...

> The nature of human reason is such that there is an intrinsic plausibility about any hypothesis which seeks to explain the manifold in terms of unity, to reduce apparent multiplicity to essential identity.[2]

It is fair to say that situated historically, philosophy and psychoanalytic theory have not made for exactly comfortable bedfellows. Despite the discomfort and perceived breach of taboo that is undoubtedly caused by their intercourse, they do however remain near cousins and mutual attractors. From Freud's practical neo-Platonism and Aristotelianism, in *Beyond The Pleasure Principle,* to Lacan's reworking of, for example, Plato's *Symposium* with regard to the lost object, desire and lack, sexuality and death, as well his inversion of Descartes' *cogito* with regard to a psychoanalytic theorisation of the subject, there has been a distinct inter-locution between psychoanalytic theory and philosophy. Freud in *Beyond The Pleasure Principle,* proposes a potential dualism of *Eros* and *Thanatos, Eros* being in an Aristotelian sense prime-mover, from which for Freud, the death drive emerges;[3] all the while though Freud is bemoaning the fact that by doing so, "we have unwittingly steered ourselves into the harbour of Schopenhauer's philosophy".[4] Lacan in *Seminar XI* takes up this point by offering a psychoanalytic alternative to the Platonic articulation, through *Aristophanes*' myth in the *Symposium*, that what the living being seeks in love "is the other, one's sexual other half".[5] Lacan argues that what in fact is sought is the forever lost part of the sexed living being, which he loses through reproducing himself. Immortality as exchanged for reproductive capacity, a concept which Lacan articulates through the myth of the lamella.[6] Indeed, according to Clemens, Lacan despite being an avowed "anti-philosopher", avails in his *Seminars* and *Écrits* of practically the complete Western tradition".[7] Clemens expresses Lacan's ambivalent relationship to philosophy succinctly, as that of a "deeply antagonistic commitment".[8] Freud however ultimately appears rather indifferent towards ontological philosophy, preferring a conceptualisation of underlying biochemical causation for the

event of the psychical apparatus. Freud is clear on this in his definition of *Trieb* in *Instincts and Their Vicissitudes* (1915)[9] and *The Question of Lay Analysis* (1926).[10]

In a contemporary contextualisation of philosophy and psychoanalytic theory there has been a clear resurgence of the Metaphysical tradition. I believe that this is a response to the failed expectation that epistemology and scientific discourse might finally answer some of the big *recurring-questions* regarding the nature of existence, the status of knowledge and truth, or being versus non being. Situated in the ontic rather than the ontological, epistemology is a retreat, or as Heidegger might say a *fallenness*, the finding-of-oneself in a position, thereby precluding the question of Being-in-itself. Verhaeghe, in *On Being Normal and Other Disorders,* articulates this position clearly in his discussion regarding the impotence of epistemology. Verhaeghe situates the fundamental problem of epistemology as a question: What the relationship is between the word and the thing? He identifies how this question is treated in the contradictory Metaphysical approaches of *idealism* and *materialism* and their corresponding epistemological opposition between *nominalism* and *realism*. In particular, in relation to the differences in linguistic considerations associated with each.[11] Science, for example, is a symbolic system (as well as mathematics, ethics, aesthetics, music, etc.) through which we can represent a study of the real as perceived. This implies that science, because it is a symbolic system, cannot be realised outside of signifiers. There clearly must be at least two signifiers in order to represent difference, and thus the *modus operandum* of science must be displacement. The relationship of signifier to signifier, Lacan's S_1 and S_2, as well as that of signifier to signified, occurring in a temporal facticity, with signification being an arbitrary contextually dependent event, founded on difference.[12] Verhaeghe argues that what makes it possible for humans to reflect from a "mediated meta-standpoint" is a combination of displacement and lack. Lack as conceived of as that structure which facilitates, the occurrence of displacement. (I will expand on this point in Section Five with regard to the relationship between the *subject*, the "logic of the signifier and Frege's theory of numbers: around what Verhaeghe describes as a "logical need for lack".[13]) For the sake of brevity, Verhaeghe's broad conclusion is that:

> The lack of object is both the cause and possibility of every symbolic system and therefore also of science. It is the cause because it is precisely the loss of the Real effected through language that drives our endless attempts to recover the Real. It is the condition of possibility because it maintains the necessary opening of the Symbolic system that enables displacement to take place.[14]

The consequences of this are that expressly no symbolic system can appropriate the thing-in-itself, but the realisation here allows us to approach the traditional philosophical impasse, represented by the juxtaposition of nominalism and realism in a different way.[15] We can conceive of the question as follows: Is there a constitutive relationship, with structural underpinnings, between the subject and the thing-in-itself? And if so what are the roles of The Symbolic order, language and lack in that structure?[16]

From a contemporary philosophical perspective, in the speculative realism of Meillasoux, for example, we can see an anti-hegemonic thought, a thorough questioning of what is essentially an epistemological egocentric position, where the "individual human subject" is given, in the context of structured thought, a situational, or an *a priori* primacy over other objects/entities, because of our perception of an a-parent, or singular consciousness.[17] In *Time Without Becoming* Meillasoux outlines "correlationism" as the contemporary opponent of any realism, the general form of the correlationist argument being that "there are no objects, no events, no laws, no beings which are not already correlated with a point of view, with a subjective access."[18]

We can see a response to the mainstream continuation of, in my reading of it, the flawed Aristotelian logical dualism of either/or as opposed to both/and in the work of Derrida. In terms of his engagement with phenomenology and also the "structuralist project", he makes two interesting determinations on this point which are relevant here. The first, a direct argument against dualism, made in his reading of Rousset's aesthetics found in *Writing and Difference.* The tendency towards analysis of "structure" in itself as the main object of study Derrida names as "ultra-structuralism".[19] Derrida's counterfoil to this is not to further the existing binary oppositions by arguing for more time rather than space or for force over form, but for a new set of concepts, a radical move away from the traditional binary oppositions of Metaphysics.[20]

In Derrida's paper *Pour l"amour de Lacan,* he states that "lack has no place in dissemination".[21] In *Dissemination* we can read Derrida's argument that Lacan proposes lack as a transcendental signifier and in doing so engenders a reinterpretation of traditional Metaphysical values:

> If dissemination cannot simply be equated with what castration entails or entrains (one should not become [en]trained in reading this word) this is not only because of its affirmative character but also because, at least up to now, according to a necessity that is anything but accidental, the concept of castration has been metaphysically interpreted and arrested. The lack, the void, the break etc., having been given the value of a signified or, which

> amounts to the same, a transcendental signifier: the self-presentation of truth (veiled/unveiled) as *Logos.*[22]

One aspect of this is certain, namely that Derrida is clear that Lacanian theory has firmly engaged with Metaphysics in such a manner as to effect a displacement in philosophical thought.

Following critiques of the *cogito* from Nietzsche, Heidegger, Kant and Husserl, post-Cartesian theories of the subject have broadly taken two strands. Contemporary philosophers and psychoanalytic theorists Althusser, Lacan, Badiou and Žižek have taken an interest in the Cartesian subject in terms of the attempted production of a surpassment which has generated according to Laruelle, "a major disjunction on the synchronic plane".[23] On the one hand Lacan, Althusser and their followers producing a mathematical psychoanalytic subject of the unconscious, based in the concept of lack (Zero, having the proper name *one* representing *a concept of that thing which is not identical to itself*) and on the other hand, Henry after Husserl, according to Laruelle, argues for a "undivided immanence of the Ego",[24] a not scientific and not objectifying view. The resultant production has been what Laruelle describes as an antimony, "the new antimony of the philosophical subject".[25] The current situation we find ourselves in, being that of a generalised "transcendental dialectic" of the modern versus post-modern subject.[26]

The introduction of Frege's theory of numbers into the Lacanian concept of the subject in Miller's paper *the Suture*, what Badiou describes as "the first piece of Lacanian theory not written by Lacan himself",[27] is an important event which merits a closer look. A recent renewed interest in this important exchange between Lacan and Miller, has been generated by the publication of *Concept and Form, volume one and volume two* (2012)[28] as well as the recent announcement from Miller that *Cahiers pour L'Analyse* is to be revived in 2014.[29] Lacan theorises in *Seminar XI* the subject as "grounded in the structuring function of a lack"[30] and posits that the "unconscious cannot be questioned in ontological framework because it is pre-ontological".[31] Miller, in *Action of the Structure* and *The Suture* attempts to provide us with a logical/mathematical structural foundation for this Lacanian argument.

It seems clear that Freud's invention of psychoanalysis has produced some interesting theoretical entanglements between philosophy and psychoanalytic theory. In particular it seems that the *subject* has once again taken centre stage. It is the purpose of the following sections of this essay to examine and elucidate this interface, with regard to a theorisation of the Lacanian subject, using the following parameters or themes: *Eros*, *Trieb*, The Logic of the Signifier and Lack. The study is oriented by the

compass of structuralism and Lacan's considerations of the subject as produced, as representation, by language.

3. Freud's Biological Bedrock

> The subject matter of the Perennial Philosophy is the nature of eternal, spiritual Reality; but the language in which it must be formulated was developed for the purpose of dealing with phenomena in time. That is why, in all of these formulations, we find an element of paradox. The nature of Truth-the-fact cannot be described by means of verbal symbols that do not adequately correspond to it. At best it can be hinted at in terms of *non sequiteurs* and contradictions.[32]

To situate our discussion in historic particularity, for example, Heidegger's *Dasein,* and the Lacanian subject are not really an equivocal juxtaposition. Conceptually *Dasein* does not represent the particular subject for Heidegger, no more than the Lacanian subject, for Lacan, represents the individual as "one" human being. Miller in his "*Theory of Turin"* states that: "The individual and their subjectivity are not equivalent. The subject is not undivided nor is it situated at the level of the undivided. What is individual, is a body, it is the *ego*. The subject-effect that is produced within the individual, and which disturbs its functions, is articulated with the big Other".[33] This is a concise but detailed statement which encompasses the body problem and a link to the subject as effect rather than cause. The subject is *represented* as an effect of language, as articulated in the field of the Other, or the Symbolic order.[34] What is of particular importance for this essay is the conceptualisation that the subject, as an articulated-effect, causes disturbance in the functions of the body or at the level of the *individual.* Is Miller alluding to the possibility that language effects a disturbance in the real of the body? And if the subject is an effect then what is its cause? These are important questions with regard to both philosophy and psychoanalytic theory, which I will try to interrogate in the following sections, in terms of clarifying a theorisation of the status of subject conceptually and with regard to the themes as outlined in Section Two.

To say something of ontology in a Heideggerian sense, when the necessary question of Being is asked, as Miller puts to Lacan in 1964: "What is your ontology?" What is he asking? Is he asking Lacan, the psychoanalyst; how, in psychoanalysis, do we organise our *logos* on the basis of the question of *ontos*: that of our existence or being? Or perhaps the question is in the context of *Da-sein:* the *Da* being the *topos* or place where the question of being is unconcealed. The "there" where *sein/is,* as

being-questioned. Interestingly Lacan remarks in *Seminar XI* that he ought to have asked for a definition of the question from Miller.[35] In any case Lacan offers Miller a quintessentially *Lacanian* juxtaposition, by way of answer to his question: "[…] in that when speaking of this gap one is dealing with an ontological function, by which I thought I had to introduce, it being the most essential, the function of the unconscious."[36] Lacan continues by stating that: "The gap of the unconscious may be said to be pre-ontological."[37]

The juxtaposition seems to be articulated in terms of the treatment of the "concept of lack",[38] its correlation to desire, what Lacan designates as *manque-à-être* (a want to be) and its structuring function in relation to the second gap; Lacan refers to a gap in the capacity of ontological function which is not articulated as that of the unconscious, as the gap related to subjectivity. I will come to a more detailed treatment of this problematic in Section Four when dealing with Lacan on language, the subject and the "logic of the signifier", as well as in the Conclusion of the essay with a discussion of Verhaeghe's treatment of the emergence of the subject, namely "… the constitution of the subject is based on the interaction between life and death, two different lacks, and their overlap".[39]

Verhaeghe in "*Causation and Destitution*" refers to what he considers three key Freudian texts (*Beyond The Pleasure Principle* is the one to which I will refer here) which contain the structural elements of Freud's move away from the universality of the pleasure principle and a singular irrevocable lack around which the Freudian drive revolves, around which the ego was considered to be constituted. The drive is described as insisting on the impossible restoration of the original homoeostasis, which was disturbed by the pre-genital loss.[40] As is clear in the footnote here taken from Freud's *Analysis Terminable and Interminable* (1937) castration, the fear of loss or lack of a penis is linked for Freud to the original pre-genital loss and therefore the irrevocable lack around which every drive revolves. Verhaeghe argues that Freud's introduction of the concept of the death drive into psychoanalytic theory, is that which enables both Freud and Lacan to move beyond the pessimism of Freud's "biological bedrock"[41] of castration as the limit of psychoanalysis and will serve Lacan as a starting point in terms of his theorisation of two lacks, four forms of object a (the original lost object) and the conceptualisation of death as the price paid for human sexuality, or phylogenetic reproductive capability.[42]

For a contextualisation of traditional ontology and psychoanalytic theory with regard to lack we can look to a metaphysical discussion of Love or *Eros*, to see how psychoanalytic theory combined with philosophy

might potentially operate at the interface of ontological difference and thinking-in-itself. It is possible to engender a dialectical unconcealing of "thinking as love-in-itself", which reveals something of the philosophical origins of Freudian/Lacanian analytic discourse as originated in Greek philosophy. This however ultimately can be contrasted with Freud's reading of Eros and therefore the Freudian pleasure principle, which is seen as something which in fact disturbs the self-preserving tendency of life. According to Clemens: "Pure pleasure ultimately implies the death of the organism driven by it."[43]

Jean-Luc Nancy in *Four Little Dialogues* makes an interesting observation regarding the articulation of love: He says "the statement I love you" is absolute, detached from everything from every measurement and comparison. "True love begins beyond every possibility of setting up quantities or degrees of comparison. True love begins on the order of the absolute."[44] For me Nancy is emphasising the articulation of love as a question which is ontological, as opposed to ontic. It belongs to the order of a fundamental questioning of our Being-in-itself and our Being-in-the-world-with-others.[45] The question of love as ontological has a distinct relevance to contemporary psychoanalytic theory and praxis. Juan-David Nasio, in "*The Book of Love and Pain*", speaks of love as absolute, in terms of an insurmountable paradox which is constitutive of our being, yet renders us entirely vulnerable. He writes that in human nature love remains the incontrovertible premise of our suffering.[46] Nasio, as psychoanalyst, is perhaps here operating at the interface of thinking and ontological difference, or pure-difference. In employing the dialectal resources of ontology, Nasio prepares the ground for a psychoanalytic unconcealing of the question regarding love and pain and their correlatives, desire and lack.

Nasio says of pain that "pain in-itself has no value or signification [...] the psychoanalyst is an intermediary who takes an in-assimilable pain and transforms it into pain that is symbolised."[47] To situate such thinking in its traditional Western origins we can look to Aristotle's Metaphysics and Plato's Symposium. In his *Metaphysics VII* Aristotle articulates the idea of the divine, absolute, or whole as *Eros*; or erotic mover for thought-as-being. Aristotle argues that the desire towards articulation of thought-as-being-in-itself announces an underlying erotic principle. An erotic longing which belongs to all living things which is expressed differently according to particular ability.[48] For Aristotle the touching power of desire is rooted in logos: a saying which assiduously seeks to articulate the being-of-that-which-appears. He writes of a correlation between desire and thought when he says that "thinking is the beginning".[49] He says of love and

thought that to articulate what is thought in terms of the beloved is to suggest at once the erotic nature of the first principle and the peculiar manner in which, not only is it related to the whole, but also relates the whole somehow to itself.

In *Metaphysics VII, 8,* Aristotle asserts a theorisation of subject and object in a relatedness to thought, from which I think, we could take an Aristotelian reading of the psychoanalytic theorisation of Lacan's object *a* and the analyst's desire/position in the transference, as detailed in Lacan's Schema L. The primary object of thinking with which Aristotle is concerned, is that primary desire which is at work holding itself. To clarify: We are not to understand the object of thinking as some definite entity in an ontic sense, rather the object of thinking is in this case "a mode of being which is the paradigm of being in general" and therefore might occupy an ontological primacy in our questioning.[50]

Aristotle defines this as self-holding, as an activity, "being-at-work at work being".[51] Its objectivity is the activity of self-holding that poignantly expresses the cooperation between subject and object, which is the possibility for the condition of an encounter. This is potentially comparable to the analyst's desire that Lacan describes in his seminar on *Transference* when he says that the difference between the analyst and one who has not been analysed is that the analyst has undergone a mutation in his or her desire,[52] with relation perhaps to an ontological thinking, that facilitates this Aristotelian position of "self-holding" in the transference. The analyst desires the articulation of the particular truth of the subject, as a saying, in the encounter between subjectivity, need/lack and demand/desire. This analytic encounter suspends all the assurances of ordinary inter-subjectivity. The ordinary inter-subjectivity which Lacan represents on the imaginary axis of Schema L, as per ego to other ego.[53]

Aristotle is essentially following on from Plato, who in *The Symposium* has Socrates establish some correlations between the object of longing and that of love.[54] Freud posits an opposition, therefore a dualism, of life and death drives and argues that object-love offers up a complementary polarity: that of love and hate. The task he then sets for himself is to relate these two polarities to each other and at the same time essentially to derive one from the other. To accomplish this he references the recognition of a sadistic element of the sexual instinct which "emerges as a predominant component drive in one of the "pre-genital organisations" and poses the question as to how this sadistic instinct could possibly be derived from Eros, "the preserver of life"?[55] Freud hypothesises that this sadism is actually a death drive "which under the influence of the narcissistic libido has been forced away from the ego and has only consequently emerged in

relation to the object."[56] The death drive is essentially appropriated by the libido and in the same sense as it functions during the oral stage of the organisation of the libido, is now put to service in the sexual reproductive aim of mastery over the object, in terms of an overpowering function necessary to carry out the sexual act. So in effect for Freud, the sadism wrapped up in the death drive is that which provides compass and orientation for human sexual capacity.

To say that desire is comprised of tension and unpleasure would be accurate. In the ordinarily situated unconscious system we find a tolerable state of dissatisfaction, of a desire that is never totally realised. Juan-David Nasio describes this ever-present psychical tension as in no way expressing a pessimistic view of the human condition. He argues that: "On the contrary, this statement amounts to declaring that throughout our existence we will fortunately be in a state of lack".[57] Nasio conceives of desire as a helixical movement of energy, spiralling around a central void in our being, circumscribing an irreducible lack. Nasio continues by saying that this ever-present "degree of insatisfaction is thus vital for us in order to conserve our psychical stability".[58]

It is exactly here again that we could situate the role of the analyst, as Nasio conceives of the relation of the subject to their love-object: "*he or she plays the role of the unsatisfactory object of the analysand's desire and thereby of the organising pole of desire*".[59] The analyst has this castrating function of limiting the analysand's satisfaction thus allowing the analysand the space to re-inscribe their relation and tolerance to their fundamental lack or *manque à être*, the dissatisfaction or pre-ontological lack which "fortunately", according to Nasio, is a requirement in order for us to live.

De Kesel makes the point that in dealing with a neurotic symptom such as Anna O"s, Freud noted that despite her complaints of the pain of her paralysis she nevertheless took pleasure in what was said to be hurting her. In point of fact, Anna O derived an unconscious pleasure from her symptom. For Freud thus, a neurotic symptom is the result of a persisting conflict between two opposing principles, the "*Ich trieb*" ("ego-drives") and the libido (pleasure principle).[60] Freud in *Formulations on the Two Principles of Mental Functioning* will therefore argue that it is the pleasure principle which in fact is that which at its most basic perverts the human life function.[61] This according to De Kesel is a crucial novelty of psychoanalytic theory which however, does not quite fit with our reading of Eros as prime mover and thought as love-ontology.[62]

4. Take *apart*/ take *a part*...

> St. Paul distinguished between the letter that kills and the spirit that gives life. And throughout the centuries that followed, the masters of Christian spirituality have found it necessary to harp again and again upon a theme that has never been outdated because *homo loqax*, the talking animal, is still as naïvely delighted by his chief accomplishment, still as helplessly the victim of his own words, as he was when the Tower of Babel was being built.[63]

I am returning to Verhaeghe's question as cited in Section Two: "What is the relationship between the word and the thing?" in order to try and situate it within the specificity of the Lacanian hypothesis as outlined by Colette Soler and to look at something of its origin within Freud's *Trieb* theory. Soler argues of the Lacanian hypothesis that, "It concerns more than the function of speech in the field of language, it defines the function of speech and language in the field of living *jouissance*."[64] Soler contends that Lacan's hypothesis diverges from what he showed us with regard to the Freudian Unconscious being structured like a language, "since it asserts fundamentally that the unconscious and its effects on human beings are consequences of language.[65] There is an effect of language which we can recognise in the drive, which implies that language is operative in the Real and capable of effecting transformation therein.[66]

Homo loquax becomes parl-être: from talking-man to speaking-being.

Therefore it seems that the Lacanian argument in relation to our question is that language is the cause of *das Ding* (the thing), which Soler describes as "something like a hole in the real, something that creates a will to *jouissance*, a constant pressing towards satisfaction". Language is thus not only the cause of human de-naturation but also perhaps the only way we have of satisfying, at least partially, the demands of *das Ding.*[67]

The hypothesis has a direct relation to Freud's drive theory and his distinction between two types of drive satisfaction: that of the symptom, implying repression and that of sublimation which does not suppose repression, but implies a resolution of conflicts. In a very straightforward sense we are here oriented by language where in the case of repression we suppose a fixation of *jouissance* produced by the first encounter with sexuality, which returns through metonymy or displacement (Lacan's S_1 to S_2). In the case of sublimation where the lack or gap of *das Ding* was there is a production or invention, an object which provides partial satisfaction.[68] Citing Joyce's suggestion from Finnegan's Wake that a letter

is also "a litter" Soler argues that Lacan was forced to recognise that any signifier could in fact be an object, particularly in the context of the *jouissance* contained within the symptom.[69] In theory, in the void of *das Ding* "we can put anything that will function as an associate of *jouissance*, but it will always be an invention of the unconscious."[70]

In *Seminar XI* Lacan engages us in a discussion of the Freudian unconscious, the understanding of which he privileges as a precursor to treating "the law of the signifier" in the domain of causality. This is the locus in which this gap is produced, which leads to a reading of Lacan delivering up the concept of the pre-ontological gap of the unconscious being the order of the non-realised.[71] Therefore the "law of the signifier" for Lacan has a causal effect in the place/spot/position where that gap of the unconscious is produced and effects the production of "something other which demands to be realised".[72] In the phenomenon of parapraxes, flashes of wit, dreams etc. Lacan identifies a common element which he variously describes as: "impediment", "rupture", "split", "failure", producing surprise in the subject as if by way of a discovery, something which overtakes the subject but becomes lost only to be rediscovered. There is a temporality at work here which involves a discontinuity or a disjunction, in which a *wavering-between* emerges. I will try to illustrate this somewhat with a clinical example of the production of the non-realised in the pre-ontological gap in relation to the concept of lack:

Analysand: It's about finding out...
Analyst: Finding out?
Analysand: Yes finding out. When I was a young boy I was compelled to take things *apart*...to see how they worked
Analyst: Mmhm
Analysand: Isn't that what we humans do? *Take a part*
Analyst: We'll leave it there.

Lacan's return to Freud and in particular his treatment of Freud's *second topography* in relation to his own theorisation of the subject, is of exceptional relevance here:

> The doctrinal revamping known as the second topography introduced the terms *ich*, *uber-ich* and even Es without certifying them as apparatus, introducing instead a reworking of analytic experience best defined as what structuralism has since allowed us to elaborate logically: namely, the subject – the subject caught up in a constituting division.[73]

According to Johnston there is a substratum in the above quotation which on the one hand is theorising the subject as barred, divided by its very non-being, pre-ontological, carved up by language of the Symbolic order, the language of the Other. On the other hand the subject is here however, decidedly irreducible to any one, two or three, or combination of, or all of Freud's topographical agencies of the psyche. The Lacanian subject is bound up in what Johnston calls the "quasi-insubstantial negativity of intra-psychical rifts".[74] If Lacan engages in a broad diachronic structuralism coming from Levi-Strauss, then ultimately he returns to Freud's theory of *Trieb*. The psyche and soma linked (theoretically at least) and in doing so can we argue that Lacan moves away from the reliance on a pure dialectical structuralism, based on language as the "horizon of being".[75]

Can we begin to think of Lacan's most commonly cited aphorism: the unconscious is structured like a language as: the un-conscious, as/like a language, is structured? In the causality of the subject therefore it is the division, or as we will see: place of the lack, which constitutes the subject; not the positivity of the psychical agencies. The negativity of the barred subject is correlative to these agencies but it is hardly irreducible to them. According to Johnston it "circulates amongst them as their conflicts and clashes between one another."[76]

Lacan's structuralist logic is capable of accounting for the subject thus far as carved out of the Symbolic as a representation, one signifier to another, a product of language. A synchronous temporal dialectical logic, perhaps we might say a *synchronologos*, the subject as produced by the temporal facticity of language in the field of the Other. This positions Lacan to articulate that "there is no such thing as a science of man because science's man does not exist, only its subject does".[77] This period, according to Johnston, appears to represent something of a progression in Lacan's theorisation of the subject which perhaps is correlative to the view we have been exploring between psychoanalysis and science generally. As Lacan is keen to point out, he views the status of the unconscious as pre-ontological as opposed to ontic and therefore by logical inference, the ontological status of the body is not what is at stake in psychoanalysis.[78] Lacan's focus on the Real and the real of the unconscious, in a relation to *Trieb*, is to become evident from *Seminar XI* onwards.[79]

We can now say that, for Lacan, the id is the real and therefore not only is the real the exterior world to our consciousness, it is also the real of anatomy. It is important to clarify that the id and the unconscious are not the same thing: the id being the seat of the drives, a quasi-somatic-interface which affects the workings of the unconscious as the

representational order. Johnston here summarises: "the chains of linguistic associations, body images, and various mnemic traces focused on by the analyst are situated as part of the Imaginary and Symbolic unconscious – not the real of the embodied id."[80]

The ego risks being destroyed by an explosion of repressed drives and must duly defend itself. Anxiety operates as a *warning-beacon* lit when repressed drives menace the ego from within the psychical interior. Anxiety is not therefore a transformation of libidinal forces into an affective state i.e. "the repressed drive itself is not transformed into anxiety".[81] When a repressed drive conflicts with the reality principle and an appropriate repression and subsequent sublimation are not found, the ego's stability is threatened. Unable to flee from what is an internal psychical threat with a somatic origin "[…] the ego projects the internal danger outward and transforms an object or state of affairs in its *Umwelt* into an anxiety laden phobia".[82]

Johnston describes two causal elements as to why the individual finds danger in the drives. Firstly the Law, external prohibition in the *Umwelt*, and secondly the fact that the drive-source insists on recovering the initial homoeostasis in which the *cathexis* pertaining to which that source belongs, was first forged. That which Johnston calls the *objet a* effect has already guaranteed the loss of the initial object, making it impossible for the subject to satisfy the drive-source demand.[83] The drive-source is a compulsive repetitive insistence, demanding the impossible task of the recovery of *das Ding*. The defences utilised in projecting inner dangers outwards, avail of the *excuse* of "castration", as the external prohibition of the Law, which prevents the drive-source achieving its aim. If the signal of anxiety has a direct link to the object of desire, then the production of anxiety in analysis is useful in locating the partial object associated with the original repression. According to Johnston: "What the ego misrecognises in a phobia, is the proximity of an unconscious desire."[84] Paradoxically when the subject experiences anxiety, it is as the destabilising surprise in an encounter, when it appears that the Real Thing of *jouissance* might actually be obtained:

> What is feared is the "lack of a lack", namely the evaporation of the subjects desire through the closing of the gap separating the Imaginary object from the Real *Ding an ich*- anxiety occurs not when the object-cause of desire is lacking: it is not the lack of the object which gives rise to anxiety but, on the contrary, the danger of our getting too close to the object and thus losing the lack itself. Anxiety is brought on by the disappearance of desire. [85]

In approaching a discussion of the subject and the "logic of the signifier" and in terms of furthering an understanding of the relationship between the word and the thing, it becomes important to note the difference between two Lacanian concepts regarding language: *la langue* and *le langage. La langue* is used with regard to the speech of the analytic session – a certain spoken tongue common to analyst and analysand – the linguistic system of the Symbolic order which pre-exists the birth of the individual. That is to say signifiers, as well as the rules for signification and general grammatical form, which Johnston aptly describes as "a transcendent domain of linguistic and sociocultural meanings external to the individual that she/he acquires in becoming a subject."[86]

Le Langage by contrast refers to the *manner* in which strata of subjective significance are accumulated, as a consequence of the complex interactions between the individual and the Symbolic order, as life is lived. Johnston delineates this as a "process or movement", rather than a definite accumulation of contingent historical materials. The Lacanian subject, as we have seen in this section of the essay, is therefore neither reducible to a quasi-automatic product of the Symbolic order, nor to a definite psychical element capable of being isolated and studied, as detached from the "matrices of representation in which the subject is granted its existence".[87]

5. The Number *Zero*

> To suppose that people can be saved by studying and giving assent to formulae is like supposing that one can get to Timbuctoo by poring over a map of Africa. Maps are symbols, and even the best of them are inaccurate and imperfect symbols. But to anyone who really wants to reach a given destination, a map is indispensably useful as indicating the direction in which the traveller should set out and the roads which he must take.[88]

Something essential emerges when we construct the argument that what is integral to the drives, is a matrix of ideational traces which form "the finely woven fabric of the unconscious".[89] Namely, that the concept of the signifier, is indispensable to any apprehension of the mechanisms of the libidinal economy. The signifier understood, thus in Lacanian terms, is as a formal function which specifies the character of *Vorstellung* as ideational, mnemic traces, which impact *Trieb*. Drive objects can therefore be thought of as representations *qua* signifiers which mediate the source and pressure of the drive and are as such then, psychical representations, which according to Lacan, obey the "logic of the signifier".[90]

To return here to Derrida's critique of Rousset's aesthetics and of a dualism in metaphysics, we can place an emphasis on the signifier as

having two distinct but correlative elements: a spatio-synchronic difference and a temporal-diachronoic difference. Spatio-synchronic difference meaning that at any juncture in time each signifier assumes a value *qua* the synchronous coexistence of the other signifiers, in a relationship of temporal-diachronic difference. That is to say that relationship is necessarily one of deferral, since the final meaning of the signifier is always *à venir*. The import of language for the emergence of the subject; which we now begin to understand in Lacanian terms, is not therefore to be understood as a saying as showing, in terms of a dialectical unconcealing of truth as *Logos*, but instead as the "the residual after effect of an inherently unpresentable, mobile network of synchronic difference and diachronic deferrals".[91]

The ground of the Lacanian subject *qua* consciousness, in terms of the logic of the signifier, is explicated and summed up by J Miller in his paper "*Suture*":

> When Lacan faces the definition of the sign as that which represents something for someone, with that of the signifier as that which represents the subject for another signifier, he is stressing that in so far as the signifying chain is concerned, it is on the level of its effects and not of its cause that consciousness is to be situated. The insertion of the subject into the chain is representation, necessarily correlative to an exclusion which is a vanishing [évanouissement].[92]

Miller attempts to conceive of a general relation of the subject to the "logic of the signifier" that both expresses, and is formed by, the subject's lack of identity with itself; this is to say a logic in opposition to a formalised conception of logic which traditionally (taking the example of Frege's Logic as a case in point[93]) contains no reference to the subject. In Lacanian terms however, the correlation of the subject with the thing-not-identical-to-itself, that is to say lack or nothingness is in fact that which facilitates the structuring of the structure in the first instance. This conceptual nothingness, as we have seen, is expressed by Lacan in *Seminar XI* as "a pre-ontological lack".[94]

In our discussion of the difference in Lacanian thinking, between *la langue* and *le langage* we find something of a subversion of Saussurian Structural Linguistics. Lacanian psychoanalytic structuralism privileges a subjectivity which is essential in a definition of structure.[95] Hallward summarises this as follows: "Such "representations are put into play by what they conceal" (i.e. their own structuring structure) "such that they exist in order to hide the reason for their existence" They accomplish this by including in the continuum of representations not a representation of

the lack itself (which is unrepresentable by definition) but an element which "takes the place of the lack" a sort of decoy [*leurre*]."[96]

Structure thus must have *by Lacanian definition,* some such place-holder for the inherent lack. The place-holder functions as a "suture", stitching the gap and in essence, by assigning *a place* to lack allows it to be represented, as something that shows itself as that which it is not, allowing an incorporation into the Imaginary, which is in effect a concealment.[97] This allows for a resolution of the contradiction between the topology of the structure and its dynamic: that which is articulated in the displacement of its elements. We see therefore that it is structure then "which puts in place an experience for the subject that it includes." He continues: Structure then has two qualifying functions, "structuration, or the action of the structure and subjectivity, subjected [*assujettie*]".[98] Such "displacement of determination" Miller argues has its causality in *metonymy.* The cause being *metaphorised* in a discourse and more generally, in any structure the necessity of the functioning of structured causality is: "that the subject takes the effect for the cause". This is described in terms of being operative as "the fundamental law of the action of the structure".[99]

To establish the connection between displacement and lack (as with Verhaeghe's conceptualisation referred to in Section Two: that which allows reflection from a "mediated meta-standpoint") Miller draws on Frege's theory of numbers and in doing so offers a *formalisation* of the concept of the *suture*, as that which binds the subject to the lack in a structure. Namely: the subject governed by "the logic of the signifier". It is beyond the remaining scope of this essay, to do more than summarise his argument. The utilisation of Frege's *Theory of Numbers* allows Miller to express the aforementioned relationship formally in terms of logic. Employing the elementary difference between the numbers one and zero, Miller argues that in terms of concept and identity any concept can only subsume an object to the extent that any object can be treated as self-identical, a thing identical with itself: *one*. Science, as *true discourse*, excludes from its object anything which cannot be counted in this manner. The number *zero* being thought of as representing the number of things which are not identical with themselves and of course there are no such things. The argument is furthered by positing that there is however only one number that actually quantifies the number of things that are not self-identical; namely the number *zero*. Miller argues thus, that to the number zero, we can assign the proper name *one. By repeating this derivation, that is to say the exclusion of the non-identical,* it is possible to generate the infinite numerical succession: 1+1+1...

A constitutive place for lack in the Lacanian theory of the subject is developed thus by identifying this impossible object, summoned and summarily rejected, by the discourse of logic, as the thing-not-identical-to-itself. This impossible object is precisely then the *subject*, if we recognise the *zero* as suturing or standing in place of the lack. Exactly the place-holder described in *Action of the Structure* and all that is represented of the subject *qua* subject is "the place-holder of the gap in the structure."[100] If we are cognisant that a signifier can represent this gap - one gap, for another signifier - and so on indefinitely, as per the correlation between 0 to 1 producing 1+1+1... and then consider how that sequence is produced in terms of metaphor and metonymy, we may outline a general relation between subject and signifier as Miller does in the *Suture*:

> If the series of numbers, metonymy of the zero begins with its metaphor, if the 0 member of the series as number is only the standing-in-place suturing the absence (of the absolute zero) which moves beneath the chain according to the alternation of a representation and an exclusion – then what is to stop us from seeing in the restored relation of the zero to the series of numbers the most elementary articulation of the subjects relation to the signifying chain?[101]

To clarify this we can say that in the metonymic movement of the chain, from signifier to signifier; a signifier sutures, or counts-as-one-place for another signifier. This is the essential lack of self-identity or place which is all that can be represented of the subject *qua* subject: "Suture names the relation of the subject to the chain of its discourse."[102] The subject's absence, or lack of place, is subsumed in the form of a place-holder [*tenant-lieu*]. Miller argues that by "crossing logical discourse at its point of least resistance, that of the suture, you can see articulated the structure of the subject: as a flickering in ellipses"".[103] It is this movement which opens and closes up the number, as each successive number subsumes and abolishes its predecessor and in doing so delivers up the all important lack. What is perhaps important for psychoanalytic praxis in all this is that the analysis of the place or lack that is sutured at the point of least resistance in the metonymic chain, points to a "causality in the structure in so far as the subject is implicated in it" and in doing so points to desire or the want-to-be and thus a potentiality for transformation in terms of a relation to structure.[104]

6. Conclusion. The *subject* at the *bar*.

One of Lacan's expressions of the relationship of the subject and the "logic of the signifier" can be found in his *Écrits* in the *Position of the Unconscious*.[105] We can look back here to the earlier cited analytic

example (Section 3) of "take *apart/take a part*" which serves to aptly highlight the kind of *disjunction* I think Lacan is referring to, when the subject, as produced by representation, one signifier to another, has the question turned back on himself; as the analyst does not get lost in the *stays of the question* itself and in fact by scansion, inverts the question into a message. The analyst thereby "introducing the effective disjunction on the basis of which the question has a meaning". The example serves here to remind us that psychoanalysis is first and foremost a praxis, and therefore has a goal or an *end*.

There is a curious, perhaps confusing, element in the idea of transformation within structure to which Lacan points in *Seminar XI*, which I think merits some further consideration. In particular with regard to the closing of the *gap* and the disappearance of the unconscious. Lacan relates here the nature of the constitution of the subject in the field of the Other, where the characteristic of the subject of the unconscious is that of being, beneath the signifier that develops its networks, chains and its history, at an indeterminate place.[106] The task remains therefore to sketch out the constitutive, theoretical links (by way of findings) in relation to the subject and the Other, with regard to the main concepts already discussed: the drive, the signifier, the unconscious, *das Ding* and lack. In doing so it is also important that we bear in mind the main questions which have been raised. What is the relationship between the word and the thing? Is there a constitutive relationship, with structural underpinnings, between the subject and the thing-in-itself? And if so what are the roles of The Symbolic order, language and lack in that structure? Does language effect a disturbance in the real of the body? If the subject is an effect then what is its cause? What is the relationship between psychoanalysis and ontology?

Lacan says that "the subject is born in so far as the signifier emerges in the field of the Other".[107] This statement is of the utmost importance here. The relation of subject to the Other is characterised precisely as unconcealing what is represented by the lamella.[108] Thus for Lacan every drive has a dual aspect which on the one-hand represents the presentation of sexuality (not sexuality as per masculine/feminine polarity, but sexuality as that which is *subtracted* due to sexual reproduction) in the unconscious and on the other hand "represents in its essence death".[109] The unconscious opens and closes because it essentially inscribes the time of the subjects division, divided by being born with the signifier. Lacan establishes that there is a constitutive, direct relation between the subject in the field of the drive and the field of the Other, which is characterised by division and the repetitive attempt to join oneself together. This is

dependent on the idea that there is a relation of the sexes represented at the level of the unconscious and that there is no *other*.

In terms of the "logic of the signifier" the unique particularity of the subject of the unconscious, is established through the relation of the subject in the field of the Other, as the locus of truth and in the engendering of the zero from the thing-not identical-with-itself. This for Lacan is a matrical relation which cannot be included in any definition of objectivity.[110] In other words there is no relation of subject to the thing-in-itself without the logic of the signifier: the word. The subject is excluded outside of the field of the Other, which is what Lacan marks in his algebra by the bar which strikes the S of the subject in front of the capital A. The Lacanian "Unary" trait whereby this exclusion of the subject is displaced onto the Other according to the "logic of the signifier"; by a displacement which effects the emergence of signification signified to the subject.[111]

I will return to the analytic example I have given you of "take *apart*/take *a part*" in an attempt to engender one further meaning from its structure, because of course the definition of the subject comes down to *the possibility of one signifier more*. Lacan speaks of alienation as a *vel* which is characterised by a choice which has as one of its outcomes, a case of *neither one*, *nor the other*. The choice then for the Analysand in the example "is a matter of knowing whether one wishes to preserve *one* of the parts" - to take *a part* - as the other will disappear in any case.[112] If the choice is *being* then the subject disappears in an *évanouissement* into non-meaning. If the choice is *meaning* then the meaning is engendered at a cost *of the part* of non-meaning. Lacan emphasises that it is this non-meaning which is of course precisely, for the realisation of the subject, the unconscious, or the order of the *non-realised*. This is the subject-effect which is related, in Lacanian terms to its origin in demand and Drive. The relation of the subject-effect to *Trieb* represents a further line of work which is unfortunately outside the scope of this essay. All I can say here is that Johnston, for example, draws out an excellent discussion of the axiom that "no signifier can signify itself", in relation to how constellations of *Vorstellung* ceaselessly revolve around *das Ding*. Lacan's *Unary* trait, as a signifier, acts as a symbolic coordinate with regard to the subject's repetitive attempts to re-find the lost-object. Repetition of the *representation* of the drive-object can of course never deliver up the Real Thing as present or re-presented.[113] This is because libidinal-iteration (where d represents *das Ding* and V signifies *Vorstellung*) does not produce a series d/V^1, d/V^2, d/V^3... because that which is repeatable is only the representation of object *qua* object and not at all in fact the Real-Thing. The correct series is thus: $d/\ V^1/\ V^2/\ V^3$... where each repetition of

the signifier like *Vorstellung* of the drive-object introduces an ineliminable difference. The signified of V^1 is *d* whereas the signified of V^2 is d/V^1 and that of V^3 is $d/V^1/V^2$ and so on, where the only thing repeated without modification or difference is the bar itself.[114] The key for Johnston in all this is that the barring of *das Ding* is an effect which is constitutive of the temporal logic of the symbolic mediation of *Trieb*.

So we can see that the key to grasping the "logic of the signifier", in relation to the divided subject and the thing-in-itself, is that the barred subject also symbolises the impossibility, governed by the logic of the signifier, of the signifier ever signifying itself.[115] Thus we might say that in relation to *Being* and in relation to *das Ding, the subject at the bar,* as divided by language and produced by representation, *is always in the wrong place at the wrong time.* Therefore it seems that Derrida is correct, at the time of Lacan's *Seminar XI* at any rate, that Lacan by giving the lack, the break, the void, the value of a transcendental signifier, is squarely engaged in ontological thinking: a *logos* as veiling/unveiling of truth (even if it does have its locus in the field of the Other). The hypothesis that this changes in the thought of the *later Lacan*, represents study for another place in time.

Notes

[1] Aldous Huxley, *The Perennial Philosophy*, (Harper, London, 2009), 35. Huxley continues: "Consider for example those negative definitions of the transcendent and immanent Ground of being. In statements such as Eckhart's, God is equated with nothing. And in a certain sense this equation is exact; for God is certainly no thing. In the phrase used by Scotus Eriugena God is not a what; he is a That. In other words the Ground can be denoted as being there, but not as having defined qualities. This means that all discursive knowledge *about* the Ground is not merely, like all inferential knowledge, a thing at one remove, or even at several removes, from the reality of immediate acquaintance; it is and, because of the very nature of our language and our standard patterns of thought, it must be, paradoxical knowledge. Direct knowledge of the Ground cannot be had be except by union, and union can be achieved by the annihilation of the self-regarding ego, which is the barrier separating the 'thou' from the 'That'".

[2] Aldous Huxley, op. cit. 157.

[3] Take for example the following quotation: "For it is some time since Arthur Schopenhauer, the philosopher, showed mankind the extent to which their activities are determined by sexual impulses - in the ordinary sense of the word. It should surely have been impossible for a whole world of readers to banish such a startling piece of information so completely from their minds. And as for the "stretching" of the concept of sexuality which has been necessitated by the analysis of children and what are called perverts, anyone who looks down with contempt

upon psycho-analysis from a superior vantage-point should remember how closely the enlarged sexuality of psycho-analysis coincides with the Eros of the divine Plato."
Sigmund Freud, S.E. XVIII. *Beyond The Pleasure Principle, Group Psychology and Other Works*. 1-64.

[4] Freud's reading of Schopenhauer is evident here: "There is something else, at any rate, that we cannot remain blind to. We have unwittingly steered our course into the harbour of Schopenhauer's philosophy. For him death is the "true result and to that extent the purpose of life", "[...] while the sexual instinct is the embodiment of the will to live." Schopenhauer (1851; Sämtliche Werke, ed. Hübscher, 1938, 5, 236). Ibid., 1-64.

[5] Jacques Lacan, *The Four Fundamental Concepts of Psychoanalysis*, ed. J.-A. Miller, trans. A. Sheridan (Karnac, London), 2004, 205.

[6] Ibid.

[7] Justin Clemens, *Love as Ontology* in *Psychoanalysis Against Philosophy*: *Origins and Ends of the Mind*, ed. C. Kerslake and R. Brazzier (Leuven University Press, Belgium), 2007, 188.

[8] Ibid., 193.

[9] Take for example the following quote: "We thus arrive at the essential nature of instincts in the first place by considering their main characteristics - their origin in sources of stimulation within the organism and their appearance as a constant force". Sigmund Freud. S.E. XIV. *On The History of the Psycho-Analytic Movement, Papers on Metapsychology and Other Works*. 117-141.

[10] Freud describes Trieb as follows: "We give these bodily needs, in so far as they represent an instigation to mental activity, the name of "*Triebe*", a word for which we are envied by many modern languages. Well, these instincts fill the id: all the energy in the id, as we may put it briefly, originates from them. Nor have the forces in the ego any other origin; they are derived from those in the id. What, then, do these instincts want? Satisfaction - that is, the establishment of situations in which the bodily needs can be extinguished. A lowering of the tension of need is felt by our organ of consciousness as pleasurable; an increase of it is soon felt as unpleasure. From these oscillations arises the series of feelings of pleasure-unpleasure, in accordance with which the whole mental apparatus regulates its activity. In this connection we speak of a "dominance of the pleasure principle".
Sigmund Freud. S.E. XX. *An Autobiographical Study, Inhibitions, Symptoms and Anxiety, The Question Of Lay Analysis*. 183-251.

[11] Paul Verhaeghe, *On Being Normal and Other Disorders*, trans. S. Jottkand (Karnac, London, 2008), 44-46.

[12] Ibid., 54.

[13] Ibid.

[14] Ibid., 57.

[15] Author's Note: impasse of nominalism and realism is as follows: realism essentially says nothing semantic other than to negate the proposition that our semantic capacities constitute the real of the world. Nominalism on the other hand implies the rejection of abstract objects and universals as independent of a

subjective viewpoint or perceptual perspective. (The philosophical arguments are far more nuanced than my descriptions here. It is however enough for the purpose of this essay that the disjunct is highlighted in a general way.)

[16] Ibid., 58. Author's Note. Ontology in a Heideggerian sense for example, is a question of structure, which given the role of language and the creation of symbolic systems through lack, is to be situated socio-historically and not something that has a linear solution in any temporally-equivocal sense.

[17] Q. Meillassoux, *Time Without Becoming*, (presented at Middlesex University, London, 2008), speculativeheresey.files.wordpress.com/2008/07/3729-time_without_becoming.pdf,

[18] Ibid., 1. Author's Note: The argument from the circle is usually used to defend the hypothesis that: There can be no X without a givenness of X, and no theory about X without a positing of X. If you articulate an objection to the correlationist argument, the objection is the product of your situated thinking and a performative contradiction results, in which you are refuting what you articulate by the very fact that you have thought it. A vicious circle. For Meillassoux the consequence for the correlationist is that therefore it is impossible to conceive of an absolute X, a Real which is separate from a subject. In Time Without Becoming he attempts a refutation of this position, maintaining that a reality absolutely separate from the subject – can be thought by the subject. It is beyond the scope of this introduction to go into detail on Meillasoux's argument here. It is enough for now to note that he articulates it.

[19] Author's Note. Derrida argues that Rousset, in his analysis of Corneille's Polyeucte, despite defining structure as the union of formal-structure and intention, neglects the immanence of structure by focusing on the geometric. This produces, in Derrida's view, a one-dimensional analysis affording primacy to space over time. The example given is that beauty, value and force are not susceptible to geometry and are therefore excluded from Rousset's structural analysis.

[20] Jacques Derrida, *Writing and Difference*, trans. A. Bass (Routledge London and New York, 2002), 29-35.

[21] Jacques Derrida, *For the Love of Lacan*, trans. B. Edwards and A. Lecercle, in Cardozo Law Review, Vol. 16, 1995, 669-728.

[22] Jacques Derrida, *Dissemination*, trans. B. Johnson (The University of Chicago Press, Chicago, 1981), 26.

[23] François Laruelle, *The Principles of Non-Philosophy*, trans. N. Rubczak and A.-P. Smith (Bloomsbury, London and New York, 2013), 80.

[24] Ibid.

[25] Ibid., 81.

[26] Ibid., 80. Author's Note. The Lacanian turn away from a Heideggerian language based theorisation of the subject occurs from Seminar XI onwards where it seems that the interference of the ontological question as bluntly articulated by Miller "What is your ontology?" is the focal point of a rethinking for Lacan of the relation between his three registers, Real, Imaginary and Symbolic.

[27] Alain Badiou, *Numbers and Numbers* (Polity Press, Cambridge, UK, 2008), 25.

[28] Author's Note. A set of translations of (in part at any rate) and a set of accompanying contemporary essays, regarding *Cahiers pour L'Analyse.*

[29] Authors Note. *Cahiers pour L'Analyse* is the philosophical journal, edited by a group of students at the Ecole Normale Supérieure containing work by intellectual luminaries including Lacan, Derrida, Althusser, Foucault and Irigaray. The students involved included Miller, Badiou and Duroux. Produced in ten issues between 1966 and 1969 and containing vital articulations of the "structuralist project", delineating a clear disembarkation from the primacy of the lived experience and a hermeneutic phenomenology in favour of an orientation towards truth as structure, and a topographical, mathematical theorisation of the subject.

[30] Jacques Lacan, *The Four Fundamental Concepts of Psychoanalysis*, ed. J.-A. Miller, trans. A. Sheridan (Karnac, London, 2004), 29.

[31] Ibid.

[32] Aldous Huxley, op. cit. 128.

[33] J.-A. Miller. *Theorié de Turin sur le sujet de l'Ecole.* Aperçus du Congrès de l'AMP à Buenos Aires (EURL Huysmans, Paris, 2001), 62-63. My translation.

[34] Heidegger in the 1929 debate with Cassirer at Davos is remarkably prescient on this point when he says: "I believe that what I described by Dasein does not allow translation into a concept of Cassirer's. Should one say consciousness, that is precisely what I rejected. What I call Dasein is essentially codetermined—not just through what we describe as spirit, and not just through what we call living. Rather, what it depends on is the original unity and the immanent structure of the relatedness of a human being which to a certain extent has been fettered in a body and which, in the fetteredness in the body, stands in a particular condition of being bound up with beings."

Martin Heidegger, *Kant and the Problem of Metaphysics*, trans. R. Taft (Bloomington: Indiana University Press, USA, 1990), 181.

[35] Jacques Lacan, *The Four Fundamental Concepts of Psychoanalysis*, ed. J.-A. Miller, trans. A. Sheridan (Karnac, London, 2004), 29.

[36] Ibid.

[37] Ibid. Author's Note. Upon initial consideration there appears an inherent contradiction in the juxtaposition of these two remarks. Which, perhaps in keeping with Huxley's proposition of the potential insight to be gained through the analysis of non sequiteurs and paradoxes, offers us an excellent starting point with regard to what the Lacanian hypothesis regarding the subject actually is, and how we might situate the relationship between psychoanalysis and ontology generally.

[38] Ibid., 26.

[39] Paul Verhaeghe, *Causation and Destitution of a Pre-ontological Non-entity: On The Lacanian Subject*, in: *Key Concepts of Lacanian Psychoanalysis* (London, Rebus Press, 1998), 5.

[40] Ibid., 4.

[41] Freud states the following: "We often have the impression that with the wish for a penis and the masculine protest we have penetrated through all the psychological strata and have reached bedrock, and that thus our activities are at an end. This is probably true, since, for the psychical field, the biological field does in fact play

---

the part of the underlying bedrock. The repudiation of femininity can be nothing else than a biological fact, a part of the great riddle of sex".
Sigmund Freud, S.E. XXIII. *Moses and Monotheism, an Outline of Psycho-Analysis and Other Works*, 216-254.

[42] See Stijn Vanheule, *Lacan's Construction and Deconstruction of the Double Mirror Device*, in *Frontiers In Psychology*, Volume Two, Article 209, 2011, where he discusses four objects a: the gaze, the voice, taking in nothing and giving nothing: as defined by Lacan in Seminar XI.

[43] Justin Clemens, *Love as Ontology: Psychoanalysis Against Philosophy*, in *Origins and Ends of the Mind*, ed. C. Kerslake and R. Brazzier (Leuven University Press, Belgium, 2007), 188.
Clemens discusses the Freudian death drive in terms of Freud's substitution of love for sexuality and interestingly references Lear on the point that transference-love in a Freudian sense can be understood as a "world-making operation of worlding or worldliness." "Phenomena show up in the world, the world itself is not another phenomenon. Nor is worldliness. So if transference is worldliness itself, then "it" is not a phenomenon in the world. Rather it is more like the structuring condition in which phenomena show up for us." This is an interesting point regarding transference-love as structure, which possibly can be framed as Aristotle's conceptualisation of Eros as prime mover.

[44] Jean-Luc Nancy, God *Justice Love Beauty, Four Little Dialogues*, trans. S. Clift (Fordham University Press, New York, 2011), 2.

[45] Author's Note. Perhaps love cannot be measured as an ontic phenomenon or situated in the realm of the epistemological: either that of the Master Discourse or the University Discourse. We should not presume to tell another what or whom to love, no more than we would (at least I hope) presume to tell another what to think. In traditional Greek ontology, in particular Aristotle's Metaphysics, it is possible to interpret Eros as a structure which facilitates thinking, or the Being of being-at-thought. In itself, for Aristotle, Eros is situated as an ontological question, or in primordial structuring framework.

[46] Juan.-David. Nasio, *The Book of Love and Pain. Thinking at the Limits of Freud and Lacan*, trans. D. Pettigrew and F. Raffoul (SUNY Series, NY. 2004), 26.

[47] Ibid., 5. Author's Note. Nasio describes pain as articulated in having been worked through, by being-as-thought-in-itself. There is something of a primordial pain in the questioning for the particular subject regarding their being versus lack of being (or want to be), which the analyst must be prepared for. A preparation, or a prior thinking, at the limits of love and pain would seem to be a pre-requisite. Perhaps a structure of thinking conceived of as love-in-itself and therefore a philosophizing which we may construe in terms of "thought as love-ontology".

[48] Christopher.-P. Long, *Aristotle on the Nature of Truth* (Cambridge University Press New York, 2011), 209.

[49] Ibid., 210.

[50] Ibid., 214.

[51] Ibid.

---

[52] Jacques Lacan, *Seminar VIII, Transference* (lesson of 8th March 1961), my translation

[53] Author's Note. It is an odd subjectivity therefore in psychoanalytic praxis and not an even inter-subjectivity as we would usually understand it, but rather a subject/object a relation, where the analyst is situated in the transference as object cause of desire (object a). The particular truth of the divided subject then, articulated in relation to their own desire, as the subject appears through representation: one signifier to another. This concept has distinct implications for contemporary analytic praxis, in opposition to say, ego-psychology and as we can see, not without its philosophical underpinnings in traditional ontological thinking.

[54] Author's Note. What, for Plato, longing and love have in common is that they are both directed towards that which one lacks. Plato's point is ultimately, that even the actual possession of the desired object does not do away with the dimension of lack. In relating this to Freud we can say that the Freudian conceptualisation of Eros as primordial is explicated throughout his work. To explore this relationship further we can take a short relevant example from Beyond the Pleasure Principle where Freud expands the theory of *Eros* as a prime mover to encompass *Thanatos* or the "death drive".

[55] Sigmund Freud, S.E. XVIII. *Beyond The Pleasure Principle, Group Psychology and Other Works*, 1-64.

[56] Ibid.

[57] Juan-David Nasio, *The Book of Love and Pain...*, 26.

[58] Ibid., 26.

[59] Ibid., 27. My rewording from original text.

[60] Marc De Kesel, *Psychoanalysis: A Non-Ontology Of The Human*, in *Psychoanalysis Against Philosophy*, *Origins and Ends of the Mind*, ed. C. Kerslake and R. Brazzier (Leuven University Press, Belgium, 2007), 5.

[61] Sigmund Freud, S.E. XII. *The Case Of Schreber, Papers on Technique and Other Works*. 218-226.

[62] Marc De Kesel, *Psychoanalysis: A Non-Ontology Of The Human*, 5.

[63] Aldous Huxley, op. cit., 128.

[64] Colette Soler, *The Paradoxes of the Symptom in Psychoanalysis, Chapter 6*, in: *The Cambridge Companion to Lacan*, ed. J.-M. Rabaté (Cambridge University Press, U.K., 2003), 90.

Authors Note: An example of jouissance being Anna O's symptom of paralysis as something which encompasses paradoxical elements of pleasure/unpleasure. In other words the practically masochistic enjoyment of something which is fundamentally unpleasurable but therefore pleasurable at the same time.)

[65] Ibid. Soler refers to the origin of the drive as follows: "If we ask, "Where does the drive come from?" we have only one answer: the drive is produced by the operation not of the Holy Ghost but of language. The drive derives from needs; the drive is a transformation of natural necessities produced by language, through the obligation of articulating demands. Such is the Lacanian thesis without which no one can be called a Lacanian: language is not an instrument that we can use as we

want, is not just an organ allowing one to express oneself or to communicate with others, as it is often believed, but language is fundamentally inscribed in the real."

[66] Ibid.

[67] Ibid., 13.

[68] Ibid.

[69] Authors note: the literal translation of the English word letter, In the Irish language is: "litir".

[70] Ibid.

[71] Jacques Lacan, *The Four Fundamental Concepts of Psychoanalysis*, 29.

[72] Ibid., 25.

[73] Jacques Lacan, Seminar IV, "La relation d'objet et les structures freudiennes", (1994), citation in Adrian Johnston, *Time Driven: Metapsychology and the Splitting of the Drive*, (Northwestern University Press, USA, 2011), 265.

74 Adrian Johnston, *Turning the Sciences Inside Out: Revisiting Lacan's Science and Truth*, in *Concept and Form*, *Volume Two*, ed. P. Hallward and K. Peden (Verso, London, 2012), 107.

[75] Ibid.

[76] Ibid.

[77] Jacques. Lacan, *Écrits* , trans. B. Fink (Norton, USA,2002), 730.

[78] Adrian Johnston, *Time Driven: Metapsychology and the Splitting Of the Drive*, 268-269.

[79] Author's Note. Freud's theory of Trieb has four components: source – thrust (pressure) – aim – object. The drive-source is an a priori meta-psychological assumption based on the consistent quality of recognition associated with a reiterative demand for satisfaction, providing a consistent undercurrent to a series of otherwise seemingly disparate object choices. In conjunction with the reiteration of the drive-source there is also a recurrence of drive-pressure, a build up of unpleasurable affectively experienced tension, stemming from the unsatisfied drive source. The drive-source and drive-pressure are the aspect or Trieb that are constituted in a temporal structural repetition. It is important here to note that Freud considers Trieb to be homogeneous and that drive-pressure results in a negative-affective state namely anxiety, which arises, as Freud theorises it, when a repressed drive becomes two powerful. The affective-anxiety is not somatic in itself, but arises in the ego.

[80] Ibid.

[81] Ibid., 274.

[82] Ibid., 279. Author's Note. The ego engages in a self-deception attributing the anxiety it experiences to an external cause, a thing in reality which can therefore be avoided. The recognition or connection is not made that the anxiety is a warning component with regard to a repressed drive, and therefore something internal. Anxiety is in essence object-less, the initial or original fear, in terms of the contradiction between the drive and the reality principle remains unconscious. The ego, as self, merely displaces the anxiety onto phobic substitutes in reality.

[83] Ibid.

[84] Ibid., 280.

---

[85] Ibid.
[86] Ibid., 311.
[87] Ibid., 312.
[88] Aldous Huxley, op. cit. 135.
[89] Adrian Johnston, *Time Driven: Metapsychology and the Splitting Of the Drive*, 315.
[90] Ibid., 318.
[91] Ibid., 316.
[92] Jacques.-Alain. Miller, *Suture* (*Elements of the Logic of the Signifier*), in *Concept and Form Volume One*, *Selections from The Cahiers Pour L'Analyse*, ed. P. Hallward and K. Peden (Verso, London and N.Y., 2012), 101.
[93] See Edward Kanterian, *Frege A Guide for the Perplexed* (Continuum, London, 2012), 27.
[94] Jacques Lacan, *The Four Fundamental Concepts of Psychoanalysis*, 29.
[95] Author's Note. Any conceptualisation of structure must, in Lacanian theory, include the subject. What is important to recognise here is the function of a gap, or lack in the structuring process. On the level of a hermeneutic phenomenology this gap is arguably concealed on the level of the imaginary/ideological by an illusion of coherence, or in other words a representation of immanence.
96. *Concept And Form Volume One*, *Selections from The Cahiers Pour L"Analyse*, ed. P. Hallward and K. Peden (Verso, London and N.Y., 2012), 45.
97. Ibid. Author's Note. According to Miller, unless traditional Structuralism can annul the alteration inherent in the exclusion of the speaking subject it remains in a position where linguistic structures cannot extend beyond their localisation. Psychoanalytic Structuralism on the other-hand, conceived of as having an ineliminable subjectivity which is situated in the experience which it takes for its object.
[98] Jacques-Alain Miller, *Suture* (*Elements of the Logic of the Signifier*), 101.
[99] *Concept And Form Volume One*, *Selections from The Cahiers Pour L"Analyse*, ed. P. Hallward and K. Peden, (Verso, London and N.Y., 2012), 47-48.
[100] Ibid.
[101] Jacques-Alain Miller, *Action of the Structure*, in *Concept And Form Volume One*, *Selections from The Cahiers Pour L'Analyse*, ed. P. Hallward and K. Peden (Verso, London and N.Y., 2012), 75.
[102] Jacques-Alain Miller, *Suture*, 101.
[103] Ibid.
[104] Ibid.
[105] When it is directed back at what calls us into question (as much as at he who questions us, if he is not already lost in the stays of his question)—namely, the subject—the alternative [language or speech] proposes itself as a disjunction. Now it is this very disjunction that provides us with the answer, or, rather, it is in leading the Other to constitute itself as the locus of our answer—the Other furnishing the answer in a form that inverts the question into a message—that we introduce the effective disjunction on the basis of which the question has meaning. The effect of language is to introduce the cause into the subject. Through this

effect, he is not the cause of himself; he bears within himself the worm of the cause that splits him. For his cause is the signifier, without which there would be no subject in the real. But this subject is what the signifier represents, and the latter cannot represent anything except to another signifier: to which the subject who listens is thus reduced. One therefore does not speak to the subject. It speaks of him, and this is how he apprehends himself; he does so all the more necessarily in that, before he disappears as a subject beneath the signifier he becomes, due to the simple fact that it addresses him, he is absolutely nothing. But this nothing is sustained by his advent, now produced by the appeal made in the Other to the second signifier. As an effect of language, in that he is born of this early split, the subject translates a signifying synchrony into the primordial temporal pulsation that is the constitutive fading* of his identification. This is the first movement. But in the second, desire—bedding down in the signifying cut in which metonymy occurs, the diachronic (called "history") that was inscribed in fading— returns to the kind of fixity Freud grants unconscious wishes (see the last sentence of the Traumatize [The Interpretation of Dreams]). This secondary subornation not only closes the effect of the first by projecting the topology of the subject into the instant of fantasy; it seals it, refusing to allow the subject of desire to realize that he is an effect of speech, to realize, in other words, what he is in being but the Other's desire. Jacques Lacan, *Écrits*, 709.

[106] J. Lacan, *The Four Fundamental Concepts of Psychoanalysis*, 207.

[107] Ibid., 199.

[108] Author's Note. The lamella is a concept to which I have referred in Section Two, but now wish to further address here, in the context of the subject, the drive and the unconscious. The lamella represents the libido qua pure life instinct, that which is subtracted from the living being as a necessary result of the sexual reproductive cycle. It is this, the original lost object, that is represented by all forms of Lacan's object a.

[109] Ibid.

[110] Jacques-Alain Miller, Suture, 100.

[111] Ibid.

[112] Jacques Lacan, *The Four Fundamental Concepts Of Psychoanalysis*, 211. My italics.

[113] Adrian Johnston, *Time Driven: Metapsychology and the Splitting Of the Drive*, 319.

[114] Ibid., 320.

[115] Ibid., 321.

References

Badiou, Alain. *Numbers and Numbers*. Translated by Robin McKay. Polity Press, Cambridge. 2008.

Clemens, Justin. "Love as Ontology: Psychoanalysis Against Philosophy". in *Origins and Ends of the Mind*. Ed. C. Kerslake and R. Brazzier. Leuven University Press, Belgium. 2007. 188.

—. *Concept And Form Volume 1, Selections from The Cahiers Pour L'Analyse*. Ed. P. Hallward and K. Peden. Verso, London and N.Y. 2012. 45.

De Kesel, Marc. "Psychoanalysis: A Non-Ontology Of The Human". In *Psychoanalysis Against Philosophy, Origins and Ends of the Mind*. Ed. C. Kerslake and R. Brazzier. Leuven University Press, Belgium. 2007. 5.

Derrida, Jacques. *Dissemination*. Translated by B. Johnson. The University of Chicago Press, Chicago. 1981. 26.

Derrida, Jacques. "For the Love of Lacan". (1993) Trans. B. Edwards and A. Lecercle. In *Cardozo Law Review*, Vol. 16, 1995. 669-728.

Derrida, Jacques. *Writing and Difference*. (1967) Translated by A. Bass. Routledge, London and New York. 2002. 29-35.

Freud, Sigmund. S.E. XII. *The Case Of Schreber, Papers On Technique and Other Works*. 218-226.

Freud, Sigmund. S.E. XVIII. *Beyond The Pleasure Principle, Group Psychology and Other Works*.

Freud, Sigmund. S.E. XIV. *On The History of the Psycho-Analytic Movement, Papers on Metapsychology and Other Works*. 117-141.

Freud, Sigmund. S.E. XX. *An Autobiographical Study, Inhibitions, Symptoms and Anxiety, The Question of Lay Analysis*. 183-251.

Heidegger, Martin. *Kant and the Problem of Metaphysics*. Translated by R. Taft. Bloomington: Indiana University Press, USA. 1990. 181.

Huxley, Aldous. *The Perennial Philosophy*. (1945) Harper, London. 2009.

Johnston, Adrian. *Time Driven: Metapsychology and the Splitting Of the Drive*. Northwestern University Press, USA. 2005. 268-269.

Johnston, Adrian. "Turning the Sciences Inside Out: Revisiting Lacan's 'Science and Truth'". In *Concept and Form, Volume II*. Ed. P. Hallward and K. Peden, Verso, London. 2012. 107.

Kanterian, Edward. *Frege A Guide for the Perplexed*. Continuum, London. 2012. 27.

Lacan, Jacques. Seminar IV, *La relation d'objet et les structures freudiennes*. Cited In Adrian Johnston, *Time Driven: Metapsychology and the Splitting of the Drive*. Northwestern University Press, USA. 2011. 265.

Lacan, Jacques. *Écrits* . Translated by. Bruce Fink. 2006, Norton, USA. 730.

Lacan, Jacques. *Seminar VIII, Transference.* (1960-1961) Unpublished Translation.

Lacan, Jacques. *The Four Fundamental Concepts of Psychoanalysis.* (1973) Ed. J.-A. Miller, Translated by Alan. Sheridan. Karnac, London. 2004.

Laruelle, François. *The Principles of Non-Philosophy.* (1996) Trans. N. Rubczak and A.-P. Smith. Bloomsbury, London and New York. 2013. 80.

Long, Christopher-P. *Aristotle on the Nature of Truth.* Cambridge University Press New York. 2011. 209.

Meillassoux, Quentin. *Time Without Becoming.* Middlesex University, London. May 2008. speculativeheresey.files.wordpress.com/2008/07/3729 time_without_becoming.pdf.

Miller, Jacques-Alain. "Action of The Structure". (1966) In *Concept and Form Volume 1, Selections from The Cahiers Pour L"Analyse.* Ed. P. Hallward and K. Peden. Verso, London and N.Y. 2012. 75.

Miller, Jacques-Alain. "Suture (Elements of the Logic of the Signifier)". (1966) In *Concept and Form Volume 1, Selections from The Cahiers Pour L'Analyse.* Ed. P. Hallward and K. Peden. Verso, London and N.Y. 2012. 101.

Miller, Jacques-Alain. *Theorié de Turin sur le sujet de l'Ecole. Aperçus du Congrès de l"Amp à Buenos Aires.* (2000) EURL Huysmans, Paris. 2001.

Nancy, Jean-Luc. *God Justice Love Beauty, Four Little Dialogues.* Translated by S. Clift. Fordham University Press, New York. 2011. 2.

Nasio, Juan-David. *The Book of Love and Pain, Thinking at the Limits of Freud and Lacan.* Translated by D. Pettigrew and F. Raffoul. SUNY Series, NY. 2004. 26.

Soler, Collette. "The Paradoxes of the Symptom in Psychoanalysis, Chapter 6". In *The Cambridge Companion to Lacan.* Ed. J.-M. Rabaté, Cambridge University Press, U.K. 2003.

Vanheule, Stijn. "Lacan's Construction and Deconstruction of the Double Mirror Device". In *Frontiers In Psychology*, Volume Two, Article 209. 2011.

Verhaeghe, Paul. "Causation and Destitution of a Pre-ontological Non-entity: On The Lacanian Subject". In: *Key Concepts of Lacanian Psychoanalysis.* London, Rebus Press 1998. 5.

Verhaeghe, Paul. *On Being Normal and Other Disorders.* (2004) Translated by S. Jottkand. Karnac, London. 2008. 44-46.

CHAPTER FOUR

PEACE BEYOND REASON: PSYCHOANALYTICAL REMARKS ON *THE BETTER ANGELS OF OUR NATURE*

JOÃO GABRIEL LIMA DA SILVA

To Michael Brown and Amarildo,
victims of peace.

This paper will present a critique of Steven Pinker's book *The Better Angels of Our Nature* from a psychoanalytical perspective. Though our opinions diverge on some matters, there are several legitimate reasons to praise Pinker's efforts in facing the enigma of violence. His use of historical research coupled with his attempt at data interpretation by means of present-day research in psychology, anthropology, ethology and sociology reveals an attentive spirit, truly dedicated to providing answers to this complicated issue. Certainly, the sensible critic must proceed carefully so as to not become too judgmental and misunderstand an author's arguments – especially when dealing with work from a different tradition of thought and study. I will endeavor to avoid the tendency to oversimplify. However, to a large extent, simplification will be unavoidable given that Pinker's book is composed of more than 700 pages, making it considerably more lengthy than this analysis. Rather than simply critique Pinker's work, the true aim of this paper is to consider some questions on the same matter that have emerged from over a hundred years of psychoanalytical practice and theory.

The Better Angels

The main argument of *The Better Angels of Our Nature* is quite simple: violence has diminished throughout the centuries. Despite all the cases of massacres, murders, rapes, and other violent acts communicated by the

media each day, Pinker affirms that, “we may be living in the most peaceable era in our species' existence”[1]. The author clearly assumes that this major claim will be received as unlikely and somehow unacceptable. In order to prove his hypothesis to the reader, Pinker opts to provide statistics and aims to prove that violence *relative to population size* has diminished.

The author begins the book with historical research, presenting the factors that have led human beings toward a more peaceful overall existence. Pinker designates our ancestors’ transition from anarchy to a state of civil society as the first significant decline in violence rates. According to Pinker, this change would have commenced around five thousand years ago, when, “came a reduction in the chronic raiding and feuding that characterized life in a state of nature and a more or less fivefold decrease in rates of violent death”[2]. Through data analysis, Pinker compares murder rates in *non-state societies* to *state societies* and highlights the prevalence of violent acts in *non-state societies.* Then, Pinker returns to the Hobbesian theory of the Leviathan, which says that men in state of nature live in anarchy and violence[3]. Only a strong and centralized power is able to control the violence. In concordance with the philosopher, Pinker has reasons (and data) to believe that the establishment of a centralized power amongst a people – that is, the Leviathan – reduces human violence.

The author then goes on to explore behavioral changes in regards to violent acts during the medieval period and the Renaissance. Guided by the works of the renowned sociologist Norbert Elias, Pinker again stresses the centrality of the Leviathan State in the decline of violent acts during the Renaissance. However, another element is suggested as the cause for the decline, namely: the *gentle commerce* - capitalism. Pinker credits the economic reformation in which feudalism became replaced by the capitalist system as a further cause in the decline in the rate of violence. Furthermore, a notable change in the overall sensibility of individuals occurred during the Enlightenment period, during which explicitly sadistic behavior that was previously common became less frequent and some feelings of sympathy and self-control began to sprout[4].

Later, Pinker explores murder and other violent crime rates during the World Wars. Replete with data, graphics, and all sorts of percentages and statistics, the author aims to convince the reader that even the tragic events of the 20th century were not *proportionally* more violent than ordinary life in ancient, *non-state societies*. After World War II, occurred an expansion of the Leviathan State through some intergovernmental commerce organizations, such as the European Coal and Steel Community, “founded

in 1950 by France, West Germany, Belgium, the Netherlands and Italy to oversee a common market and regulate the production"[5]. Pinker contends that the international capitalist structure served as a sort of centralized and supervising power and thus credits it as being an influential factor in the decrease of violent murder rates. Furthermore, Pinker argues that legal and social manifests against violence have a complementary force in the task of restraining violent acts, citing the Universal Declaration of Human Rights, and so on.

Yet, *The Better Angels of Our Nature* is not only an extensive historical investigation. A substantial part of the book is devoted to the psychology of violence. Pinker[6] develops an understanding of this phenomenon grounded in a "synthesis of cognitive science, effective and cognitive neuroscience, social and evolutionary psychology". He provides an in-depth explanation of the psychology and neurobiology of violence, not only in humans, but also in animals and human ancestors. Perhaps it would be better to begin with an issue that has some importance for psychoanalysis. Pinker does not admit a drive towards aggression as well as an innate tendency to act peacefully. In his own words:

> "The decline of violence thereby allows us to dispatch a dichotomy that has stood in the way of understanding the roots of violence for millennia: whether humankind is basically bad or basically good, an ape or an angel, a hawk or a dove, the nasty brute of textbook Hobbes or the noble savage of textbook Rousseau. Left to their own devices, humans will not fall into a state of peaceful cooperation, but nor do they have a thirst for blood that must regularly be slaked. There must be at least a grain of truth in conceptions of the human mind that grant it more than one part – theories like faculty psychology, multiple intelligences, mental organs, modularity, domain specificity, and the metaphor of the mind as a Swiss army knife. Human nature accommodates that – under the right circumstances – impel us toward peace, like compassion, fairness, self-control, and reason"[7].

Refusing the idea of a death drive, Pinker develops a long explanation of the psychology and neurobiology of violence, not only in humans, but also in animals and our ancestors. At the very least, the structure and the division of violence according to the author must be mentioned.

Firstly, Pinker exposes the *neurobiology of violence*. There are four different brain systems that produce *violent acts*[8]. *(i)* The first one is the *Rage circuit*, which connects the periaqueductal gray, the hypothalamus and the amygdala. This circuit is present in inferior mammals and is responsible for a cat's hiss and attack. *(ii)* The second one is the *Seeking System*, localized in midbrain and lateral hypothalamus, which motivates the animal to hunt and to identify the animals to pursue. This system has a

straight connection to the liberation of dopamine. *(iii)* The third one is *Fear System*, which is very similar to the *Rage System*. Indeed, there is a powerful interaction between the Rage and Fear systems, and, according to Pinker, that is the reason why animals and humans attack when afraid. *(iv)* The last one is called *Dominance System.* This system is located near "and probably interacts strongly with both the Rage and Seeking circuits"[9]. In the *Dominance System,* there are three nuclei that have receptors for testosterone. The sort of aggressiveness triggered by this part of the brain is related with the male sexuality in mammals.

These systems are closely located within the brain as well as interconnected. All these systems that trigger violence exist in inferior mammals. The radical difference in the anatomy of human brain is that it has something similar to a sort of *brain cover*, an extra layer on top of the primitive mammal (sub-cortical) structures which serves to restrain certain impulses. As Pinker says, "The neuro-anatomy suggests that, in *homo sapiens,* primitive impulses of rage, fear, and craving must contend with the cerebral restraints of prudence, moralization, and self-control [...]"[10].

This "brain cover" is mostly responsible for the brain structures of peace. The first brain structure of peace is the *Orbital cortex*, which is an inhibitor of violence present also in inferior mammals. It is a primitive part of the cerebrum "involved in several of the pacifying faculties of the human mind, including self-control [...] and sensitivity to norms and conventions"[11]. The second part is the *junction between temporal and parietal lobe*, which makes possible the feeling that Pinker calls empathy (the ability to understand the desires of another person, to put himself in the perspective of some other human being). Finally, the third part is the *dorsolateral cortex*, responsible for the intellectual judgment and the utilitarian thought. The *dorsolateral cortex* is ambivalent, allowing the decreasing of violent acts or the justification of some sorts of violence.

Pinker is sensible enough to distinguish the neural functioning (the "hardware", in his metaphor) and the psychological reasons of violence (the "software"). Adapting from the work *Evil* of he psychologist Roy Baumeister, Pinker discern five categories of violence. Perhaps it would be useful to present Pinker's taxonomy in his own words:

> "The first category of violence may be called practical, instrumental, exploitative, or predatory. It is the simplest kind of violence: the use of force as a means to an end. The violence is deployed in pursuit of a goal such as greed, lust, or ambition, which is set up by the Seeking system, and it is guided by the entirety of the person's intelligence, for which the dorsolateral prefrontal cortex is a convenient symbol. The second root of violence is dominance—the drive for supremacy over one's rivals

> (Baumeister calls it "egotism"). This drive may be tied to the testosterone-fueled Dominance or Intermale Aggression system, though it is by no means confined to males, or even to individual people. As we shall see, groups compete for dominance too. The third root of violence is revenge—the drive to pay back a harm in kind. Its immediate engine is the Rage system, but it can recruit the Seeking system to its cause as well. The fourth root is sadism, the joy of hurting. This motive, puzzling and horrifying in equal measure, may be a by-product of several quirks of our psychology, particularly the Seeking system. The fifth and most consequential cause of violence is ideology, in which true believers weave a collection of motives into a creed and recruit other people to carry out its destructive goals. An ideology cannot be identified with a part of the brain or even with a whole brain, because it is distributed across the brains of many people"[12].

With the astonishing exception of ideology, every sort of psychological violence is produced by one or two neurobiological Systems. Ideology is the only kind of psychological violence that is somehow supra-individual.

The author stresses the idea that human beings have cerebral structures that permit violent acts but also have psychological constructs that allow for a peaceful existence. The first psychological construct of peace is the feeling of *sympathy*, which is the ability to "put oneself in the shoes of another" – that is, to see things from another person's perspective, understanding their thoughts and emotions. When an individual is "witnessing the suffering of another person," sympathy is what causes a feeling of distress in the viewer. Apparently, Pinker relates the feeling of sympathy not to a specific Brain System, but rather to hormonal plumbing (specially to oxytocin - the so-called "motherhood hormone"). This supports the idea that "maternal care is the evolutionary precursor of other forms of human sympathy"[13]. However, Pinker understands that sympathy is not a biologically-motivated sentiment. Sympathy is a psychological trait that assumes the existence of a human community. In his words, sympathy is "accompanied by guilt and forgiveness. Anything that creates a communal relationship, then, should also create sympathy"[14]. Thus, community, guilt and forgiveness are intimately connected to the feeling of sympathy.

The second psychological construct that allows for a peaceful existence is *self-control.* Pinker abundantly praises the exercise of *self-control* in the human mind. He designates the brain activity associated with *self-control* as located mainly in the frontal lobe and in the dorsolateral cortex. Analyzing some experimental studies on human *self-control*, Pinker feels confident enough to argue that individuals who demonstrate proper self-control are also good at putting things in perspective. The author states

that "contrary to the conventional wisdom that says that people with too much self-control are uptight, repressed, neurotic, bottled-up, wound-up, obsessive-compulsive, or fixated at the anal stage of psychosexual development, the team found that the more self-control people have, the better their lives are. The people at the top of the scale were the mentally healthiest"[15]. According to Pinker, *self-control* is a partially inherited characteristic. Further, it is significantly related to intelligence coefficients - that is, individuals with higher IQ's tend to demonstrate higher levels of *self-control*. He further points out that *self-control* is correlated with a decline in murder rates.

Pinker equally argues that morality has an effect on controlling violence, in spite of not necessarily having any relation to reason. "Moral norms", says Pinker, "even when ineffable, can sometimes be effective brakes on violent behaviour"[16]. These moral norms which, according to the complex models adopted by Pinker, might not always be efficient in interrupting violence, can improve this efficiency when joined with Reason. As such, the religious model of *communal sharing* can become the principle of human rights, the principle of authority present in traditional communities which "may authorize the state's monopoly on the use of violence in order to prevent greater violence"[17].

Finally, Pinker emphasizes that reason is one of the most important weapons against violence. Reason is both biologically and statistically linked to self-control. Using reason, it is possible to, "suppress some of our base instincts in the service of motives that we are better able to justify"[18]. Furthermore, reason is capable of being linked to morality – an advantageous connection. Pinker argues that reason is an instrument of peace, should he that implements his reason desires peace – that is, should he wish to exist in a community that promotes well-being.

In the final part of the book, Pinker summarizes the books contents in order to propose a process for dealing with the problem of violence. First, he maintains that the Leviathan Model is the best method of *making peace more attractive than war*. As Pinker states, "if government imposes a cost on an aggressor that is large enough to cancel out his gains – say, a penalty that is three times the advantage of aggressing over being peaceful – it flips the appeal of the two choices of the potential aggressor"[19]. Evidently, *Pinker considers a violent act a rational decision* that can somehow be measured. Second, the external instance of self-control (*the bystander*, in Pinker's vocabulary) must be more and more internalized by the individual as an ubiquitous presence of self-control. Third, individuals must transform their understanding of reality from the "zero-sum warfare" interpretation into the "positive-sum, mutual profit" understanding, by

means of the gentle commerce. In sum, Pinker advocates a strong capitalist State with self-controlled, reasonable and sympathetic people as the best path toward the task of annihilating violence in the world.

As we have seen, then, Pinker understands the phenomena of peace and violence as being grounded in a biological structure molded by evolution. This structure can develop itself with a tendency toward violent behaviors (sadism, dominance) or toward peace (self-control, sympathy) according to the environment. The protagonist of his theory is a rational individual who deals with his biological structures inherited in the process of evolution. Pinker denies the possibility of an innate drive toward violence, arguing that the human being has as many structures to produce violence as he has structures capable of engendering peace. Pinker is very immersed in his task of constructing a world without violence, claiming that the path toward this world is paved by two levels of intervention: political and psychological. The first one can be understood as the expansion of the power and scope of the Leviathan State, the dissemination of gentle commerce and the promulgation of individual rights. The second one is the intense encouragement of *self-control* in individuals, the reinforcement of sympathy and the exercise of the rational thought. To conclude our quite abbreviated panorama, Pinker fully accepts that violence is something that *must be annihilated* and further argues that the reduction of violence has little impact on the joy and pleasure that people can experience.

The Psychoanalytical Response

I must begin my critique by offering a different perspective of the problem of violence. In order to do so, it is worthwhile to reconstruct the path Freud used to approach the matters of violence, self-control, empathy and reason.

At the beginning of his clinical and theoretical work, Freud long resisted accepting the existence of an aggressive drive. In the first part of his work, which occurred between 1900 and 1920, Freud thought that the human being has an innate drive that would essentially move the human being towards pleasure. However, in face of the dangers of the environment, this drive to obtain pleasure is gradually substituted by a different principle, which permits the permanence of a lower level of dissatisfaction in order to preserve its own life. Although there is yet no designation of a death drive in this work, the sex drive itself could become a source of aggression if limitations and censorship of desire promoted by self-preservation happened to occur. Aggression is associated with the

censorship of the conscience, by being a conscience responsible for impeding and repressing these desires.

Yet, there was a problem. Certain phenomena of aggression challenged this conception, leaving Freud in a delicate situation. First, there was the cruelty found amongst children, a phenomenon that proved difficult to understand in light of this conception. Another, perhaps less artful phenomenon (due to its close link to sexuality), was sadism. In his work *Three Essays on the Theory of Sexuality*, Freud presented the concept of a dominance drive which ended up being referenced to the scope of the self. In this book, the dominance present in sadism and children's cruelty would be due to the selfish forces of auto-preservation. As Birman confirms:

> "It was in this direction that the Freudian discourse began to formulate the concept of the dominance drive, in which sadism would serve the ego in order to dominate the object. It would be for these biases, therefore, that aggression would be articulated as a problem of power and cruelty, [...] This theoretical model was further detailed in "Instincts and Their Vicissitudes", an essay of Metapsychology, in which the relationship between love and hate for the psyche is discussed in a surprising way. Indeed, hate here would not be a negative love, as one might suppose given the apparent mutation of hate into love. This would be an illusion, since hate would have its own genesis. [Yet], as Laplance and Pontalis tell us, in the Vocabulary of Psychoanalysis, "the true prototypes of hate do not stem from sexual life, but rather from the ego's fight for its own preservation and affirmation". It therefore follows that, in short, the dominance drive forms part of the self's own record of itself, that concerns itself effectively with its own preservation and affirmation"[20].

One must therefore arrive at the conclusion that the phenomenon of aggression found in neurotics initially did not manage to awake in Freud an ambition to conceive of an aggression drive. In the first phase of his work, aggression will generally be a result due to limiting the *Eros* in the form of self-censorship, with the aim of self-preservation.

Only after seeing the clinical effects of a terrible war did Freud see himself as obligated to change his conception of violence. Starting with the clinical cases of war veterans whom he treated, as explored in his 1920 work *Beyond the Pleasure Principle*, Freud becomes astonished with the fact that these war-trauma induced dreams have gone in a direction completely opposite to pleasure – be it conscious or unconscious. In his inaugural book of psychoanalysis, *The Interpretation of Dreams*, dreams were understood as hallucinatory manifestations of desire distorted by censorship. On the contrary, these traumatic dreams did nothing more than reenact both the conscious and unconscious displeasure of a traumatic

scene[21]. Those dreams characteristic of traumatic neurosis indicated to Freud that there is a part of the psyche that operates not in the search for satisfying erotic desires and the reduction of stress, but rather in the complete annihilation of the being. This impulse toward destruction – which Freud called the death drive (*Todestrieb*) – forces the organism's level of tension to return to zero in the most radical way, that is, returning to the inorganic state of matter. In this way, Freud began to conceive the death drive that, along with the erotic drive, composes the unconsciousness's dynamic. It is important to note that violence, as understood in psychoanalysis, cannot be separated into immutable categories (as does Pinker with his "five violences"). On the contrary, violence is born out of an auto-destructive impulse that has the power to transform itself into other types of violence. Its most important characteristic is its mobility.

In the final part of the work, sexual and death drives expand their meanings to principles and elevate themselves to societal movements. In the incomplete work *Abriß der Psychoanalyse*, Freud conceptualized the death drive (*Thanatos*) as a drive for disassembly, while the sexual drive (*Eros*) is destined to aggregate disperse parts and unit them as a whole.

Now that we have presented Freudian drive theory, albeit in an entirely too concise manner, we must now investigate two essential elements of psychoanalytic theory. The first is the *instance of censorship* (which Freud termed the "superego"), which responds in the most expansive way to what Pinker calls the "self-control" and "morality". The second is the *fragility of reason*, found at the base of psychoanalytic theory. This paper will not touch upon one of Pinker's fundamental themes: empathy. The theme – which, in psychoanalysis, goes from *Totem and Taboo* to the problem of tolerance with Slavoj Zizek – deserves its own article, given its complexity. This, however, will not prevent us from discussing some other considerations about violence and how it contrasts with Pinker's vision.

The Instance of Censorship

After the 1920's revision of drive theory, Freud began to reconsider several aspects of his concepts. One of the most important Freudian conceptual revisions is the new division of psychical apparatus in three instances: the id (*Es*), the ego (*Ich*) and the superego (*Über-Ich*). The *id* is the most profound and largest part of the psychic reality, motivated by the sexual and death drives, wherein reside all unconscious processes – the ones that were repressed from the consciousness and the ones that never have been in the consciousness. The ego is a structure that emerges from

the *id*, modified by the direct influence of the external world, being responsible for the rational thought. In Freud's words, "the ego represents what can be called reason and common sense, in contrast to the id, which contains the passions"[22]. It is worth-mentioning that the ego systematically interprets the action of the *id*'s drives as if it were its own desire.

And the superego – what is that? It is an instance of censorship, of self-observation, of moral conscience. The superego co-opts instinctual aggression, redirecting it via moral censorship against its own impulsive desires and against the ego. From the psychoanalytical perspective, the instance of moral censorship (also responsible for self-control) is a terrible violent instance, born out of the self-destruction drive. Moreover, it is important to state that this instance of control of the ego and of drives does not act solely upon the individual's action, but combs through each thought, instilling the auto-aggression characteristic of the feeling of guilt. Furthermore, there is no content defined *a priori* in the superego. By having originally been formed from one's identification with one's parents (which, throughout life, spreads to identification with authority figures, religious figures, professors, etc.), the superego can accumulate prohibitions and ideas – one more different than the next – leading to, in the case of neuroses-obsessed, the dedication to bizarre rituals. According to psychoanalytical theory, *the same instance that is responsible for self-control, containing violent desires and the crystallization of elevated ideas which the ego seeks to achieve, is also responsible for instilling a terrible sentiment of guilt, of inferiority in relation to the ideal, directing aggression against the ego and against desires.* It is important to state, as well, that violence and self-destruction that emanate from the drive are mobile and can strengthen the superego, now that they are directed toward external objects.

It might therefore be reasonable to be more cautious than Pinker when attributing decisive influence over the diminishment of violence to self-control. In the first place, for having dealt exactly with patients that have suffered from "side effects" of the instruments of self-control and morality for many years, psychoanalysis naturally distrusts this method. In reality, although it is absolutely indispensable for life within society, self-control is nothing more than a *rechanneling* of violence toward the individual. Its most common manifestations are self-loathing and guilt. Pinker does not seem to pay too much attention to the fact that self-control also involves a continuous and methodical self-observation, which is not limited to acts, but mainly occurs in the realm of thoughts. Thus, man no longer feels guilty for his actions, but feels the wrath of guilt and self-loathing every thought that deviates from moral ideal[23]. Unfortunately, these processes

are much less visible psychological laboratories. They rely on years of analysis in order to demonstrate their inner logic.

Encouraging the self-control means, therefore, to psychoanalysis, the strengthening of the instance of censorship and internal investigation, the superego. It is not in any way an annihilation of violence, but rather a reinvestment of violence. Increasing self-control means increasing aggression against the ego and against desire, a movement that, in turn, causes detrimental consequences. When one experiences a failure of self-control (it will inevitably fail at some point), or remembers a previous failure, or even at the mere prospect of future failure of self-control, superegoic aggressiveness will then be invested with full force, bringing the individual what Freud called *Unbehagen* (discontent). This discontent may, however, be translated into common language, such as guilt, self-loathing, suicidal thoughts and, in some cases, physical aggression against oneself. But it is above all a malaise that defies description. Put simply, in one's defense of self-control's role in suppressing violence, Pinker seems to forget to mention that self-control is also a form of violence – violence against one's very self. Were man to suppress all his aggressive desires through self-control, this morality via patrolman – what type of effect would this have on his life? Thus, with the exception of cases where there is no self-control at all, increasing self-control seems to be a mistaken strategy for dealing with the problem of violence because it actually brings violence back to the individual, often involving the amplification of malaise to a level that we might reasonably call unbearable.

Psychoanalysis has a distinct solution to this problem. Freud attempts to address this problem in his work *Civilization and Its Discontents* by devoting himself primarily to the relationship between aggression and society. In this book, Freud questions the complex action that culture must exercise over human impulses. It is quite important to stress that, from a psychoanalytical perspective, the non-realization of aggressive desires implies an increasing sensation of discontent (*Unbehagen*). Each time man fails to satisfy a desire, he will necessarily be filled with a terrible discontent, a bitter unhappiness that will only grow and compound with future instances of this failure. Since man is constituted also by a death drive (apart from the *eros*), the impulse toward aggression and violence will continue to exist – in spite of all self-control and morality stimulated by the culture. However, if the death drive remains, it does not necessarily remains the violent *act*. For Freud, society becomes not merely a way to interrupt an aggressive act via self-control and morality but it also makes it possible to realize it's deadly satisfaction through society itself. To reach this conclusion, Freud returns to his concept of sublimation – which, in

simple terms, could be described as the process of "de-sexualizing" the sex drive, re-channeling it toward an intellectual or artistic destination (i.e. academic production, scientific research, painting, sculpture, etc.). As he began to assume the existence of the death drive in 1920, Freud began to speculate on the possibility of aggression being re-channeled within society – not as aggressive acts, but rather as a kind of sublimation of the death drive.

There are many cultural battles to be fought that can serve to rechannel the death drive, rather than reprimanding it through an excess of morality and self-control. Intellectual battles are perhaps the most sublime way to productively rechannel aggression. Political and rhetorical battles are also ways to co-opt this aggression toward a cultural and social order. The plastic and literary arts have also served as a privileged avenue for re-channeling agression. There are, however, smaller and more comprehensive cultural methods for channeling agression. We cannot forget Hollywood's role in letting the world live out its aggressive impulses vicariously via the big screen as well as the essential role of *Call of Duty, God of War* and other modern emulators. From a certain perspective, Vin Diesel is more important than Woody Allen.

There is yet another avenue that is neither athletic nor artistic nor sublimatory, necessarily. This is the psychoanalytical path, with its precarious means and its aversion to totalizing explanations about the phenomenon of aggression. When considering the division (splitting) that characterizes the subject of psychoanalysis – the division between reason and desire – the French psychoanalyst Jacques Lacan synthesized, in his own way, the psychoanalyst's task and position regarding his work with aggression:

> In the 'emancipated' man of modern society, this splitting reveals, right down to the depths of his being, a neurosis of self-punishment, with the hysterico-hypochondriac symptoms of its functional inhibitions, with the psychasthenic forms of its derealizations of others and of the world, with its social consequences in failure and crime. It is this pitiful victim, this escaped, irresponsible outlaw, who is condemning modern man to the most formidable social hell, whom we meet when he comes to us; it is our daily task to open up to this being of nothingness the way of his meaning in a discreet fraternity – a task for which we are always too inadequate[24]

Unfortunately, it is unreasonable to expect that culture will provide us with all the means to sublimate violence, despite having giving us much up until now. Further, we cannot be so optimistic as to think that any psychotherapy will eradicate man's aggression, for, were it successful in this task, the effects would include the nulling of desire and the re-

emergence of the super ego – and all of the ailments associated to it. Psychoanalysis is very familiar with the errors of insisting on this path. If, in the future, we aim to live in a society with less discontent, it is essential to have more boldness in dealing with violence that goes beyond these useful, but ultimately insufficient methods. We believe this is the strategy of psychoanalysis, since peace is not just the act of refraining from violence.

The Weakness of Reason

We must now investigate a second point: the problem of the weakness of reason in psychoanalysis. Ever since its beginning with hysteric symptoms in the 19th century, psychoanalysis did not fail to find it justifiable to consider the instance responsible for rationality as constituting merely the surface of a vast sea of unconscious desires. This justification initially stemmed from treating neurotic patients, mainly hysterical patients, that physically carried out, symptomatically, that which was blocked access via the consciousness25. In the treatment of hysteria, it was discovered that throughout the entire conscious and rational process, there was a greater, dynamic process that had nothing to do necessarily with reason and the consciousness. This larger process left traces in dream analysis, in the patient's symptoms, and in slips. By gathering the traces of these phenomena in patients' cases, in dream, in literature and in the arts, Freud advanced his hypothesis that, the dynamic of the human psyche, there is something greater than the rational. The base for all rational proceedings – the "ego" – is just a small portion of all psychical activity. Unconscious processes fall within a greater scope and are much more capable of moving the psyche's dynamic.

Apart from this modest participation of the ego and of reason in the psyche's dynamic, there is another observable phenomenon in psychoanalytical clinical practice, whose effects were observed even before the invention of psychoanalysis. In one of his experiments with hysterics at the Salpetrière, Jean-Martin Charcot ordered a hysteric to do something while the latter was under a hypnotic trance. As predicted, upon awaking from the hypnotic state, the hysteric did that which he was ordered to do. Yet, when the hysteric was questioned by Charcot as to why he had done it, she did not states she was unaware of his motives. On the contrary, she affirmed his awareness of the reasons for his actions, and began to give entirely rational and legitimate explanation for his act. This act of rationalizing an order coming from an unconscious state, already present in the Charcot's hypnotic experiments, ended up revealing itself to

be as true and present as the act of providing a rational framework for unconscious desires. Freud notes that, often, the "ego" tries to take responsibility for its unconscious desires. Clinical psychoanalysis, therefore, alerts one to the fact that "conscious thought appeals to a rationalization to mask an unconscious motive"26. Put differently, rational thought often sustains itself with unconscious desires that only reveal their true reach during analysis. As such, it is difficult to say when there exists pure rationality (if such thing does indeed exist at all), and when this rationality is pervaded with desires that are not accessible to reason itself.

Therefore, there are two weaknesses of reason. The first is a *constitutive weakness*. Human reason is modest in comparison to the dominance of unconscious desires. The second is an *operative weakness*. Reason can assume as its own reality certain desires that it is incapable of seeing itself. Regarding the first, Pinker seems to be conscious that, in human history, reason has always developed in its relationship with desire. Regarding the second weakness, however, Pinker's book contains a fundamental problem. The unconditional embrace of scientific studies as the way to discover truths about man might not allow him to see a certain "desire" that is in play. We might make three observations that, at first, could seem to lack cohesion. But, they will lead to the center of an important argument.

Method. Pinker's decision to work with data proportional to the quantity of violence is a methodological choice and entirely justified from a rational standpoint. Nevertheless, from a practical standpoint, this choice makes a massively singular event in human history, such as the Second World War, comparable to tribal skirmishes. There is a general leveling of differences between the quality of violence and its strategic use, reducing almost everything to a question of quantity. The methodological choice itself should already say something to the more attentive observer – as Robert Epstein stated in one of the first critiques of Pinker's book[27]. In this critique, in addition to rejecting that the use of proportional data would be the best way to approach the problem, Epstein also pointed out that Pinker selected scientific data that corroborated his thesis while electing to leave out data that did not support his ideas and conclusions. "Pinker wants peace, and he also believes in his hypothesis; it is no surprise that he focuses more on facts that support his views than on those that do not"[28]. At the very least, we must be suspicious of this use of proportional data as a justification.

Concept. There's no doubt that Pinker takes a pragmatic approach to violence. Violence is something that can be measured, illustrated in graphics, able to have its rates extracted, in short, comparable. If, on the

one hand, this measured approach to violence allows us to see an important part of the phenomenon, it questions very little the concept of violence itself, on the other hand. There are many theories of violence found in philosophy that would see in this conception a lack of means which would result in insufficient conclusions (*e.g.* G. Agamben, W. Benjamin, S. Zizek). Despite the quotations of Hobbes, it is not a concept of violence that is in play, but a *practical definition.* We think that opting for this practical definition of violence has many motivations – but Pinker sees only scientific motivations for this choice.

Support. Lastly and oddly, Pinker hardly questions the conditions under which the hundreds of scientific studies cited in his book were performed – if they had a broad cultural reach, if they are really trustworthy. The investigations of the academic actor-network theory regarding the creation of scientific truths casts doubt up the scientific truths linked to political problems, since they are productions that come from a certain society – and for this reason they are inevitably affected by it[29]. Despite all the lessons from the philosophers of science, we are unable to see that Pinker really questioned the status of these truths. After all, for the author, the results were found through a methodologically strict, logical and rational process. Pinker accepts his results with the naturalness of one who reaches an indisputable truth (that can only be questioned if there was an error in the method.)

It is in precisely this way that reason shows its second weakness. The method (proportional), the concept (pragmatic) and the support (scientific) are works of rational thought. Yet, these tree axes, fundamental to Pinker's book, are at the service of a political desire. Pinker desires a State that controls it citizens at every moment (preferably they control themselves), allowing them, however, to maintain the impression that they are free to act as they wish. The relationship between man and his neighbor is based in the word "tolerance" – a word of order – which, as Slavoj Zizek defines it, means that another cannot manifest himself as *otherness*[30]. Supposedly, each person has his own personal space protected and guaranteed. The punishment for he who would violate the law of tolerance is established via mathematical methods and impedes physical violence between those that makeup society. No violence is permitted other than that of the State – whose intention is to suppress violence. In this context, the *method, concept, and support* of Pinker act in harmony to confirm the advances of peace and the benefits of the desired model.

Still, Pinker almost unwillingly admits that a "measured degree of violence […] in the form of police forces and armies [...]" will be necessary[31]. We do not have the same certainty as Pinker that the extent of

this violence will be reasonable or measured. The Slovenian philosopher Slavoj Zizek warns us of a recurring error:

> "When we perceive something as an act of violence, we measure it by a presupposed standard of what the "normal" non-violent situation is – and the highest form of violence is the imposition of this standard with reference to which some events appear as 'violent"'[32].

Pinker says nothing about the violence necessary in the coercions necessary to the production of capital. He also says very little about the relationship between violence and inequality found at the heart of the political model which he defends. There is equally no distrust that the authority of a police force can be used for violent purposes. And there exists no possibility of considering violence as anything other than what he thinks it is. Pinker claims the authority of modern science in order to justify his wish of a society free from a certain type of violence. Yet, the author remains silent regarding the possible element of "residual violence". They are, in short, the remnants necessary for the exploitation of "human capital", for the production of private capital and for the repression of the otherness. This last, silent part in Pinker's developmentalist epic is striking to those *on the other side* of this vision of power. It is with good reason that the book generated so much anger amongst socialist critics and indigenous theorists[33].

Conclusion

Pinker's strategy is understandable. He would like to annihilate the death drive's most obvious effects. Additionally, he would like to have a society based purely in Eros – a gentle commerce between nations, wide empathy circles, etc. As such, he attempts to strengthen the ties of Eros while, at the same time, he makes *Thanatos* part of the State's machine (and that of Reason) in order to prevent violence. He would like to have Reason command the death drive in order to avoid violence – understood here in a practical sense.

Yet, this begs many questions. How can Reason defend against something it itself cannot see or conceive? And what if Reason isn't preventing violence but rather encouraging that very violence in man? And what if, as has happened so many times in the past, Reason is being used to justify existing violence through scientific debate? What if Reason simply serves to numb the economic system that it has created? And what if it is Reason that produces the very psychological ailments that it seeks to cure?

Psychoanalysts reluctantly trust reason. They are also very aware of the counterpart, the effects of government and political intervention regarding the individual's desires. It doesn't seem that Pinker's proposed direction given to desire can produce a less violent world. It can certainly be less violent as Pinker defines the term, rooted in his methodological intelligence; but, the same does not hold for violence as defined by psychoanalysis. In psychoanalytical clinical practice, we see the death drive's every force when it fails to be sublimated, and returns in an overwhelming way over the patient and his body.

Notes

[1] Pinker 2011, xxi

[2] Pinker 2011, xxiv.

[3] In accordance with Pinker (2011, 35), Leviathan's logic could be understood as it follows. Consider an aggressor and a victim. The aggressor imposes his power and violence upon the victim, which attempts to *hit back*, to retaliate in order to escape from or destroy the aggressor. Since there is no guarantee that a stranger will not attack, the more reasonable strategy is always attack first, so that one minimizes the risks of an aggressive act. This condition of distrust and generalized aggression is the Hobbesian state of nature. Thus, the solely measure capable of reversing this scene is a powerful *bystander* whose action is to inhibit the aggressor's violence (through the use of violence). Pinker takes very seriously the Hobbesian theory, as seen in this quotation: "Violence between the combatants may be called war; violence by the bystander against the combatants may be called law. The Leviathan theory, in a nutshell, is that law is better than war. Hobbes's theory makes a testable prediction about the history of violence. The Leviathan made its first appearance in a late act in the human pageant. Archaeologists tell us that humans lived in a state of anarchy until the emergence of civilization some five thousand years ago, when sedentary farmers first coalesced into cities and states and developed the first governments. If Hobbes's theory is right, this transition should also have ushered in the first major historical decline in violence" (Pinker, 2011, 35). Therefore, the first substantial decline in the rates of violence is attributed to solid and centralized governments in ancient cities.

[4] Pinker 2011, 169.

[5] Pinker 2011, 289.

[6] Pinker 2011, xxiii.

[7] Pinker 2011, 483.

[8] Pinker 2011, 497-509.

[9] Pinker 2011, 501.

[10] Pinker 2011, 502.

[11] Pinker 2011, 507.

[12] Pinker 2011, 508-509.

[13] Pinker 2011, 579.

[14] Pinker 2011, 585.
[15] Pinker 2011, 599.
[16] Pinker 2011, 624.
[17] Pinker 2011, 637.
[18] Pinker 2011, p. 645.
[19] Pinker 2011, 680.
[20] Birman 2006, 316.
[21] Freud 1961.
[22] Freud 1996, 39.
[23] Freud 2013.
[24] Lacan 2001, 22.
[25] Freud 1964.
[26] Freud 2012, 308.
[27] Epstein 2011.
[28] Epstein 2011.
[29] Latour 2000; Latour 1997.
[30] Zizek 2008.
[31] Pinker 2011, 646.
[32] Zizek 2008, 64.
[33] Herman 2014; Corry 2014.

References

Birman, Joel. “Arquivo da agressividade em psicanálise”. *Natureza humana,* São Paulo 8, n. 2 (2006). Accessed January, 2015. http://pepsic.bvsalud.org/scielo.php?script=sci_arttext&pid=S1517-24302006000200005&lng=pt&nrm=iso

Canguilhem, Georges. Études d'histoire et de philosophie des sciences. Paris: Vrin, 1979.

Corry, Stephen. "The case of the ‘Brutal Savage’: Poirot or Clouseau?: Why Steven Pinker, like Jared Diamond, is wrong". *Survival International* (2014). Accessed January, 2015. http://assets.survivalinternational.org/documents/1081/corry-on-pinker.pdf

Epstein, Robert. Book Review: The Better Angels of Our Nature: Why Violence Has Declined. Scientific American (2011). Accessed January, 2015. http://www.scientificamerican.com/article/bookreview-steven-pinker-the-better-angels-of-our-nature-why-violence-has-declined/

Freud, Sigmund. O Ego e o Id. In: *Obras completas de Sigmund Freud Vol XIX: o Ego e o id e outros trabalhos,* edited by Jayme Salomão. Rio de Janeiro: Imago, 1996.

Freud, Sigmund. Estudos sobre histeria. In: *Obras completas de Sigmund Freud Vol II:* Estudos sobre histeria, edited by Jayme Salomão. Rio de Janeiro: Imago, 1964.

Freud, Sigmund. Contribuição à história do movimento psicanalítico. In: *Obras completas, volume 11: Totem e Tabu, contribuição à história do movimento psicanalítico e outros textos.* Edited by Paulo César de souza. São Paulo: Companhia das letras, 2012.

Freud, Sigmund. *O mal-estar na cultura.* Porto Alegre: L&PM, 2013.

Herman, Edward, and David Peterson. *Reality Denial: Steven Pinker’s Apologetics for Western-Imperial Violence.* Coldtype, 2013. Accessed January, 2015. http://coldtype.net/Assets.12/PDFs/0812.PinkerCrit.pdf

Latour, Bruno. *A ciência em ação.* São Paulo: Editora Unesp, 2000

Latour, Bruno. *Nous n'avons jamais été modernes.* Paris: La Découverte, 1997.

Law, John. *After Method: Mess in Social Science Research.* Abingdon: Routledge, 2004

Pinker, Steven. *The Better Angels of our nature.* London: Penguin, 2011.

Zizek, Slavoj. Violence: Six Sideways Reflections. New York: Picador, 2008.

Chapter Five

'Will it not be Better': Recognising the Indian Psychoanalytical Society

AKSHI SINGH

Some of the objects that populated Sigmund Freud's consulting rooms in Bergasse 19, Wien IX came with him to London. When the most precious of these, the "famous collection of Greek and Egyptian antiquities" and other "Oriental treasures" arrived, the poet and novelist H.D. sent the Professor a bunch of gardenias to "greet the return of the Gods."[1] Freud, quoting this in his note of thanks, added–"other people read: Goods."[2] These objects, both the ones that were returned to the Professor, and the ones that were lost, made another journey, coming to inhabit H.D.'s memoir of her analysis with Freud. Here they have the dual status of "Gods or the Goods."[3]

These objects have an exceptional mobility in H.D.'s account. They are symbols, hold associations that she is invited to release, and are portals into other times. Time, like the objects, is also particularly mobile–both seeming to move into each other–"Length, breadth, thickness, the shape, the scent, the feel of things. The actuality of the present, its bearing on the past, their bearing on the future."[4] A multiplicity of times and places seem to co-exist and coalesce in the analytic room that H.D. describes.

There is the present moment, in which she adjusts the rug or sneaks a look at her wristwatch. There is the childhood home evoked by the porcelain stove, which transforms Freud's room into her father's study. The objects and paintings sometimes stand for another, civilizational, time–but one that becomes part of the present again when it reappears as dream symbols that are discussed in analysis. And right outside the room, there is the historical moment, stacked with rifles on the street corner, scratched in chalk on the pavements. In H.D.'s analogy, time was like a room, with a fourth dimension to it–"described and elaborately tabulated in the

Professor's volumes."[5] In the account of her analysis, she would represent an attempt to articulate a relationship to time, to find the time that she was living through.

It is a moment of tension in the text, when Freud invites H.D. to look at the objects arranged on his desk–"I did not always know if the Professor's excursions with me into the other room were by way of distraction, actual social occasions, or part of his plan."[6] In an exchange where all gestures and words seem more than usually weighted with meaning, H.D. describes herself drawn to the objects on the desk, while at the same time trying to think of an appropriate response to them. Her response is articulated within her reading of Freud's desire–"I wanted then, as at other times, to meet him halfway."[7]

She picked a statuette of a Hindu god- (Vishnu, by her guess), to comment upon–partly incorporated into her elaborate personal mythology because of the S shaped serpents that formed a dome over the god's head in the statuette. She could not, however, easily take in the object or enter it–"this carved Indian ivory which compelled me, yet repelled me, at the same time."[8] Her expression of interest in it, despite her ambivalence towards it, was directed by her reading of its place at the centre of Freud's semi-circle of objects–its place seen as a mark of its importance to Freud.

This was desire predicated on an attempt to predict the desire of the other–the teacher, the master. In this, H.D. seemed to fail. Freud, "barely glancing at the lovely object," said that it was sent to him by his "Indian students."[9] He followed that with the remark: "On the whole, I think my Indian students have reacted in the least satisfactory way to my teaching."[10] It had then not been possible to meet him halfway. "So much for India, so much for his Indian students," she wrote.[11] In a gesture that seems to have an almost consolatory, restorative position in the text, right after this dismissal, Freud offers to H.D. a small statue of Athena ("He knew that I loved Hellas").[12] She had kept her place amongst his chosen students.[13]

The traffic in goods, the place of gods, and time–as a belief in progress as well as the intimations of its impossibility, are key to an account of psychoanalysis in India. Also unavoidable in any discussion of psychoanalysis as an institution is the question of what it meant to be Freud's students–never an easy question, let alone position, and one that was particularly complicated at the time of H.D.'s analysis–when swastikas rained like confetti on the streets of Vienna.

By this time Freud had given, in *Civilization and its Discontents,* an account of the psyche in which the agency which is meant to be the voice of conscience is intolerant, harsh and demanding of increasing sacrifice.

Civilization had made of the individual a conquered city, with an internal garrison to keep watch over it–guilt arose not just from fear of an external authority, but also from the authority that had been internalised as part of the psyche–"threatened external unhappiness–loss of love and punishment on the part of the external authority–has been exchanged for a permanent internal unhappiness, for the tension of the sense of guilt."[14] Here, Freud's description of the superego sounds like his description of the leader-as-tyrant in *Moses and Monotheism*: "jealous, severe and ruthless"[15] and "domineering, hot tempered and even violent."[16]

Mark Edmundson writes that just as Freud was offering this radical critique of authority, he was also complicit with the consolidation of authority in the persona of Sigmund Freud, as well as its entrenchment in the International Psychoanalytical Association.17 However, the ineluctable ambivalence towards authority remained unacknowledged and unanalysed in the manner in which the institutionalisation of psychoanalysis took place. As Moustapha Safouan writes, the process of the institutionalisation of psychoanalysis performed "the myth promoted by Freud in *Totem and Taboo*, of a 'fraternal' deal dictated by a murder not so much actual as unable to be acknowledged, or rather able to be so even though it had not actually taken place; it was the end-point of a set of convergent repressions."18

If psychoanalytic institutions could act as though they were oblivious to the insights of psychoanalysis, then perhaps the question to ask of Freud's "Indian students" is not *why* they were found to be unsatisfactory, but *what* it was that was wanted of them, which they failed to provide. This brings us up against the question of how an object is recognised, or constituted through what may be wanted of it–the question then, at its broadest can be: what did psychoanalysis want? A question is complicated by the contradictoriness of the object psychoanalysis–who, or what, was psychoanalysis, and who spoke in its name?

In 1921, Girindrasekhar Bose, a Calcutta doctor and lecturer in "psychoanalysis and abnormal psychology" at the University of Calcutta, wrote to Ernest Jones.19 He asked about the International Psychological Association, of which he'd heard from Freud–its conditions of membership, and whether a branch could be established in Calcutta.20 In his reply, Jones writes -

> "the conditions to any given local society becoming affiliated to the International Society depends on my having reason to think that it contains members doing serious work along psycho-analytical lines. If you are able to start such a society in Calcutta (and may I suggest that you use the title

> Indian rather than Calcutta) I shall be extremely interested to hear of its progress."[21]

It did not take long for Jones to find reason to think that "serious work along psycho-analytical lines" was being carried out. Within seven months the *Indian* Psychoanalytical Society was in existence. The group of men who formed the first cohort of the Indian Psychoanalytical Society were Calcutta intellectuals, with the exception of two English members of the Indian Medical Service. Or, as Shruti Kapila writes–"psychology in India owed much to Calcutta, the 'undisputed centre of national science'."22 Indeed the Preface to Girindrasekhar Bose's *Svapna* thanks, amongst others, his brother Rajsekhar Bose, reknowned writer of satire under the pen name "Parushram" and Acharya Prafulla Chandra Ray, the author of *Hindu Chemistry.* M.N. Banerji, the first secretary of the society, was also Bose's publishing agent. That the Calcutta Society drew its members from a small, influential section of the people who lived in Calcutta is an obvious point, but it may seem more significant given Jones's suggestion that the Society be called the "Indian" rather than the "Calcutta" society.

Calcutta indicated a city, a geographical location, but it also served as to mark a particular place in empire, and in the time of the nation.23 Calcutta was a metropolis, in contrast to provinces understood as backward, and it remains a question who the Calcutta psychoanalysts saw themselves as closer to–psychoanalysts practicing in Europe, or the inhabitants of the backward provinces of India. It is worth remembering that in 1905, during the nationalist agitation in Bengal, "the spite of the Bengali nationalist press was often directed more to the savage Assamese neighbours than to the civilized British master."24 In a book published in 1945, forty years after the agitation, Bose, discussing the "murder instinct" would write: "(i)n the child or in the savage its manifestations are more or less open. The child takes delight in killing birds and insects and the savage goes out for head hunting merely for the pleasure of it."25 In a move that was the reverse of metonymy, the whole that was still being imagined (as well as administered, annexed and taxed) into existence, India, was made to stand in for a part, Calcutta. The expansive title of the Indian Psychoanalytical Society was spread like a mantle across those who had begun by identifying themselves with a city, Calcutta.

After the Indian Psychoanalytical Society was established, the following remark by Girindrasekhar Bose was included in a report published in the *International Journal of Psychoanalysis*:

> "in India psycho-analytical investigations were likely to yield very fruitful results both from the scientific and therapeutic standpoints. The mental

> cases practically went untreated and the immense variety of social and religious customs, some of them of extremely ancient origin and others comparatively recent with the people existing in different grades of civilization from the most primitive to the most modern, offered an immense field for the psycho-analyst."[26]

If there was something imperial in the tone of Jones's reply to Bose, then the Indian analysts seemed quite willing at times to perform what seemed to expected of them–if they were situated in a place that was thought to be prior in the time of capitalism, they could offer their world up as valuable to scientific investigation, while sharing in a teleological understanding of of psychoanalysis. We can return here to H.D., who tried pick the object that she thought Freud was interested in, tried to "meet him halfway." What might an identity might be, especially when the utterances through which we know it are shaped by an attempt to read another's desire, a desire which at times may be felt as an unarticulated demand?

There is an iterative quality to the terms that are used by critics to describe Girindrasekhar Bose: he is repeatedly introduced as a psychoanalyst, the first 'Indian" or "non-western" one. Ashis Nandy calls him "the Savage Freud," while for Christiane Hartnack he is "the doyen of Indian psychoanalysis."27 The term "Indian" is used quite uncomplicatedly, often in opposition to some idea of the "western." Christiane Hartnack's book *Psychoanalysis in Colonial India* is divided into two parts: "British Psychoanalysts in Colonial India" and, "The Work of Indian Psychoanalysts". Bose is categorized as an "Indian" psychoanalyst. When the Indian Psychoanalytical Society was affiliated to the International Association, Bose was still a member of the British Psychoanalytical Society.28 The Indian Psychoanalytical Society did not distinguish, in its categories of membership, between British and Indian. The British psychoanalysts discussed by Hartnack all belonged to the Indian Psychoanalytical Society. If Hartnack's distinctions are based, then, on nationality or ethnicity, then surely these are questions rather than pre-given categories?

Hartnack's distinction serves, in her argument, to mark the consequences in psychoanalytical work of the differences in nationality/ethnicity of the members. In assuming these categories to have been already constituted and available to the people she writes about, her book obfuscates questions of self-representation and identification which are particularly important to psychoanalysis if it is to be understood as a theory of mental representations (and their undoing). This move requires the elision of the similarity in the questions that interested the various psychoanalysts working at the time, and the conceptual categories they

used–we have already noted how Bose subscribed to the binary opposition between primitive and civilised.

In this attempt at strict separation between Indian and western psychoanalysis, it is as though entire parts of Bose's work can only present themselves as remainders to a narrative which wants to use the trope of resistance to Western knowledge in order to discuss Bose's work.29 In effecting this separation, Hartnack, perhaps unwittingly, comes close to sounding like Ernest Jones, writing to Bose in 1922–"(w)ill it not be better for you to transfer your allegiance from the British to the Indian group, as one cannot belong to more than one at a time."[30]

Ashis Nandy does note that "provocative and arrogant psychoanalytic summary trials of the Indian culture and personality" were put forward as much by Indian analysts as they were by analysts of British origin affiliated to the Indian Psychoanalytical Society.31 However, it is as though the resistance to a dominant western knowledge which Nandy cannot find explicitly articulated in Bose's writing has to be recuperated from elsewhere. Thus Nandy argues that Bose's "disembedding the discipline [psychoanalysis] from its cultural moorings in the West to relocate it in Indian high culture and in the bicultural lifestyle of the urban middle classes in colonial India" was a form of "unintended dissent"– and that this "unintended dissent," though "partial" due to Bose's cultural position, was responsible for his "intellectual robustness."32 Given Bose's comment on the head hunting savage, and his categorization of people into "different grades of civilization" it is well worth asking at this point *which* "savage" the title of Nandy's essay–"The Savage Freud: The First Non-Western Psychoanalyst and the Politics of Secret Selves in Colonial India"–refers to.

It is as though commentaries on Bose's work are working on the assumption that it could be better: *will it not be better*–if the work was less ambiguous, if there was an unambivalent critique of colonialism to be found in it. Jones' "will it not be better for you" is one person making a suggestion to another, yet the suggestion is made through phrasing that suggests that the speaker not only knows the other person's best interests, but also has them at heart. In an interaction with another person, such an authoritative claim to knowledge of the other's interest can be met with a response, even if the response is structured by imbalances of power and unequal access to language. However, if such an utterance is made towards a text or historical material, it becomes remarkably easy, in the absence of a response, to shape the material to one's will–in this case, to emphasise those parts of Bose's work that are easier to align to the idea of

a native resistance to western knowledge–and to suppress those that may challenge this construct.

Girindrasekhar Bose had a keen interest in establishing, beyond doubt, the status of psychology as a science. He returns to this point repeatedly, in both his Bengali and English writings–psychology is a science of the mind, "built on the same plan as that of any other science"–though it has its own, distinct subject matter and problematic.[33] Ashis Nandy accords to Bose's Bengali writings a greater skill and authenticity than his English texts, saying that "(it) is even possible that in Bengali he could more openly reconcile Indian classical traditions and the science of psychoanalysis, not only as two cognitive orders but as two aspects of his own self."[34] However what Nandy does not discuss is Bose's stated dissatisfaction with the Bengali language–"(w)hen one sits down to write an essay in Bangla, one experiences the lack of appropriate terminology at every step."[35] Bose's Bengali writings also carry the marks of attempts to make the language 'scientific'–English equivalents are provided in brackets to limit the play of polysemic Bengali words. Regardless of his skill in the language, Bose was interested in shaping the language so that it would be a suitable vehicle for scientific writing–easily translated and precise, and precision seemed to be a quality attributed to English words.36 When Bose turned to texts in Sanskrit this material was also interpreted and contained within pleas towards scientificity.

Bose's emphasis on scientificity was accompanied by a belief in the strict separation of disciplines–the first portion of his essay "Manuser Mon" argues for the "independence" of psychology from physiology, biology and philosophy. The interest in scientificity and disciplinarity was a major influence on how Bose theorised matters relating to the mind/psyche.[37] Illustrative of this is the theory of pan psychic psycho physical parallelism, developed in Bose's first book, and discussed in most subsequent work. The theory posits a radical separation between the domains of the psychic/mental and the physical. However, since both the body and the mind seem affected in certain instances, such as when alcohol is consumed, all objects are understood to have both a physical and a psychical component to them, and these respective components influence their corresponding counterparts in the object that is being acted upon–in this case, the person consuming the alcohol.

Theoretically, this seems to make the body unavailable as an object of enquiry to psychoanalysis. This was certainly not to be the case in Bose's therapeutic practice, where the patient's body was read and commented upon. Indeed Bose's theory puts his relation with psychoanalysis in question, given the manner in which Freud theorised the instinct / drive–

"a concept on the frontier between the mental and the somatic" and "as a measure of the demand made upon the mind for work in consequence of its connection with the body."[38] Freud's words–"frontier," "demand"–indicate a conversation, a back and forth movement which has central to it the issue of translation–as though the drive is a process of translation of a source text that cannot otherwise be accessed. What could the *talking* cure be, given Bose's utter splitting of the psychic from the material? In *Svapna* Bose discusses with great enthusiasm how narrative effects a cure. However, his own theory of the separate spheres of the material and the psychic cannot account for speech–especially the psychoanalytic understanding of the body being taken as material for speech in the expression of a symptom.

In reading Bose one feels that he wrote without interlocutors–while he had the honour of being the President of Indian Psychoanalytical Society, and one of the editors of the *International Journal of Psychoanalysis*, his work never received an engaged criticism. Freud, on receiving a copy of Girindrasekhar Bose's first book, *Concept of Repression* wrote that he was "glad to testify to the correctness of its principal views and the good sense appearing in it" but in both his letter to Bose and the blurb he wrote for the publisher, what stands out is his surprise at *where* the book came from–"(m)y surprise was great that psychoanalysis should have met with so much interest and recognition in your far off country" and again, "(i)t was a great and pleasant surprise that the first book on a psychoanalytic subject which came to us from that part of the world (India) should display so good a knowledge of psychoanalysis(...)."[39] A decade later, Freud was writing to Bose, expressing his regrets for not having paid attention to Bose's work earlier–"I suspect your theory of opposing wishes is practically unknown among us and never mentioned or discussed."[40]

So far we have seen that Bose's location in India functions in such a way that the *place* in which the writing was produced comes to serve as the master sign under which all his work is placed, and for different reasons served to obscure it both in the international psychoanalytic community to which Bose tangentially belonged, and in appraisals of him by postcolonial scholars. It is as though both these moments of interest in Bose avoid inhabiting the difficulty his work poses to assimilation, first to psychoanalysis and then to anti-colonial politics.

Writing to Freud in 1912, Ernest Jones mentions the papers contributed by Freud and Jung to a congress in Australia. He follows that by writing, rather jubilantly, "(t)here now remains only Brazil, China and Greenland to be penetrated. Still I do think with all the opposition that we shall suffer like Alexander for want of worlds to conquer."[41] Implicit here is the idea

that psychoanalysis, once it had established itself, would stay in place. Easy in his use of the pronoun "we"–speaking for both Freud and himself, or speaking perhaps in the name of psychoanalysis, Jones seems untroubled by the image of greedy imperial expansion that he conjures. Yet in his enthusiasm for *conquering* Jones seems to have forgotten the trials faced in the governance of large empires–and the combination of brutality and neglect required to keep them together.

Girindrasekhar Bose was a psychoanalyst who had never been through an analysis himself. It would seem that Bose had been accepted as analyst on the basis of his theoretical work (even though, as we have seen, this work was never seriously engaged with) as well as the geopolitics which placed him far away from Europe, in a place which both seemed desirable to include in the official psychoanalytic network, but also far away enough for analytic and institutional irregularities to be ignored. A later exchange between Jones and M.N. Banerji, Secretary of the IPS, makes clear where the centre of psychoanalysis was understood to be–if analytic training was to be conducted properly in India, then according to Jones what was "urgently needed" was that someone, "provided he has the necessary gifts" go to Europe for a "full training" so as to "better judge of the differences in standard and technique than is now possible with the relative isolation from which you suffer."[42] Jones' remark flags a contradiction. It was this "relative isolation" that kept the IPS from meeting the "standards" of psychoanalysis in Europe –

> "I very fully appreciate all that you say about the variation of standards in your Society. All that you say has, I think, held and to some extent still holds, of other Societies.(...) On the other hand, the Societies more favourably situated than yours have had the opportunity of raising their standards very considerably and are intent on still doing so. The fact that there have been all the difficulties you mention in the past must not deter us in this respect, or prevent us from pushing on in the future".[43]

At the same time, this very isolation may have made the IPS a valuable outpost for a psychoanalysis that imagined itself as *pushing on in the future*. Jonathan Lear writes that having "standards" may be a way of avoiding the difficult question of how a profession may conduct itself–"because the standards present themselves as having already answered the question"–but what is of interest here is also how Jones' professional standards seem to merge with the standards that nations hoist.44 Perhaps what was being avoided here, in the raising of standards (or marching under them)–were psychoanalytic insights about how there can be no uncomplicated *pushing on in the future*, the idea that the past waits around the corner waiting to direct the steps of the future.

We do not know what "difficulties" Banerji mentioned, but difficulties there were.45 Owen A.R. Berkeley Hill was the Superintendent of the Ranchi European Mental Hospital, and a founding member of the Indian Psychoanalytical Society. In his autobiography, Berkeley Hill would describe the sixteen feet high wall that had been built around the asylum building at such great expense that "when the time came to realise that lunatics wear clothes, eat and drink and like to sleep on beds, and that beds connote bedding, there was hardly any money left to provide even the barest necessities."[46] His opinion was shared by J.V. Jameson, a visitor to the hospital, who wrote an indignant letter to *The Statesman* about the conditions in the hospital–which he thought were more conducive to creating madness than healing it.[47]

This situation of an overcrowded, understaffed and ill-maintained asylum seems to have been fairly common across the country as well as in other colonised countries.48 What attracts our attention to it is that this is the place out of which Berkeley Hill conducted his psychoanalytical work and produced his psychoanalytic writings. Indeed, some of the articles compiled in his *Collected Papers* are mentioned in the asylum report for 1921-23. In the same report, Berkeley Hill writes that "the psychological laboratory has been finished and a suitable room for psychoanalytical treatment is at last at our disposal."[49] Despite this room having materialised (at last!), infrastructure remained lacking - "the only available place in this hospital for pathological and microscopical work is a disused lavatory measuring 7'-9"— 8'-0."[50]

It would not have been easy to carry out psychoanalysis in a place like the Ranchi European Mental Hospital, which was so pressed for resources. The analyst in question, Berkeley Hill, was overworked, the patients lived in inhospitable conditions. Added to that was the widespread practice of trying to get psychiatric institutions to *pay*–by getting the inmates to take part in the labour required to sustain the institution, and by manufacturing saleable products. Freud had been skeptical about what analysis could do in a situation of crisis, when "(t)he ego's whole interest is taken up by the painful reality and it withholds itself from analysis, which is attempting to go below the surface and uncover the influences of the past."[51]

Surely the barriers to analysis in Ranchi could not have been removed by an analyst proceeding to Europe for full training? This difficulty, different from the problems in analysis in India as imagined by Jones, never became a productive difficulty–neither Berkeley Hill nor Ernest Jones were interested in raising the question of the material obstacles faced by psychoanalysis in a colonial country, questions that cut close to the question of who, in *any* unequal economic system, had access to

psychoanalysis. To do this would have meant seeing Indian and European analysts not as separated by a wide gulf in standards, institutional practice etc., but rather as mutually imbricated in violent system of economic expropriation. Instead, Berkeley Hill's psychoanalysis, when it commented on the people amongst whom he lived and worked, seemed to take refuge in an anthropological and historical speculation shorn of any reflection on the colonial system and his own place within it.[52]

Towards the end of Freud's life, the following was published in an Australian newspaper –

> "Professor Sigmund Freud, world-famous psychologist, who was ejected from Austria by Hitler's orders, is writing a new book. In his study in a red-brick Hampstead house, he is busily engaged, day and night, on what his friends expect will be his greatest book. Its theme is a closely guarded secret. But those in closest touch with the 82-year-old thinker believe that it will be a study of the Nazi psychology, which will provide a shattering answer to *Mein Kampf.* Hitler's mentality, it is believed, will be shown up as a conglomeration of morbid repressions and neuroses."[53]

Instead, *Moses and Monotheism* reflects on the time Freud was living and suffering in, through a fantastic reconstruction of a much more hazy and ancient time, in which an identity that was under threat was allowed both a capacity for violence and the possibility of recognising the other within itself. When it would have seemed most legitimate and indeed obvious to analyse the persecuting other, Freud chose perhaps to look as much at himself as at what was going on around him. Here at least, was a form of psychoanalytic reflection that did not evaporate in a time of crisis, a way of taking responsibility within the threatening confines of a historical moment.

Moses and Monotheism is, after all, a text that involves itself in the question of what it means to live a history, and to write a historical account. Demands are made upon the past, it is expected to yield something by way of explanation or consolation – "Long-past ages have a great and often puzzling attraction for men's imagination. Whenever they are dissatisfied with their present surroundings- and this happens often enough – they turn back to the past and hope that they will now be able to prove the truth of the unextinguishable dream of a golden age".[54]Both H.D. and Freud were interested in the question of the prior–the shards and statuettes of past civilizations, their myths and religions. Their response to the prior is comparable in that it involved recognising this past as a player in the present. And their return to history was not to find a golden age but to place a question over what was understood as the past–a question over

both the past as the safe bedrock of tradition to which civilization referred itself, and as a dangerous primitivity that had been long left behind.

We have seen how tropes of conquest circulated amongst practitioners of psychoanalysis. Writing to Bose in 1931, Freud would say "(t)he statuette is charming. I gave it the place of honour on my desk. As long as I can enjoy life it will recall to my mind the progress of psychoanalysis, the proud conquest it has made in foreign countries, and the kind feelings for me it has aroused in some of my contemporaries at least."55 However, there is also a way in which Freud 's writing gives identity the gift of being constituted by the stranger– in *Moses and Monotheism*, the origins of monotheism are referred further and backwards in time, and outwards in space–Moses is an Egyptian taking forward an Egyptian religion, which itself came from outside Egypt–"it is possible that direct incitements to monotheism even made their way in from Syria."56 The founding of an identity, in this account, can only refer itself to an other which refers to an other. At the same time, while this is a narrative of identity dismantling itself even as it tries to learn its own contours, Freud is alert and unsparing in how this very instability may feed a desire for violent consolidation, and how the relation to the strangers / others who constitute an identity is, at the very least, ambivalent.57 I suggest that *both* strands are woven together in the manner in which psychoanalysis presents itself as a recognisable entity–both compelled and repelled–like H.D. with the statuette, by its strangers–that it theorises the ambivalences that it also enacts. And in the history of psychoanalysis, this ambivalence seems to demand–not excision, not resolution–but a reckoning.

Notes

[1] H.D. (Hilda Dolittle) *Tribute to Freud,* rev edn. (Manchester: Carcanet, 1985) p. 11.
[2] H.D. *Tribute to Freud,* 11.
[3] H.D., *Tribute to Freud,* 11.
[4] H.D.,*Tribute to Freud,* 23.
[5] H.D.,*Tribute to Freud,* 23.
[6] H.D.,*Tribute to Freud,* 68.
[7] H.D.,*Tribute to Freud,* 68.
[8] H.D.,*Tribute to Freud,* 67.
[9] H.D.,*Tribute to Freud,* 68.
[10] H.D.,*Tribute to Freud,* 68.
[11] H.D.,*Tribute to Freud,* 68.
[12] H.D.,*Tribute to Freud,* 69.
[13] Mark Edmundson's account of Freud's last days also returns to this statuette of Athena:

"Marie Bonaparte, who sat on the stairs every day after Anna was arrested to make sure that the Gestapo did not come and take away the Professor, and who often seemed to know what Freud needed, sometimes better than he knew himself, soon smuggled away his favorite treasure: a bronze statue of Athena, a little more than four inches high. Athena's left hand is poised to grip a spear, which was lost; in her right hand she holds a libation bowl. She is wearing a Corinthian helmet, set far back on her brow, and a breastplate, decorated with the figure of Medusa, though in this rendition, Medusa is without her snakes. The statue had a special place in Freud's heart, symbolizing both wisdom and martial prowess; it was an icon of the mind as warrior, the intellect combatant. Marie Bonaparte held it for Freud at her home in Paris to present to him when he was finally free."
The Death of Sigmund Freud (London: Bloomsbury, 2007), 119.

[14] Sigmund Freud, *Civilization and Its Discontents*, trans. by James Strachey, The Standard Edition of the Complete Psychological Works of Sigmund Freud, 24 vols (London: The Hogarth Press), XXI, 128.

[15] Sigmund Freud, *Moses and Monotheism: Three Essays*, trans. by James Strachey, The Standard Edition of the Complete Psychological Works of Sigmund Freud, 24 vols (London: The Hogarth Press), XXIII, 33.

[16] *Moses and Monotheism*, SE XXIII, 63. All of these qualities are attributed by Freud to the first Moses, a man who was so demanding and ruthless as a leader that he was killed by his followers–yet the one who was the proponent of an idea of living truth and justice (Ma'at) that survived him. Ambivalence, it seems, is always to be found associated with ethical ideals.

[17] See Mark Edmundson, *The Death of Sigmund Freud.*

[18] Moustapha Safouan, Jacques Lacan and the Question of Psychoanalytic Training , trans. Jacqueline Rose (London: Macmillan 2000), 62-63.

[19] Devajyoti Das, *Girindra Sekhar Vasu* (Calcutta: Vangiya Sahitya Parisat, 1971), 61. This is Bose's designation as stated on the frontispiece of his book, *The Concept of Repression*, from the 1921 edition quoted by Devajyoti Das.

[20] Girindrasekhar Bose to Ernest Jones, July 15, 1921, Ernest Jones Collection, Correspondence, PO4/C/B/10, British Psychoanalytical Society, London. Bose's letter refers to the "International Psychological Association," Jones writes back about the International Psychoanalytic Association.

[21] Ernest Jones to M.N. Banerji, December 23, 1936, Ernest Jones Collection, Correspondence, PO4/C/B/10, British Psychoanalytical Society, London.

[22] Shruti Kapila, "The 'Godless' Freud and his Indian Friends: An Indian Agenda for Psychoanalysis" in *Psychiatry and Empire* ed. Sloan Mahone and Megan Vaughan (New York: Palgrave Macmillan, 2007),126.

[23] See Bodhisattva Kar "Can the Postcolonial Begin? Deprovincializing Assam" in *Handbook of Modernity in South Asia: Modern Makeovers* ed. Saurabh Dube (New Delhi: Oxford University Press, 2011), 43-58.

[24] Kar, "Can the Postcolonial Begin? Deprovincializing Assam", 45.

[25] Girindrasekhar Bose, *Everyday Psycho-Analysis* (Calcutta: Susil Gupta, 1945), 27. For an account of how "head hunting" was constituted as an object of enquiry and administration see Bodhisattva Kar, "Heads in the Naga Hills" in *New*

Cultural Histories of India: Materiality and Practices ed. Partha Chatterjee, Tapati Guha-Thakurta and Bodhisattva Kar (New Delhi: Oxford University Press, 2014).

[26] "History of the Indian Psycho-Analytical Society" *The International Journal of Psychoanalysis,* 4 (Jan- Apr, 1923), 250. n.a.

[27] See Ashis Nandy, "The Savage Freud: The First Non-Western Psychoanalyst and the Politics of Secret Selves in Colonial India" in *The Savage Freud and Other Essays on Possible and Retrievable Selves* (New Delhi: Oxford University Press, 1995) 81-145; Christiane Hartnack, *Psychoanalysis in Colonial India* (New Delhi: Oxford, 2001), 94. See also Kalpana Seshadhari Crooks, "The Primitive as Analyst: Postcolonial feminism's access to Psychoanalysis" *Cultural Critique,* 28 (Autumn, 1994) 175-218. Seshadhari Crooks refers to Bose as the "first Indian Freudian" and "the only non-western analyst of note" (p.183).

[28] Girindrasekhar Bose to Ernest Jones, 30 March 1922. Ernest Jones Collection, Correspondence, P04/C/B/10, British Psychoanalytical Society, London.

[29] Christiane Hartnack writes: "Since their own culture was not worth much in colonial circles, it had to be elevated and demonstrated to be at least equal to, if not better than, the imposed colonial one. Thus, in a way, the colonial conditions nourished intellectual resistance to Western theories, and the challenge of juxtaposing indigenous cultural elements and Western imports encouraged productivity." *Psychoanalysis in Colonial India,* 121.

[30] Ernest Jones to Bose, 8 May 1922, Ernest Jones Collection, Correspondence, P04/C/B/10, British Psychoanalytical Society, London.

[31] Nandy, "Savage Freud", 101..

[32] Nandy, "Savage Freud", 131. Later in the essay, Nandy argues that Bose "unwittingly-probably against himself-owned up this dual responsibility of the Indian psychoanalyst – the dual responsibility of being self critical at two levels by de-mystifying both 'Indian culture' and 'the proxy-West, constituted by the interlocking cultures of the colonial state and westernized middle-class Indians." ,140.

[33] Girindrasekhar Bose, *A New Theory of Mental Life,* reprint (Calcutta: Indian Psychoanalytical Society, *n.d.* [1933]), 4.

[34] Nandy, "Savage Freud", 119.

[35] Girindrasekhar Bose, *Svapna*, (Kolkata: Vivekananda Book Centre, 2013 [1928]), 3. Translation mine.

[36] See Devajyoti Das, *Girindra Sekhar Vasu,* for list of bengali 'scientific' terminology coined by Bose.

[37] Girindrasekhar Bose, 'Manuser Mon', *Prabasi*, Asad, 1337. (Volume 30, Part 1,1930) 339-353. Despite Bose's interest in a standardised, scientific terminology in Bengali, the word "mon"in the title of his essay is very difficult to translate, as it could indicate mind, soul, psyche etc. This alerts us to how the problem of translation seems to be built into how psychoanalysis has been received and developed. For a discussion of this, see Bruno Bettelheim, *Freud and Man's Soul* (London: Pimlico, 2001).

[38] Sigmund Freud, 'Instincts and their Vicissitudes', in *Papers on Metapsychology*, trans. by James Strachey, The Standard Edition of the Complete Psychological Works of Sigmund Freud, 24 vols (London: The Hogarth Press), XIV, p. 122.

[39] Sigmund Freud to Girindrasekhar Bose, 20 February 1922 in *The Beginnings of Psychoanalysis in India* (Calcutta: The Indian Psychoanalytical Society, 1999), 7.
[40] Sigmund Freud to Girindrasekhar Bose, 1 January 1933,7.
[41] Ernest Jones to Sigmund Freud, 10 May 1912, in *The Complete Correspondence of Sigmund Freud and Ernest Jones 1908-1939* ed. R. Andrew Paskauskas (London: Harvard University Press, 1993), 141-142.
[42] Ernest Jones to M.N. Banerji, 23 December 1936,Ernest Jones Collection, Correspondence, P04/C/B/10, British Psychoanalytical Society, London.
[43] Ernest Jones to M.N. Banerji, 23 December 1936
[44] Jonathan Lear, *Open Minded : Working Out the Logic of the Soul* (Cambridge: Harvard University Press, 1998), 3.
[45] Only one page remains of the letter that M.N. Banerji wrote to Ernest Jones, dated December 12, 1936, Ernest Jones Collection, Correspondence, P04/C/B/10, British Psychoanalytical Society, London.
"We were obliged not to push the qualification of being psycho-analysed to the utmost depth and control work for membership to suit the local conditions in India. We are now faced with assigning some objective limit for the depths of psycho-analysis for a member and a would-be analyst. Recently the Rules of the New York Psycho-analytical Society seem to assign a minimum of 300 analytical hours for the guidance of the analyst. I am thinking of assigning two limits in our Indian society for the guidance of analysts: 125 for membership and 250 for an (sic) would-be analyst, though I personally consider that in the latter case the minimum should be rather higher. I shall be obliged by your expressing an opinion on this point."
[46] Owen A.R. Berkeley Hill, *All too Human* (London: Peter Davies, 1939), 244
[47] J.V. Jameson, letter to the Editor of *The Statesman* dated September 19, 1920, 1922 Home Department, Jails Branch, File No. 88, National Archives of India, New Delhi.
"(i)s it to be wondered at that a man accustomed to the ordinary amenities and comforts of life, whose brain has been affected by illness or accident, should imagine that he has been put into jail for some unknown offence, when he finds himself confined to a small grey prison cell? For a prison cell it is in all but name, its door with a barred opening covered by a wooden slide to enable the keepers to see in."
[48] See Sanjeev Jain and James Mills "The History of modern psychiatry in India 1858-1947" *History of Psychiatry* 12 No. 48 (December 2001): 431-458. See also Megan Vaughan *Curing their Ills: Colonial Power and African Illness* (Cambridge: Polity Press, 1991).
[49] Owen A.R. Berkeley Hill, *Report of the European Mental Hospital at Ranchi for the Triennium 1921-23* (Patna: Superintendent, Government Printing, Bihar and Orissa 1924) Home Department, Jails Branch, File no.11/II/25, National Archives of India, New Delhi.
[50] Owen A.R. Berkeley Hill, *Report of the European Mental Hospital at Ranchi for the Triennium 1921-23*
[51] Sigmund Freud, "Analysis Terminable and Interminable", SE XXIII, 231-232.

[52] See "The Anal Erotic Factor in the Religion, Philosophy and Character of the Hindus" and "A Short Study of the Life and Character of Mohammed" in Owen A.R. Berkeley Hill, *Collected Papers.*

[53] 'Reply to Mein Kampf' Daily Clarion, Sydney, 24 December 1938, Press Cuttings, Sigmund Freud Archive, Freud Museum, London.

[54] *Moses and Monotheism*, SE XXIII, p. 71. The quote continues - 'They are probably still under the spell of their childhood, which is presented to them by their not impartial memory as a time of uninterrupted bliss.'

[55] Sigmund Freud and Girindrasekhar Bose, *The Beginnings of Psychoanalysis in India: Bose Freud Correspondence* , reprint (Calcutta: The Indian Psychoanalytical Society, 1999) p. 21. Sigmund Freud to Girindrasekhar Bose, 13th December 1931.

[56] *Moses and Monotheism*, SE XXIII, pp 21-22.

[57] For a discussion of Freud's conceptualisation of identity in *Moses and Monotheism* see Edward W. Said, *Freud and the Non-European*, with an Introduction by Christopher Bollas and a response by Jacqueline Rose (London: Verso, 2003).

References

Berkeley-Hill, Owen A.R. –

All Too Human: An Unconventional Autobiography, (London: Peter Davies, 1939)

Collected Papers (Calcutta: Book Company, 1933)

Bose, Girindrasekhar –

A New Theory of Mental Life, reprint (Calcutta: Indian Psychoanalytical Society, *n.d.* [1933])

Svapna, (Kolkata: Vivekananda Book Centre, 2013 [1928])

'Manuser Mon', *Prabasi*, Asad, 1337. (Volume 30, Part 1,1930) 339-353

*Concept of Repression (*Kolkata: Bangiya Kala Kendra, 2009 [1921])

Everyday Psycho-Analysis (Calcutta: Susil Gupta, 1945)

Das, Devajyoti *Girindra Sekhar Vasu* (Calcutta: Vangiya Sahitya Parisat, 1971)

Edmundson, Mark, *The Death of Sigmund Freud* (London: Bloomsbury, 2007)

Freud, Sigmund, *Civilization and Its Discontents*, trans. by James Strachey, The Standard Edition of the Complete Psychological Works of Sigmund Freud, 24 vols (London: The Hogarth Press), XXI

—. “Instincts and their Vicissitudes”, in *Papers on Metapsychology*, trans. by James Strachey, The Standard Edition of the Complete Psychological Works of Sigmund Freud, 24 vols (London: The Hogarth Press), XIV

—. *Moses and Monotheism: Three Essays*, trans. by James Strachey, The Standard Edition of the Complete Psychological Works of Sigmund Freud, 24 vols (London: The Hogarth Press), XXIII

—. “Analysis Terminable and Interminable”, trans. by James Strachey, The Standard Edition of the Complete Psychological Works of Sigmund Freud, 24 vols (London: The Hogarth Press), XXIII

Freud, Sigmund and Girindrasekhar Bose, *The Beginnings of Psychoanalysis in India: Bose Freud Correspondence*, reprint (Calcutta: The Indian Psychoanalytical Society, 1999)

Freud, Sigmund and Ernest Jones *The Complete Correspondence of Sigmund Freud and Ernest Jones 1908-1939* ed. R. Andrew Paskauskas (London: Harvard University Press, 1993)

Hartnack, Christiane, *Psychoanalysis in Colonial India* (New Delhi: Oxford, 2001)

H.D. *Tribute to Freud,* rev edn. (Manchester: Carcanet, 1985)

“History of the Indian Psycho-Analytical Society” *The International Journal of Psychoanalysis,* 4 (Jan- Apr, 1923) 249-252. n.a.

Kar, Bodhisattva, ‘Can the Postcolonial Begin? Deprovincializing Assam’ in Saurabh Dube (ed.), *Handbook of Modernity in South Asia: Modern Makeovers* (New Delhi: Oxford University Press, 2011)

—. 'Heads in the Naga Hills' in Partha Chatterjee, Tapati Guha-Thakurta and Bodhisattva Kar (eds.), *New Cultural Histories of India: Materiality and Practices* (New Delhi: Oxford University Press, 2014)

Lear, Jonathan, *Open Minded: Working Out the Logic of the Soul* (Cambridge: Harvard University Press, 1998)

Nandy, Ashis, 'The Savage Freud: The First Non-Western Psychoanalyst and the Politics of Secret Selves in Colonial India', in *The Savage Freud and Other Essays on Possible and Retrievable Selves* (New Delhi: Oxford University Press, 1995)

Safouan, Moustapha, *Jacques Lacan and the Question of Psychoanalytic Training* trans. by Jacqueline Rose (London Macmillan 2000)

Seshadhari Crooks, Kalpana, 'The Primitive as Analyst: Postcolonial feminism's access to Psychoanalysis', *Cultural Critique,*28 (Autumn, 1994), 175-218

Archival Sources

London, British Psychoanalytical Society, Ernest Jones Collection.

London, Freud Museum, Sigmund Freud Archive.

New Delhi, National Archives of India.

Chapter Six

Anti-Melancholia: The Failure of Melancholy Gender and its Alternative

Chenyang Wang

Since its birth two decades ago, Judith Butler's "melancholy gender" has been one of the most celebrated theories in studies of gender and sexuality. By utilizing Freud's notion of melancholia to analyze the formation of gendered and sexed identities, melancholy gender, as Meg Jay comments, "bridged disciplines by becoming one of the most influential psychoanalytic theories in gender studies as well as one of the most recognized psychoanalytic concepts in the feminist lexicon."[1] However, an interdisciplinary endeavor like this is not without risk. As Wendy Cealey Harrison and John Hood-Williams point out in "Beyond Sex and Gender", the purpose for which and manner in which different approaches are brought together "is fundamental to the success or failure of the enterprise."[2] In this paper, I provide a critique of Butler's theory not by drawing on different theoretical resources or introducing new disciplinary perspectives, but more fundamentally, by examining the way Butler reads Freud and the purpose her reading serves for. Through a close reading of the same texts of Freud to which Butler refers, I suggest that the so-called "melancholic identification" on which Butler's whole theory is premised might come from a non- or even anti-Freudian interpretation. In so doing, I argue for a recognition of Freud's original idea on melancholia and its possible contribution to future studies of subjectivity.

Before presenting my critique of melancholy gender, I would like to first review Butler's theory in detail. Heavily relying on Freud's texts, in particular "Mourning and Melancholia" (1917) and "The Ego and the Id" (1923), Butler's developing of melancholy gender starts from a transition she suggests in Freud's theory, that is, from melancholia as a pathology to melancholia as the foundation to ego formation and character. In

"Mourning and Melancholia", Freud clearly draws a boundary between these two mental states. Mourning, as he defines, is "regularly the reaction to the loss of a loved person, or to the loss of some abstraction which has taken the place of one."[3] Such a loss results in the withdrawal of libidinal cathexes from the object which no longer exists, and will be soon followed by a displacement of libido towards another object. Freud thus suggests that mourning is only a temporary departure of the normal life which will be "overcome after certain lapse of time", and "it never occurs to us to regard it as a pathological condition and to refer it to medical treatment."[4] Melancholia, by contrast, is different at first sight for its overwhelmingly emotional intensity: "a profoundly painful dejection, cessation of interest in the outside world, loss of the capacity to love, inhibition of all activity, and a lowering of the self-regarding feelings to a degree that finds utterance in self-reproaches and self-revilings, and culminates in a delusional expectation of punishment."[5] The cause of these symptoms, explained by Freud, might be the inability of the ego to reorient the libido to the outside but instead turns an object-loss into an ego-loss by identifying the ego with the lost object.

Butler then argues that this distinction between normativity and pathology becomes blurred in Freud's later work. In "The Ego and the Id", melancholia is highlighted in relation to the ego formation. Freud admits that in the earlier work he "did not appreciate the full significance of this process (melancholia) and did not know how common and how typical it is."[6] The characteristic identification with the lost object of love, which is used to be regarded as the pathological nature of melancholia, now becomes the precondition for the work of mourning: "The two processes, originally conceived as oppositional, are now understood as integrally related aspects of the grieving process."[7] This identification may indeed be "the only condition under which the id can give up its objects."[8] This theoretical transition enables Butler to foreground loss and incorporation as the core elements and the universal basis of being as a subject. To understand the Freudian notion of the ego, thus is to see it as a precipitate of abandoned object-cathexes, the sedimentation of those objects loved and lost, and "the archaeological remainder, as it were, of unresolved grief."[9]

Turning her attention to the Oedipus complex, Butler suggests that the connection Freud postulates between identification and the lost object backfires on his own theory of psychosexual development. Freud's declaration that the boy-father identification and the girl-mother identification are the more normal resolution of the Oedipus complex seems to be unfounded, because considering his postulation of the

primitive bisexuality, there is no reason to devalue the homosexual love of the son for the father. How could Freud so insist on this specific heterosexual attachment as the "positive" form, if it is not because his notion of primitive bisexuality, namely the mixture of masculine and feminine traits in every individual, has already contained heterosexual aims? As Butler goes on to question, "To what extent do we read the desire for the father as evidence of a feminine disposition only because we begin, despite the postulation of primary bisexuality, with a heterosexual matrix for desire? "[10] Normative masculinity and femininity are constructed by a heterosexual logic that only permits attraction between opposites. Therefore, she concludes that the Oedipus complex not only endorses normative heterosexuality, but presumes the accomplishment of heterosexual desire from the very beginning in the sense that the homosexual attachment has already been prohibited and rendered unthinkable. In other words, reaching the normal Oedipus complex presupposes the impossibility of the negative Oedipus complex: "The taboo against homosexuality must *precede* the heterosexual incest taboo."[11] This unnamed prohibition "represses the expression of desire for that parent, but also founds an interior 'space' in which that love can be preserved," [12] which, as Butler suggests, brings us to the consolidation of gender identity. Instead of understanding gender and sexuality as two categories independent of each other, Butler suggests that gender identification has already required the establishment of a certain sexual desire and a refusal of the other: "gender is produced as a ritualized repetition of conventions and that this ritual is socially compelled in part by the force of a compulsory heterosexuality."[13] In other words, a boy's homosexual attachment must be repudiated in order for him to become a "man", whose return would not only threaten heterosexuality as normativity, but also threaten his gender.

Guided by a Foucauldian perspective, Butler does not stop at revealing the melancholic construction of heteronormativity, but goes further to criticize any production of identity that requires the exclusion of its exceptions. Even for people who identify themselves as gay and lesbian, their disavowal of heterosexuality might also be problematic, which, however it can be understood as a political necessity, misses the opportunity "to work the weakness in heterosexual subjectivation and to refute the logical of mutual exclusion by which heterosexism proceeds."[14] According to Butler, any attempt to sustain an identity as coherent is suspicious for rejecting the possibility of alternatives. "There is no necessary reason for identification to oppose desire, or for desire to be fueled through repudiation."[15] To deconstruct the logic of repudiation,

Butler's strategy is to introduce the "outsider" back into the focus of contemporary political domain that can subvert the conventional understanding of sexuality. For instance, she encourages the emergence of collective institutions for grieving homosexual desire that has been foreclosed as never-having-loved and never-having-lost. However, how to realize this goal in practice remains unclear in Butler's theory. After all, changing our understanding of gender from the natural disposition to social construction does not change much. As long as such a construction is not fictional but formative, not a superficial performance but the materialization of power which highly regulates practices, it leaves little space for the subversion Butler expects from melancholy gender.

Even though Butler herself admits that the theory she has charted here is "in some ways a hyperbolic theory, a logic in drag, as it were, that overstates the case,"[16] melancholy gender, nevertheless, is fundamental to her claim that gender troubles and is also one of her most significant contributions to queer theory. While Butler's theory has received both complaints from psychoanalysts for inadequately theorizing lived experience of everyday individuals, or critiques from academics for its privileging of the pre-discursive intentionality of the autonomous individual and the master narrative of increasing self-consciousness, [17] the correctness of her reading of Freud seems to be generally accepted. It is precisely this part that my article aims to challenge. The failure of melancholy gender, as I would argue, starts from the very beginning, where Butler selectively reads Freud's texts to construct the false premise of melancholic identification without which the entire theory of melancholy gender would not be possible. More importantly, in so doing, she misses the gist of Freud's theory, later illustrated and developed by Lacan, that has the potential to provide an alternative to deconstruct heteronormativity in a different way.

In "Melancholy gender – refused identification", Butler starts by reminding the reader that Freud himself acknowledged that melancholy "is central to the formation of those identifications which form the ego itself,"[18] then she moves on exploring what the lost object is that will later be incorporated in the ego. However, this logical process is flawed because the object-cathexes in Freud's theory is never the starting-point of the ego formation, despite Butler's reading trying to make the reader believe so. "On narcissism: An introduction", a key essay in which Freud makes this point clear, is not even mentioned in Butler's discussion of melancholy gender. Therefore, she misses an important passage which I will quote here at length:

> The question arises: What happens to the libido which has been withdrawn from external objects in schizophrenia? The megalomania characteristic of these states points the way. This megalomania has no doubt come into being at the expense of object-libido. The libido that has been withdrawn from the external world has been directed to the ego and thus gives rise to an attitude which may be called narcissism. But the megalomania itself is no new creation; on the contrary, it is, as we know, a magnification and plainer manifestation of a condition *which had already existed previously.* This leads us to look upon the narcissism which arises through the drawing in of object-cathexes *as a secondary one,* superimposed upon *a primary narcissism* that is obscured by a number of distinctive influences.[19] (emphasis added)

The concept of primary narcissism is what Freud names the primitive state of the child prior to any object-choice. It is an initial investment of libido into an undifferentiated unity of the child and its parent when the notion of the object has not yet been developed. It governs the formation of later attachments to others, which can be sent out and drawn back again and named by Freud "object-libido". Comparing Butler's terminology with Freud's in "On Narcissism", we can easily find out that the psychic mechanism of her so-called "melancholic identification" is nothing new but the same as Freud's secondary narcissism, both of which are in part "an attempt at recovery, designed to lead the libido back to objects."[20] However, what Butler has missed out is crucial. In Freud's original theory, the role of primary narcissism profoundly influences the target to which object-libido is oriented and the way in which the loss of the object is experienced by the ego. Not only is Freudian object-choice less concerned about the object itself but more about its ability to resemble the self, but also Freudian mourning "involves less a lament for the passing of a unique other, and more a process geared toward restoring a certain economy of the subject."[21] Therefore, rather than what Butler suggests, that melancholy, narcissistic self-love comes from previous object-love, Freud actually reverses the sequence by reducing object love to primary narcissistic love.

As we shall see later, Freud's understanding of primary narcissism remains unchanged in his later essays "Mourning and Melancholia" and "The Ego and the Id", yet Butler, for some reason, ignores its presence. In order to serve her already established theoretical standpoint which might completely contradict Freud's original idea, Butler often reads Freud selectively by abstracting some sentences out of the context they belong to. For example, in "Gender Trouble", Butler quotes Freud to support her argument:

> "The narcissistic identification with the object then becomes a substitute for the erotic cathexis, the result of which is that in spite of the conflict with the loved person the love-relation need not be given up" (170). Later, Freud makes clear that the process of internalizing and sustaining lost loves is crucial to the formation of the ego and its "object-choice."[22]

Whereas this isolated sentence Butler cites seem to support her interpretation, the original paragraph in "Mourning and Melancholia" expresses an opposite meaning:

> The narcissistic identification with the object then becomes a substitute for the erotic cathexis, the result of which is that in spite of the conflict with the loved person the love-relation need not be given up. This substitution of identification for object love is an important mechanism in the narcissistic affections; Karl Landauer (1914) has lately been able to point to it in the process of recovery in a case of schizophrenia. It represents, of course, a *regression* from one type of object-choice to *original narcissism.* We have elsewhere shown that identification is a *preliminary* stage of object-choice, that it is the first way—and one that is expressed in an ambivalent fashion—in which the ego picks out an object.[23] (emphasis added)

Even through Freud has made a direct claim that "If we could assume an agreement between the results of observation and what we have inferred, we should not hesitate to include this regression from object-cathexis to the still narcissistic oral phase of the libido in our characterization of melancholia" [24] and has further defined the three preconditions of melancholia as "loss of the object, ambivalence, and regression of libido into the ego," [25] the idea of regression has never been included in Butler's discussion of melancholy gender. Instead, she seems to replace it with the phrase "turning back" that reflects a totally different nature. While "regression" implies a specific root of object-choice that can be discovered, "turning back" covers a more basic question: Why does the libidinal energy "turn forth" in the first place? The answer appears to depend on Butler's own subjective interpretation conveniently.

In "The Ego and the Id", Freud indeed emphasizes the importance of identification with the lost object of love in building one's ego and character, but meanwhile, he also puts forwards the concept of primary identification. According to Freud, primary identification is the "first identification made in earliest childhood."[26] Different from other secondary identifications, primary identification does not presume an earlier establishment of the relationship between the individual and the object, nor does it rely upon the existence of a recognizable other, as Freud declared that "it is a direct and immediate identification and takes place

earlier than any object-cathexis."[27] As I would explain later with the help of Lacan's theory, primary identification in essence is exactly primary narcissism. They are the two sides of the same coin. The neglect of the "coin" as a whole causes confusion when Butler reads this part in "The Ego and the Id": "But, whatever the character's later capacity for resisting the influences of abandoned object-cathexes may turn out to be, the effects of the first identifications made in earliest childhood will be general and lasting. This leads us back to the origin of the ego ideal; for behind it there lies hidden an individual's first and most important identification, his identification with the father in his own personal prehistory,"[28] which she interprets as follows:

> In the first formation of the boy-father identification, Freud speculates that the identification takes place without the prior object cathexis (21), meaning that the identification is not the consequence of a love lost or prohibited of the son for the father. Later, however, Freud does postulate primary bisexuality as a complicating factor in the process of character and gender formation. With the postulation of a bisexual set of libidinal dispositions, there is no reason to deny an original sexual love of the son for the father, and yet Freud implicitly does.[29]

Because Butler fails to distinguish primary identification from melancholic identification, the latter of which, in her opinion, is the only form of identification in Freud's theory, she is unable to find logical coherence in this text. As a result, she concludes by suggesting that there must be a prior homosexual attachment that has been prohibited for the emergence of the boy-father identification, and the only reason Freud does not mention it is ideological, a reflection of culturally sanctioned heterosexuality which requires the foreclosure of the homosexual cathexis. Unfortunately, Butler's accusation is misplaced for a simple reason: The so-called father the boy identifies primarily is not the father as a gendered object, because in Freud's theory, the child has no knowledge of sexual difference at this stage. This point has become more clear in this very important footnote to this sentence:

> Perhaps it would be safer to say 'with the parents'; for before a child has arrived at definite knowledge of the difference between the sexes, the lack of a penis, it does not distinguish in value between its father and its mother. I recently came across the instance of a young married woman whose story showed that, after noticing the lack of a penis in herself, she had supposed it to be absent not in all women, but only in those whom she regarded as inferior, and had still supposed that her mother possessed one.[30]

So, what is identified primarily can be either the mother or the father, a suggestion reemphasizing the basic point that primary identification has nothing to do with gender, but essentially speaking, it is neither the father nor the mother, but a person who is supposed to possess a penis. This discovery corresponds with Freud's use of the phrase "the father in his own personal prehistory". According to Freud's description in "Totem and Taboo" (1913) and "Moses and Monotheism" (1939), the father in the prehistory is the almighty male in the primal horde, who always possess a penis and never faces the threat of castration. Nevertheless, questions immediately arise: Why does a child need to identify primarily with such a figure? How does it relate to primary narcissism and/or primary identification? And how can the introduction of this new dimension help us reconfigure the relation between mourning and melancholia? Freud's own conceptual framework is simply inadequate to answer these questions. Here, as we shall see, Lacan provides a crucial missing link that can help clarify and further elaborate Freud's original theory.

In order to argue the rationality of introducing Lacan's reading of Freud, let us reexamine some unresolved problems in Freud's conceptualization of primary narcissism. By Freud's definition, primary narcissism designates the initial stage of human development, when the infant without developed self-consciousness is unable to differentiate the outside from the inside, the other from the self, and ego from id. The original libidinal cathexes work as a pre-object emotional attachment to maintain this symbiotic, self-absorbing state. Nonetheless, a logical impossibility emerges the moment we start to think the end of this stage, when an object forms out of an objectless state, a relationship appears from the total absence of any relationship, or to reframe it as a more philosophical statement, when something, mysteriously, comes out of nothing. The dilemma we are facing here is that in order to make the formation of otherness possible, we must presuppose the formation of the self, which once again, requires an already established boundary between the self and the other that is not supposed to be there. Thus try as we may, solving the origin myth must require a logical leap, which bluntly inserts something in nothing without explanation. It is worth noting that Butler herself is fully aware of this problem. In her critique of Althusser's theory of interpellation, which argues that the subject comes into being when he or she turns around to answer the call made by an officer of "the law", Butler raises the same question: How can Althusser account for the intentionality to turn around prior to the subject formation but nevertheless suggesting a conscious anticipation of something to be gained from such a turn? As she explains later: "naming cannot be accomplished without a

certain readiness of anticipatory desire on the part of the one addressed. To the extent that the naming is an address, there is an addressee prior to the address; but given that the address is a name which creates what it names, there appears to be no 'Peter' without the name 'Peter'."[31] In this sense, we end up with a desire both subjectless and subjective. In Butler's opinion, this dilemma is impossible to solve due to the grammatical rule that shapes our thinking:

> The grammar of the subject emerges only as a consequence of the process we are trying to describe. Because we are, as it were, trapped within the grammatical time of the subject (e.g., "we are trying to describe," "we are trapped"), it is almost impossible to ask after the genealogy of its construction without presupposing that construction in asking the question.[32]

Perhaps this is the reason why Butler gives up the whole idea of primary narcissism, which for her is too difficult to handle. But the truth is Freud has already solved this dilemma successfully, and we can see this point through the lens of Lacan's theory. It is well known that one of Lacan's major contributions to psychoanalysis is his theory of the mirror stage. Lacan illustrates a metaphorical scene in which the infant comes to see and recognize an external image of its own body in the mirror in order to explain how the fragmented and objectless state of being is replaced by a sense of mastery and wholeness, even though it depends on a misrecognition of otherness as oneself. When comparing the mirror stage with Freud's theory, one way of misreading is to situate the mirror stage at the end of the phase of primary narcissism, to see it as a way out of the primitive, undifferentiated state by starting perceiving the other and the self, and then to apply the same critique we have already used on Althusser's theory: How can the infant see anything at all since there is nothing before the identification with the mirror image, unless "it presupposes some ante-specular apprehension of the other, and of the ego"?[33] However, Lacan's theory of the mirror stage is fundamentally different from Althusser's theory of interpellation, since he introduces otherness into the subject formation without relying on any real other. The imaginative identification with the mirror image Lacan proposes occurs not *after* primary narcissism, but *during* primary narcissism, when the original overinclusion seems to alienate itself. Defining this identification as "the rootstock of secondary identifications, this latter term subsuming the libidinal normalization functions,"[34] Lacan simply rephrases Freud's theory of primary identification in a different way. Therefore, instead of being the end of primary narcissism, the mirror stage corresponds to the

onset of primary narcissism and further complicates the meaning of the latter. In other words, Freud and Lacan do not attempt to answer how does something comes from nothing, as they suggest that nothing is always already something.

But is it not a bigger dilemma to say that the infant has already identified something when there is nothing? As we shall see, there is a key concept that will help us understand Lacan's and also Freud's theory: the notion of lack. Disappointed by the contemporary philosophy which "grasps that negativity only within the limits of a self-sufficiency of consciousness,"[35] Lacan in his paper "The Mirror Stage as Formative of the I Function as Revealed in Psychoanalytic Experience" urges us to fully comprehend "existential negativity" embedded in the term "primary narcissism". In this sense, to say there is nothing is equally to say there is a lack of anything, which grammatically turns a negative sentence into an affirmative proposition where the lack acquires its own positive meaning. What happens here is not a reversal of content but a shift of perspective. Instead of understanding lack as a pure form through which we expect something else, we now existentialize lack as something, a non-thing. The reader might wonder if it is sophism to linguistically disguise a real negation with a pseudo-affirmation, but this mode of thinking has already presupposed its own definition of the "real" that can only be substantial within a priori form. What Lacan tries to do here is to deconstruct precisely this kind of binary thinking: To the extent that lack is not the opposite of being but a part of being that must be repressed as if it is the opposite, lack stands for the unconscious of being, whose persistence regardless of content in a substantial sense becomes an intrinsical cut into being per se. Applying this understanding to Freud's theory, we can easily conclude that primary identification is the other side of primary narcissism, which does not require a bounded object that prepares to be recognized or a conscious subject with the ability to recognize, but suggesting that even the purest sameness has to live with the otherness as its own production from the very beginning. In regard to the mysterious ending of primary narcissism, there is nothing from outside to disturb the original harmony by forcing a distinction between the self and the other, alterity comes from inside, from the very existence of nothing that is always already the thing-in-itself. As Slavoj Zizek has put it, "the answer to 'why is there something rather than nothing? ' is thus that there is only Nothing. […] However, this nothing is not the Oriental or mystical Void of eternal peace, but the nothingness of a pure gap, the pure form of dislocation ontologically preceding any dislocated content."[36]

We are now in a better position to understand why Freud insists "the father in his own personal prehistory" as the very object of primary identification. Such a figure, as well as the image of totality with which an infant would primarily identify in Lacan's mirror stage, most fundamentally reveals the difference between lack as form and lack as content: the almighty, primordial father lacks nothing except the lack per se. Whilst this kind of omnipotent image is named by Lacan the imaginary other or more essentially the imaginary phallus, identification with which sustains the infant's fantasy to escape castration; lack as such illustrates perfectly another Lacanian notion, the *objet petit a*, which is nothing but a place-holder that conflates being and the lack-of-being. As the object-cause of desire, it sets desire in motion by seducing endless attempts to fulfill this impossible void. Meanwhile, it remains both interior and exterior of any particular object that can be attached and identified emotionally. For lack excluded from being can only return in a fantastic form as "lacking something", it simultaneously marks the impossibility of complete fulfillment from the inside and the surplus of *jouissance* from the outside.

Introducing the object *a* and the imaginary other *i(a)* allows a theoretical clarification of Freud's understanding of object-choice, mourning and melancholia that is radically different from Butler's theory. To begin with, let us rethink a fundamental question: what makes one's love of another possible in the first place? Butler's reading of Freud cannot answer this question. Interestingly, she attempts to circumvent it by introducing a Lacanian term "foreclosure". Whilst repression applies to a desire which emerged before and is only repressed "subsequently", foreclosure is "an act of negation that founds and forms the subject itself." It turns out that the way Butler answers this question is to deny the existence of it, because according to her, the subject does not love originally, but only retrospectively. Both the aim and the object of original love are foreclosed: "it cannot happen and, if it does, it certainly did not; if it does, it happens only under the official sign of its prohibition and disavowal."[37] Butler's solution appears to be brilliant, but it is problematic for a good reason. Not only because, as critics have correctly pointed out, the moment Butler eagerly claims that the foreclosed love is homosexual love, she has already been trapped by the same logical dilemma with which she accuses Althusser: How is it possible to say that before the gendering of the subject, the subject has lost the desire for a same already-gendered object? Desire defined by certain identities is also what confers identity - this vicious circle props up Butler's whole theory of melancholy gender;[38] but also because it is far from Freud's original standpoint, or the

way Lacan would interpret it. Instead of suggesting any work of foreclosure, Lacan emphasizes the point that "Freud qualifies the passage from love to identification using precisely the term regression" (Lacan 2014, 117) and goes on further to indicate the destination of this regressive path: the object *a*. Even though Freud never comes up with this term, his postulation of the coexistence of primary narcissism and primary identification has already been calling for this concept. Essentially speaking, object-choice and following identification with the object are all attempts to fill the primary lack with certain content, to repair a rupture in the real in an imaginary or symbolic way. The other attracts the subject not because of its own unique character or personality, but because of the lack in the other which mirrors the lack in the subject itself. By representing its lack to the subject, the other makes the subject wonder if his being can fill this lack by pretending that he has something to give. This misrecognition characterizes the impossibility of love in Lacan's theory: "One loves, when one is a lover, with what one hasn't got."[39] So if we reconsider Freud's original argument that the grown up boy seeks to find in the outside world "the new form of an ego ideal", the substitution "for the lost narcissism of his childhood in which he was his own ideal," [40] we can now see why his searching is endless and why his desire cannot be fully satisfied, because the ego ideal has always already been contaminated by the object *a*, the lack in oneself.

Just as her failure to understand object-choice comprehensively, we are hardly surprised to see that Butler's conflation of identification with melancholia is also a serious simplification of Freud's theory. Identification with the lost object is only part of the mechanism of melancholia. As Freud makes it clear:

> The melancholic's erotic cathexis in regard to his object has thus undergone a double vicissitude: part of it has regressed to identification, but the other part, under the influence of the conflict due to ambivalence, has been carried back to the stage of sadism.[41]

This other part, as Freud notices, reflects "something else besides which is lacking in mourning." The extraordinary diminution in the patient's self-regard and a dramatic impoverishment of one's ego explain the high tendency to suicide among melancholics. But why do melancholics show these symptoms? Butler stops wondering about this question perhaps because she thinks it does not matter. Insofar as both of them replace the lost object with identification, mourning and melancholia are only different in their emotional intensity but same in the psychic mechanism. However, this understanding is mistaken as it runs counter to the entire

thrust of Freud's larger argument. Compared with mourning, these unique symptoms of melancholia suggest more than a different degree of intensity but a different nature. Consider this passage in "Mourning and Melancholia":

> Let us now apply to melancholia what we have learnt about mourning. In one set of cases it is evident that melancholia too may be the reaction to the loss of a loved object. Where the exciting causes are different one can recognize that there is a loss of a more ideal kind. *The object has not perhaps actually died, but has been lost as an object of love* (e.g. in the case of a betrothed girl who has been jilted). In yet other cases one feels justified in maintaining the belief that *a loss of this kind has occurred, but one cannot see clearly what it is that has been lost,* and it is all the more reasonable to suppose that the patient cannot consciously perceive what he has lost either. This, indeed, might be so even if the patient is aware of the loss which has given rise to his melancholia, but only in the sense that *he knows whom he has lost but not what he has lost in him.* This would suggest that melancholia is in some way related to an object-loss which is withdrawn from consciousness, in contradistinction to mourning, in which there is nothing about the loss that is unconscious.[42] (emphasis added)

A common understanding of melancholia, including Butler's theorizing, which assumes a loss of a positive entity that can be recognized by the subject in order to compensate the loss by identification with the same one, is fully refuted by Freud here. On the contrary, what he suggests in this passage is not just the inability of the subject to know what he has lost, but whether or not there is a lost to be known. And even when the object he once loved is still there, paradoxically, the subject would still feel a strong sense of loss. The problem here seems to concern less about the object but more about the subject. As Freud further summarizes: "In mourning it is the world which has become poor and empty; in melancholia it is the ego itself." It is the melancholic's own ego, which is incapable of love, that draws self-criticism and self-mutilation. But why?

Equipped with a more succinct conceptual framework, Lacan's theory is able to explain well the difference between mourning and melancholia. In his 1962-1963 seminar on Anxiety, Lacan claims that "unless we distinguish between the object *a* and the *i(a)*, we cannot form a conception of the radical difference that lies between melancholia and mourning." [43] Following Freud's spirit, he formulates the loss in mourning as the loss of the *i(a)*, the imaginary other. "We mourn but for he of whom we can say *I was his lack.*"[44] Such a loss closes the lack it used to represent for the subject, which made the subject feel that "we were precious and indispensable for him." However, loss in mourning does not affect the

subject's capability to love, because "desire is suspended, not from the object *a*, but from *i(a)*."[45] The bond between the subject and the object a still maintains, cultivating the next formation of object-choice. In terms of melancholia, the whole dialectic is different. The melancholic losses not the *i(a)* but the object *a*, the object-cause of desire, which is why "he knows whom he has lost but not what he has lost in him". Put simply, the melancholic losses nothing but lack. He would feel melancholia even when the object is well preserved in front of him, because it means nothing to him as long as he cannot find the lack in it which seduces his desire. But something more profound is at stake here. By losing the object *a*, the melancholic ends up with the *i(a̶)*, the over-presence of the imaginary other that not only denies lack as form, but also cancels lack as content, as the non-thing. Indulging in the fantasy of never-having-lacked, a state the subject did not even experience in primary narcissism, the melancholic loses the last evidence of subjectivity and is completely objectified. In this sense, Lacan concludes by saying "the object takes the helm. The object triumphs". All those self-destructive symptoms are indeed caused by this pathological objectification:

> Initially he attacks this image so as to reach, within it, the object a that transcends him, whose control escapes him – and whose collapse will drag him into the suicide-rush, with the automatism, the mechanism, the necessary and fundamentally alienated character with which, as you know, these suicides of melancholics are committed.[46]

It is at this point we can try to provide an alternative to Butler's theory of melancholy gender, a theory which not only misreads Freud's theory of melancholia, but becomes a melancholic fantasy itself. While we can easily appreciate Butler's intention to explore the reproduction of heteronormativity not only at the sociopolitical level but also at the unconscious level, her reading of Freud is simply inadequate to support her argument. Ironically, by ignoring the notion of lack that is crucial to Freudian-Lacanian psychoanalysis, Butler falls prey to the same illusion melancholics have experienced, that is, as Zizek has put it, "the confusion between loss and lack: insofar as the object-cause of desire is originally, in a constitutive way, lacking, melancholy interprets this lack as a loss, as if the lacking object was once possessed and then lost."[47] The misrecognition that there is no lack but loss unavoidably leads to the objectification of the loss, as if there is truly something repudiated, without which the subject cannot emerge." While the belief that this lost object can be "a resource in the struggle to rearticulate the very terms of symbolic legitimacy and intelligibility,"[48] drives Butler to look outward, to locate more subject

positions that are available to desire, to rescue "something more" behind the heteronormative prohibition, and ultimately, to achieve a supreme form of fulfillment without a loss, it has almost become a variant of today's desire-driven consumerism that keeps demanding insatiably. Meanwhile, the lesson Freudian-Lacanian psychoanalysis would teach us is exactly the opposite, an anti-melancholic one: There is nothing behind the prohibition. It is nothing but lack that must be repressed in order to suture a coherent identity, be it male or female, heterosexual or homosexual. Against the melancholic maneuver which transforms inherent lack into exterior loss in order to sustain an illusion that we are prohibited from getting enough, it is the duty of psychoanalysis in postmodern times to remind us that we have already got too much. Such an alternative to Butler's theory of melancholy gender, as I would argue, might open new space for a reconfiguration of subjectivity.

Notes

[1] Meg Jay, "Melancholy Femininity and Obsessive—Compulsive Masculinity: Sex Differences in Melancholy Gender," *Studies in Gender and Sexuality* 8 no. 2 (2007): 117

[2] Wendy Cealey Harrison and John Hood-Williams, *Beyond Sex and Gender*, 1 edition, (London: SAGE Publications, 2002), 190

[3] Sigmund Freud, "Mourning and Melancholia." In *S.E. XIV*, (1917), 243

[4] Ibid., 243-44

[5] Ibid., 244

[6] Sigmund Freud, "The Ego and the Id." In *S.E. XIX*, (1923), 28

[7] Judith Butler, *Gender Trouble: Feminism and the Subversion of Identity (Routledge Classics)*. (London & New York: Routledge, 2006), 84

[8] Freud, Mourning, 29

[9] Judith Butler, "Melancholy Gender—refused Identification." *Psychoanalytic Dialogues* 5 no. 2 (1995): 167

[10] Butler, *Gender*, 82

[11] Ibid., 87

[12] Ibid., 85

[13] Butler, Melancholy, 175

[14] Ibid., 179

[15] Ibid.

[16] Ibid.

[17] Geoff Boucher, *The Charmed Circle of Ideology: A Critique of Laclau and Mouffe, Butler and Zizek (Anamnesis)*. (Melbourne: Re.press, 2008)

[18] Butler, Melancholy, 166

[19] Sigmund Freud, "On Narcissism : An Introduction." In S.E. XIV, (1914), 74-75

[20] Ibid., 74

[21] Tammy Clewell, "Mourning Beyond Melancholia: Freud's Psychoanalysis of Loss." *Journal of the American Psychoanalytic Association* 52 no. 1 (2004): 47
[22] Butler, *Gender*, 78
[23] Freud, Mourning, 241
[24] Ibid., 250
[25] Ibid., 258
[26] Freud, Ego, 31
[27] Ibid.
[28] Ibid., 31
[29] Butler, *Gender*, 80
[30] Freud, Ego, 31 footnote
[31] Judith Butler, *The Psychic Life of Power: Theories in Subjection.* (California: Stanford University Press. 1997): 111
[32] Ibid., 117
[33] Mikkel Borch-Jacobsen, *Lacan: The Absolute Master.* (California: Stanford University Press. 1991): 66
[34] Jacques Lacan, "The Mirror Stage as Formative of the I Function as Revealed in Psychoanalytic Experience." In *Ecrits*, (London & New York: W. W. Norton & Company. 2006), 76
[35] Ibid., 80
[36] Slavoj Zizek, *Less Than Nothing: Hegel and the Shadow of Dialectical Materialism,* (London: Verso Books. 2012), 38
[37] Butler, Melancholy, 171
[38] Boucher, 143
[39] Jacques Lacan, *Anxiety (Book X) (The Seminar of Jacques Lacan).* Edited by Jacques-Alain Miller. (London & New York: Polity Press. 2014), 117
[40] Freud, Narcissism, 94
[41] Freud, Ego, 251-52
[42] Ibid., 245
[43] Lacan, *Anxiety*, 335
[44] Ibid., 141
[45] Ibid., 335
[46] Ibid.
[47] Slavoj Zizek, "Melancholy and the Act." *Critical Inquiry* 26 no. 4 (2000): 659-60
[48] Judith Butler, *Bodies That Matter: On the Discursive Limits of Sex (Routledge Classics)*. (London & New York: Routledge. 2011), xiii

References

Borch-Jacobsen, Mikkel. 1991. *Lacan: The Absolute Master*. Stanford University Press.

Boucher, Geoff. 2009. *The Charmed Circle of Ideology: A Critique of Laclau and Mouffe, Butler and Zizek (Anamnesis)*.

Butler, Judith. 1995. "Melancholy Gender—refused Identification." *Psychoanalytic Dialogues* 5 (2): 165–180.

—. 1997. *The Psychic Life of Power: Theories in Subjection*. Stanford University Press.

—. 2006. *Gender Trouble: Feminism and the Subversion of Identity (Routledge Classics)*. Routledge.

—. 2011. *Bodies That Matter: On the Discursive Limits of Sex (Routledge Classics)*. Routledge.

Clewell, T. 2004. "Mourning Beyond Melancholia: Freud's Psychoanalysis of Loss." *Journal of the American Psychoanalytic Association* 52 (1): 43–67.

Freud, Sigmund. 1914. "On Narcissism : An Introduction." In *S.E. XIV*, 67–102.

—. 1917. "Mourning and Melancholia." In *S.E. XIV*, 237–258.

—. 1923. "The Ego and the Id." In *S.E. XIX*, 1–66.

Harrison, Wendy Cealey, and John Hood-Williams. 2002. *Beyond Sex and Gender*. SAGE Publications.

Jay, Meg. 2007. "Melancholy Femininity and Obsessive—Compulsive Masculinity: Sex Differences in Melancholy Gender." *Studies in Gender and Sexuality* 8 (2): 115–135.

Lacan, Jacques. 2006. "The Mirror Stage as Formative of the I Function as Revealed in Psychoanalytic Experience." In *Ecrits*, 75–81. London & New York: W. W. Norton & Company.

—. 2014. *Anxiety (Book X) (The Seminar of Jacques Lacan)*. Edited by Jacques-Alain Miller. London & New York: Polity Press.

Zizek, Slavoj. 2000. "Melancholy and the Act." *Critical Inquiry* 26 (4): 657–681.

—. 2012. *Less Than Nothing: Hegel and the Shadow of Dialectical Materialism*. Verso Books.

CHAPTER SEVEN

VICTORIAN VISIONS OF YOUTH: THE CHILD IN ART AND PSYCHOANALYSIS

MELISSA L. GREENBERG

Introduction

Differing conceptions of childhood as a stage of human development have prevailed in different socio-cultural and historical contexts. In tracking the history of these shifting ideas about childhood, popular and academic writers have identified two opposing notions that supposedly take turns dominating and shaping historical eras and discourse: at some points in time, children have been seen as inherently good and sexually pure, at others, as inherently bad and morally corrupt.[1] It is often said that the former view—that children are innocent and pure—defined the Romantic and Victorian outlooks on children and childhood. According to historian Paul Robinson, the belief in childhood innocence was "the most cherished belief of nineteenth-century sexual ideology."[2] It is also said that the alternative view—that children are inherently bad and morally corrupt—dominated the preceding centuries. Protestant reformers of the 16th century, for example, maintained that children bear the mark of original sin and so are innately depraved. As such, children in this context were viewed as "faulty small adults, in need of correction and discipline."[3]

Historians of childhood trace the origins of the Romantic and Victorian belief in childhood innocence to the writings of Jean-Jacques Rousseau. Rousseau's *Emile* and other texts like it prompted a shift in ideas about childhood during the 18th century. While the view that children are "faulty small adults" faded, the idea that childhood is an important stage of social and moral development gained popularity.[4] At the end of the following century, another theorist's writings would prompt another shift in Western ideas about childhood: the early psychoanalytic writings of Sigmund Freud introduced the idea that childhood was not just a period of social

and moral development, but also one of psychological and sexual development.

Freud's idea that sexual development takes place during the childhood years is often framed as a dramatic break with the popular and scientific thinking of his time, which so "cherished" the belief in childhood sexual innocence.[5] Framing Freud's contribution in this way has led scholars to think of the past several centuries of Western history in two distinct eras: the blissfully naïve pre-Freudian era, a time when children were seen as sexually pure, and the sex-crazed post-Freudian era, in which all aspects of life and culture are infused with sex. To think of history in this highly schematized way, however, oversimplifies the matter and creates a false schism between "pre-" and "post-Freudian" thought. This schism obscures the degree to which supposedly "post-Freudian" ideas, like the recognition of childhood sexuality, pre-dated Freud and played a role in shaping cultural, intellectual, and scientific discourses before Freud's time.

This paper examines the diverse ways in which children were viewed during the second half of the 19th century—in the public eye, in the medical literature, and in the arts—with the aim of better understanding the socio-cultural context in which Freud wrote his seminal works on childhood sexuality. Such an exploration reveals that children, their bodies, and their sexuality were subjects of intense study even in the years before Freud's first writing on this subject.

19th-Century Theories of Childhood Sexuality

Several early psychoanalytic texts are devoted to investigating the psychological significance of childhood sexual experiences. In the years following the publication of *Studies on Hysteria*, Freud's landmark 1895 collaboration with Josef Breuer, Freud wrote several papers on the etiology of hysteria.[6] In these papers, Freud articulated his famous seduction theory—a theory that postulated that childhood sexual abuse was the root cause of hysteria. Freud's work in this area focused on an unsettling social reality: children can be the objects of adult sexual desire, and childhood sexual experiences have lasting, often pathogenic psychological sequelae.

Psychoanalytic historian Jeffrey Moussaieff Masson has written that, in developing his seduction theory, Freud was influenced by growing recognition of the frequency of childhood sexual abuse in the legal and medical fields.[7] The second half of the 19th century saw an expansion of the literature on childhood sexual abuse, with contributions by influential figures like Auguste Ambroise Tardieu, Alexandre Lacassagne, and Paul

Bernard, who all held prestigious positions on the medical faculties of French universities. In 1857, Tardieu published a book entitled *Etude médico-légale sur les attentats aux moeurs*, a study of childhood sexual assault and rape.[8] In 1886, Lacassagne published an article on the rates of sexual assault of young girls, which included an alarming statistic: one-third of cases brought to criminal court in France involved the sexual assault of young girls. The same year, a similarly alarming statistic emerged from the researches of Bernard: 36,176 cases of "rape and assaults on the morality" of youths aged 15 years or younger were reported in France in the years between 1827 and 1870.[9]

The literature on childhood sexual abuse continued to grow in the 1880s, along with awareness of the physical trauma associated with such abuse. As this awareness mounted, so did public efforts to protect children. Governments across Western Europe and North America introduced new laws and agencies intended to protect children's rights. Several countries established new laws regarding the age of sexual consent. In England, for example, the age of consent was raised from 12 to 13 in 1875. Ten years later, it was raised again to 16.[10] In 1874, the first American child-protection organization was founded.[11]

Freud's seduction theory offered a unique contribution to the growing awareness of childhood sexual abuse: his theory introduced the idea that childhood sexual abuse could have psychological repercussions in addition to physical ones. The seduction theory is based on a trauma model. It takes as its point of departure a non-sexual child who is vulnerable to precocious sexualization by alien, adult sexuality. This theory offered a vision of childhood that was compatible with that which supposedly dominated Victorian times: children are sexually naïve and pure, but they are vulnerable to attack and corruption by external forces.

It was not long, though, before Freud's thinking about the nature of childhood sexual experiences changed. In 1905, he published a reworked theory on this topic in the essay "Infantile Sexuality," one of the *Three Essays on the Theory of Sexuality*.[12] In this 1905 essay, Freud broke away from the trauma model of his seduction theory and proposed instead that all infants are born with a drive towards erotic gratification. That is, sexuality is not imposed on children by alien, adult forces; rather, it is endogenous in all children and infants. This theory implied that children are not merely the passive *objects* of adult sexual interest but that they are also sexual *subjects*.

Many historical accounts of early psychoanalysis characterize Freud's theory of an innate sexual drive that is active during infancy and childhood as a radical break from previous scientific ideas on the subject.[13] Indeed,

this was Freud's own position on the subject. In the first paragraphs of the essay on infantile sexuality, Freud claimed that, despite frequent reports of sexual behavior in children, this topic had been under-investigated and underdeveloped. In keeping with Freud's claim, George Makari, a historian of psychiatry, wrote, "Most nineteenth-century sexologists did not even believe children were sexual" and that Freud's 1905 essays on sexuality were "a bombshell" that completely redefined sexological discourse.[14]

On the other hand, Henri Ellenberger, another historian of psychiatry, asserts that there was more continuity between 19th-century notions of childhood sexuality and the ideas advanced in Freud's essay on infantile sexuality. He cites a number of 19th-century scientific and popular sources to support this point: In the 1840s Father Debreyne, a French theologian and physician, wrote about infantile masturbation and sexual play between young children.[15] In the 1860s Jules Michelet, a widely read French historian, asserted that the infant has sexual impulses from the time of birth.[16] In 1879 the Hungarian psychiatrist S. Lindner published a study on thumb sucking as an expression of infantile erotic gratification, a study that Freud himself cites in the essay on infantile sexuality.[17]

Ellenberger points to textual sources to support his assertion that doctors, scientists, and lay people alike were interested in investigating the sexual acts and experiences of children, even in the years before Freud wrote his major works on the subject. In the remainder of this paper, I will expand upon this point and examine artworks from the period in question, which lend further support to the idea that Freud was not alone in his interest in exploring children's sexual subjectivity. On the contrary, 19th-century depictions of children reveal that many artists and audiences of this time shared Freud's interest in children, their bodies, and their experiences of sexuality.

The Child in Art: 18th to 19th Centuries

Over the course of the 18th century, children became increasingly popular subjects of secular art. By the beginning of the 19th century, the most popular paintings at Salons pictured peaceful, happy families with young children.[18] These images of family life appealed to wide audiences and were not only produced as paintings, but were also circulated in large numbers as prints.[19]

Around this time there was a similar shift in Christian art, with renewed interest in images of the Madonna and Child. While images of Mary in the preceding generation emphasized her virginal qualities, 19th-

century images more often highlighted her maternal qualities. The bond between Mary and her son became a model for all mother-child bonds, and the mother-child relationship was endowed with a "sacred aura."[20]

Fig. 7-1: Mary Cassatt *Peasant Mother and Child*, ca. 1894

Many secular mother-child portraits of this time convey that holy reverence for the mother-child bond. Mary Cassatt (1844-1926), an American artist who spent much of her career in France, was famous for

her works in this genre, which were referred to by her contemporaries as "Modern Madonnas."[21] Cassatt's 1894 *Peasant Mother and Child* (Fig. 7-1) is one example of such a work. In this print, a peasant mother holds her child on the left side of her lap and touches his torso with her right hand. The composition is remarkably similar to a *Hodegetria*, a type of Christian icon that shows Mary holding her son on her left side while pointing toward the child with her right hand, a gesture that gives the icon type its name (*Hodegetria* means "she who points the way").[22] Cassatt's composition recalls this classic Christian iconography and suggests a likeness between her subjects and the holy family.

Portraits of children solo, *sans* parents, also appeared with increasing frequency during this time. One especially popular image in the 19th century was that of the mob-capped little girl.[23]

Fig. 7-2: John Everett Millais *Cherry Ripe*, 1879

Cherry Ripe (Fig. 7-2), painted in 1879 by British artist John Everett Millais (1829-1896), is a prime example of this image type. The painting shows a young girl in 18th-century costume seated in a child-like pose, feet not quite touching the ground, in a peaceful woodland setting. She wears a soft white dress accented with a pink sash, a floppy mob-cap, and pink shoes. Her arms, gloved in shiny black fabric, lay in her lap.

Cherry Ripe was a sensation in its time. It was reproduced as the centerfold in the *Graphic* Christmas Annual of 1880, which sold 500,000 copies that year. It was also widely circulated as a stand-alone print.[24]

Speculations about why *Cherry Ripe* became such a popular image vary and have become the subject of art historical debate. Anne Higonnet and Laurel Bradley, both experts on Victorian art, attribute the painting's success to its subject's expression of purity and innocence.[25] Bradley writes, "this pretty child in old-fashioned dress is meant to embody the positive attributes of English culture. Her benign, Madonna-like presence, multiplied through modern printing, spreads peace and goodness."[26]

Other scholars read Millais' work quite differently. Pamela Tamarkin Reis acknowledges that "Purity, innocence, and culture sell pictures," but she argues that another, more powerful marketing tool accounts for *Cherry Ripe's* success: sex.[27] According to Reis, the "bold gaze" and "half-smile" of the little girl who appears in *Cherry Ripe* are "sexual cues."[28] Reis also sees the positioning of the girl's gloved arms as sexualized symbols: her arms frame her genitalia, and the dark color of her gloves imply "mature pubic hair around the depicted labia." More, Reis argues that the title *Cherry Ripe* alludes to the girl's sexuality, for "the word 'cherry' meant young girl and referred also to the hymen and virginity."[29]

Higonnet and Bradley resist this sexualized reading of *Cherry Ripe*. They argue that to read eroticism in this picture is anachronistic, an imposition of a 21st-century, "post-Freudian" perspective on these works. Bradley even declares that she consciously chose not to address the possible sexual allusions in *Cherry Ripe* in order to avoid "retroactively psychoanalyzing an artist or (worse) a whole category of viewers (Victorian men)."[30]

Higonnet and Bradley are right to point out that our 21st-century perspective may lead us to see things differently than did our 19th-century counterparts, and their caution against uncritically employing a "post-Freudian" lens to examine the original cultural meanings of Victorian art is justified. But need we out of hand dismiss our own observations of artworks from previous eras as anachronistic and therefore entirely inapplicable? Might we instead use our observations to steer our scholarly efforts and investigate whether they can shed any light on the art and culture of the period in question? The remainder of this paper explores whether our 21st-century perception of sexuality in 19th-century child portraits, like Reis' reading of *Cherry Ripe*, are in fact at odds with 19th-century responses to those artworks. To that end, this paper will examine select portraits from the second half of the 19th century along with contemporary responses to those portraits. This examination reveals that

19th-century audiences did indeed recognize the sexualized nature of some child portraits. Thus, seeing 19th-century art in this way is not necessarily unique to a "post-Freudian" age.

19th-Century Child Portraits: Sex and Scandal

Giovanni Boldini's 1892 painting of a 10-year-old girl (Fig. 7-3), one that provoked scandal in its own time, provides a good starting point for this study. Boldini (1842-1931) was an Italian-born painter who spent most of his career in Paris. Though his art is not very well known today, he was one of the most renowned and sought-after portraitists of his time, best known for his glamorous and fashionable portraits of "high society" women.[31] The girl who appears in Boldini's painting shown here (Fig. 7-3) is Giovinetta Errazuriz, the daughter of wealthy Chilean art collectors who lived in Paris in the 1890s.[32]

Fig. 7-3: Giovanni Boldini (Italian) *Portrait of Giovinetta Errazuriz*

Boldini's portrait of Giovinetta, which shows the sitter in a ruffled bonnet, recalls the images of mob-capped little girls that were so popular in the late 19th century, like Millais' *Cherry Ripe* (Fig. 7-2). There are a number of differences, however, between the subjects of Boldini's and Millais' paintings. For example, Giovinetta, at 10 years old, is significantly older than the girl who appears in *Cherry Ripe*. Whereas the subject of *Cherry Ripe* wears a quaint, old-fashioned costume, Giovinetta's outfit is ill-fitting and oddly put together. The type of bonnet she wears was meant for girls much younger than 10. In contrast, the black cape that gathers around her shoulders and the matching umbrella that extends in front of her were components of a "walking costume" for older women.[33] More, Giovinetta's long and angular legs, encased in sleek black stockings, are distinctly un-childlike. Her precocious gaze that confronts the viewer is also startlingly adult.

Giovinetta's manner of dress stands out for another reason as well: her white skirt is hiked up beyond the limits of her black stockings, revealing a stretch of her bare thigh.

Giovinetta's exposed thigh did not go unnoticed by Boldini's contemporaries. When the painting was exhibited at the Paris Salon of 1892 and the Venice Biennale of 1895, this detail became the subject of scandal. In a posthumous biography of the artist's life, his widow Emiliana Cardona wrote the following about the critical response to Giovinetta's portrait:

> The notorious centimeter of skin between the top of the black stocking and the hem of the white dress created a much greater scandal in the audience than some of the opulent nudes.
>
> This discreet glimpse of a child's leg, hardly visible and purely artistic, became the reference for 'l'art diabolique' attributed to Boldini and which was soon to be widespread... It is probably as a result of this ambiguous reputation that Queen Marguerite of Italy did not offer Boldini the opportunity to paint her portrait...
>
> And it's too bad! The first queen of the young Italy should have been painted by the first Italian portrait painter of its time.[34]

Though Cardona saw the glimpse of Giovinetta's bare thigh as "hardly visible and purely artistic," others interpreted that display of flesh as an unsettling allusion to the young girl's sexuality. This allusion was more scandalous and disturbing to the public than the "opulent nudes" shown in the same exhibitions, and it permanently affected the way that people understood Boldini as a painter. Before this portrait was exhibited, Boldini

had a reputation for being able to portray his female sitters with irresistible elegance and grace. Because of this portrait, however, he was vilified, called "diabolical."[35]

Though Cardona diminishes the significance of Giovinetta's "notorious centimeter of skin," there is evidence that Boldini recognized this detail as an important and distinctive component of his composition. A preparatory drawing for the painting, one that includes only a rough sketch of the painting's major compositional features, clearly shows the raised skirt and exposed thigh. These details are also clearly articulated in a painting that Boldini executed that pictures Giovinetta's completed portrait in the artist's studio—a kind of "portrait of a portrait." Clearly, for Boldini, the exposed thigh was an essential element of the portrait.

How, then, can we characterize the 19th-century response to Giovinetta's portrait? On the one hand, in the years immediately after it was painted it was selected for exhibition in important European artistic venues, suggesting that curators esteemed it as worthy of show. In addition, the passage cited above from Boldini's biography is evidence that Giovinetta's exposed thigh could be seen as "discreet," "hardly visible," and "purely artistic." On the other hand, many critics regarded the portrait as an eroticized depiction of a prepubescent girl that was scandalous and diabolical.

In this case, we have evidence that the public response to Giovinetta's portrait was not unitary but instead included diverse, even divergent, interpretations and reactions. We need not impose a 21st-century, "post-Freudian" lens on this work in order to conclude that viewers in the years preceding Freud's writing on childhood sexuality acknowledged the erotic character of Giovinetta's portrait. We also need not assume that this erotic interpretation was universal among 19th-century viewers. Rather, we may understand that Victorian audiences had varying reactions to this painting, as audiences in our own time likely do.

Art historian David Lubin has commented on the seemingly self-contradictory quality of some Victorian paintings, which appear simultaneously "buoyantly innocent" and "teasingly erotic."[36] Lubin explains that the concepts of childhood innocence and eroticism, though they seem mutually exclusive, coexisted during the 19th century. He cites the 1867 painting *Making a Train* by American artist Seymour Joseph Guy (1824-1910) to support his point. The painting[37] shows a prepubescent girl, her nightgown having slipped off her shoulders to expose her bare chest, making a train like that of a bride out of bright red fabric. The girl seems to play an innocent game of make believe in her attic bedroom, safe within the domestic sphere. Yet the way she admires her bare shoulder and

the train that symbolizes her future entrée into adult relations also seems to allude to her own awareness of and appreciation for her sexuality. According to Lubin, "the line between innocence and depravity is not clear-cut" in paintings like *Making a Train*, and it is not necessary to settle on any one, static interpretation of the image. The painting is multivalent, "dualistic, and contradictory": it captures both the young girl's innocence and her sexuality.[38]

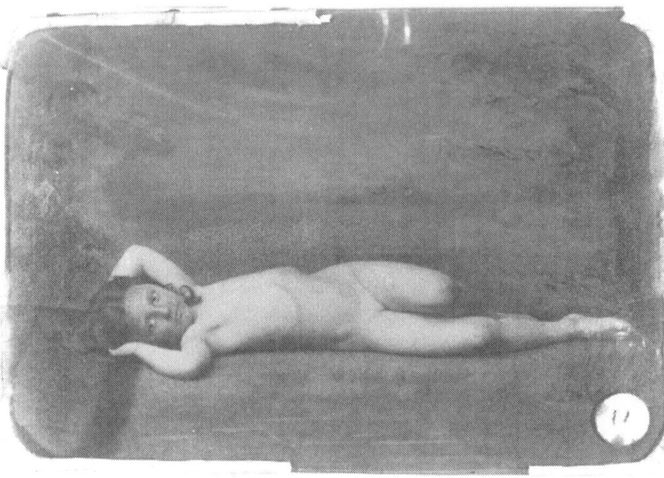

Fig. 7-4: Charles Lutwidge Dodgson (Lewis Carroll) *Portrait of Evelyn Hatch*, ca. 1879

The line between the innocent and the erotic also appears blurred in the photographs of Charles Lutwidge Dodgson (1832-1898), better known by his pen name Lewis Carroll. Though he achieved most fame for his literary depiction of a young girl in *Alice's Adventures in Wonderland*, Carroll was also a prolific photographer who favored young female subjects, such as Evelyn and Beatrice Hatch, who are pictured nude in Figs. 7-4 and 7-5. Carroll was friendly with the Hatch family, and Evelyn and Beatrice were regular subjects of his photographs.

The nature of Carroll's relationships with the young girls who inspired his writings and photographs has been the subject of much commentary and speculation. Carroll scholars Helmut Gernsheim and Morton N. Cohen both defend the "innocence" of Carroll's interactions with his young female friends. They cite excerpts from Carroll's letters, in which he describes children as good and close to God, as evidence that Carroll intended for his pictures of undressed children to be seen as visions of the spiritual purity and innocence of children. They argue that the photographs

should be read and understood in ways that are consistent with the artist's intention.[39]

Fig. 7-5: Charles Lutwidge Dodgson (Lewis Carroll) *Portrait of Beatrice Hatch*, 1873

Other scholars criticize the methodology employed by Gernsheim and Cohen. They argue that focusing on an artist's explicitly stated intentions limits what we see in works of art.[40] Focusing on the formal qualities of Carroll's photographs rather than on the artist's own commentary, such scholars do not see Carroll's images of young girls as innocent or naïve.[41] Rather, they see girls who "look immensely knowing" and "disturbingly adult, aware, self-absorbed."[42] Art historian Carol Mavor sees Evelyn Hatch (Fig. 7-4) as "a tiny odalisque" or as "a child-woman, posed like a courtesan."[43]

To some 21st-century eyes, images like those of Evelyn and Beatrice Hatch carry such an erotic charge that they cross the line from art into pornography. While to those who view these nude pictures as representations of innocence and purity this may seem like an extremist position, it is one that today carries significant political weight. The much-publicized 2008 controversy over a photograph by Australian artist Polixeni Papapetrou (b. 1960), entitled *Olympia as Lewis Carroll's Beatrice Hatch Before White Cliffs* (Fig. 7-6), is a case in point. Papapetrou's photograph, modeled after Lewis Carroll's picture of Beatrice Hatch (Fig. 7-5), shows the artist's 6-year-old daughter nude, seated on a rock in front of a painted seascape, just as Beatrice appears in Carroll's work. This photograph was published on the cover of the July 2008 issue of Australia's *Art Monthly* magazine shortly after controversy erupted over the photographs of another Australian artist, Bill Henson (b. 1955), which showed a nude adolescent girl. In May 2008, police seized Henson's photographs from a Sydney art gallery where they were on display. State prosecutors threatened the artist with obscenity and child pornography charges.[44] Though the case was eventually dropped, with no charges pressed, this event sparked a heated public debate over the artistic and legal status of nude child portraits.

Fig. 7-6: Polixeni Papapetrou *Olympia as Lewis Carroll's Beatrice Hatch Before White Cliffs*, 2003

When Papapetrou's photograph of Olympia appeared on the cover of *Art Monthly*, it was similarly controversial. Children's rights activists attacked Papapetrou's integrity both as an artist and as a mother.[45] Australian Prime Minister Kevin Rudd even had a voice in this debate: he argued that underage children should not be used in debates about the boundaries between art and pornography and at one point said he "can't stand" Papapetrou's picture of Olympia.[46] On the other side of the debate, those who defended the artistic merit of Papapetrou's picture declared "Nudity is not obscenity" and argued that photographing children in the nude is not necessarily an act of pedophilia or child exploitation.[47]

The controversies over Papapetrou's and Henson's pictures are not the only ones of their kind in recent memory. A similar debate took place in the US over the child portraits of American artist Sally Mann (b. 1951).[48] There is a tendency to view these controversies as present-day phenomena, symptoms of our sex-obsessed 21st-century culture. Writing for the July 2008 *Art Monthly* issue in which Papapetrou's *Olympia* appeared, artists Denise Ferris and Martyn Jolly lamented, "Every photographic act is now more readily viewable through the prism of victim and abuser, rather than artist and subject."[49] Art historian Anne Higonnet expressed a similar concern when she wrote, "No subject is as publicly dangerous now as the subject of the child's body."[50] Both comments use the adverb "now" and suggest that "now," our time, is different from others. Behind this suggestion lies the idea—perhaps the fantasy—that there was a time when things were different, when public audiences did not respond so fearfully or aggressively to depictions of child nudity. But are these 21st-century concerns regarding child pornography and exploitation unique to "now"? Or did previous eras, including the Victorian one that supposedly saw only the innocence and sexless purity of the child's body, share our concerns about these types of images?

Another look at Carroll's letters provides some answers to these questions. While, as Gernsheim and Cohen tell us, Carroll explicitly refers to the spiritual purity and goodness of children, certain passages from his letters indicate that his correspondents, even some friends and peers, expressed concerns about his photographic practices and intimacies with children. Not all parents immediately acquiesced to his request to photograph their children, for example. Indeed, many of Carroll's letters include "elaborate negotiations with parents about whether they will permit their daughters to be depicted in 'primitive costume.'"[51]

Carroll was well aware that others might object to his pictures of nude children. In an 1887 letter addressed to the mother of one of the girls he photographed, he wrote that he wanted to ask a professional painter to add

color to some of his nude portraits, which were all originally black-and-white.[52] He hesitated, though, anticipating the painter's response to his pictures. He wrote, "But I am shy of asking her [the painter] the question, people have such different views, and it *might* be a shock to her feelings if I did so."[53]

Here Carroll acknowledges the "different views" his colleagues had about his photographs and their potential shock value. Carroll's reluctance to shock his peers seems to have contributed to his decision to end his career as a photographer and to destroy the negatives of his nude portraits, along with most of the existing prints.[54] Explaining his plan to destroy his work to a friend, Carroll wrote, "There is really *no* friend to whom I should wish to give photographs which so entirely defy conventional rules."[55] Though Carroll may have regarded his photographs as wholly innocent, the excerpts from his letters cited here are evidence that not all of his contemporaries shared his views. More, the letters are evidence that Carroll himself was aware that his pictures "entirely defied conventional rules" of his time.

The contemporary responses to Carroll's photographs and Boldini's painting show us that 19th-century audiences were very sensitive to the ways in which children and their bodies were depicted in the arts. That is, it is not only "now" in our "post-Freudian," sex-crazed society that the child's body is a dangerous subject in art, as some writers suggest.[56] On the contrary, even our 19th-century forebears, not yet introduced to Freudian theories of seduction and infantile sexuality, responded with passionate objection to images of children that could be construed as sexual or sexualized, even when the sexual nature of the images was ambiguous and difficult to distinguish from the "pure" or "innocent."

Within the Maternal Sphere: Eros Domesticated

Fig. 7-7: Julia Margaret Cameron *Venus Chiding Cupid and Removing His Wings*, 1872

This study would not be complete without a consideration of the works of Julia Margaret Cameron (1815-1879), a British contemporary of Carroll's. Like Carroll, Cameron was a photographer, and many of her photographs show child subjects in various states of undress. Unlike Carroll, Cameron is known for her family life: she was a mother of 6 when she took up photography in her late 40s.[57] Also unlike Carroll, many of Cameron's child photographs explicitly reference erotic love. Her *Venus Chiding Cupid and Removing His Wings* (Fig. 7-7), for example, shows a nude child posed as Cupid, the Roman god of desire and love.

Interestingly, despite her overt allusions to the erotic, Cameron's work "has managed to escape the label of 'perversion' that has encumbered

Carroll's photographs." Mavor attributes Cameron's escape from such labels to her "maternal life-style, which included a house full of children."[58] That maternal, domestic quality does seep into some of Cameron's photographs. There is a maternal presence, for example, in *Venus Chiding Cupid and Removing His Wings*: Venus, Cupid's mythological mother, appears in the photograph, hovering over her reclining child. But not all of Cameron's photographs so obviously manifest that maternal presence. In some of her photographs, nude children posed as Cupid appear in the absence of parental figures or allusions to a domestic context. In others, like *Turtle Doves* (Fig. 7-8), children with exposed bodies engage in a sensual embrace—again, no parents or other disciplining figures are present, aside from the mother behind the camera.

Fig. 7-8: Julia Margaret Cameron *The Turtle Doves*, 1864

Though Cameron and her photographic practices remain relatively immune from accusations of perversion and pedophilia, most who comment on her photographs do acknowledge their erotic qualities.[59] Indeed, Cameron's *Venus Chiding Cupid and Removing His Wings* (Fig. 7-7) has a distinctly different feel from other mother-child portraits of the time, like Cassatt's *Peasant Mother and Child* mentioned above (Fig. 7-1). While in Cassatt's work the mother's voluminous presence dominates the composition, in Cameron's work the luminescent, exposed skin of "Cupid" shines. While in Cassatt's work a blousy costume obscures the child's body and shape, in Cameron's the shape of the child's pale body and long limbs stands out against a dark background. In addition to these formal differences, the two works also employ markedly different performative frames. Modeling her image after devotional icons of Mary and Jesus, Cassatt situates her mother-child dyad in a Christian context, evocative of a divine love that has much more to do with the spiritual realm than the corporeal. Cameron, on the other hand, models her dyad after Pagan gods of love and desire, and in doing so she evokes the physical and sometimes violent passion that those gods represent.

Whether or not Cameron's photographs have been labeled "perverse" or "pedophiliac," they reveal the artist's "fascination with the allure of childish bodies."[60] Her photographs, together with the works by Millais, Boldini, and Carroll presented in this paper, are evidence that children, their bodies, and their sexuality were subjects of intense artistic study and interest in the 19th century, during the decades leading up to Freud's writings on childhood sexuality. 19th-century responses to those artworks—particularly the scandal that erupted over Boldini's portrait of Giovinetta and the backlash against nude child portraits that Carroll feared and took measures to avoid—show us that discomfort with such explorations of children and their sexuality is not unique to our own time. Indeed, this discomfort was common even among our "pre-Freudian" forebears, those who were supposedly naïve to childhood sexuality.

Neither-Nor

This study of the socio-cultural context in which Freud formulated his ideas about sexual development in children helps us understand that Freud did not introduce his ideas to a society that was completely unacquainted with thinking about childhood sexuality, as the case is sometimes made. On the contrary, in Freud's time—as in our own—varying, sometimes opposing, perspectives on childhood innocence and sexuality existed simultaneously. It is therefore impossible to describe one unitary Victorian

perspective on childhood sexuality, for the matter is more complex and ambiguous. Images like Carroll's portrait of Evelyn Hatch (Fig. 7-4) embody this ambiguity: Evelyn appears as a "child-woman," simultaneously both child and courtesan.[61] Mavor uses the concept of the *neutre* to elucidate the contradictory nature of works like this. Following French philosophers Roland Barthes and Louis Marin, she uses the word *neutre*, which literally means "neither one nor the other," to refer to "a series of neither-nor ambiguities." She argues that, in her portrait, Evelyn Hatch embodies the "neither-nor sexuality of the Victorian girl."[62]

These neither-nor ambiguities, not a monolithic view of children as innocent, shaped the cultural and artistic discourse around children in the Victorian Era. These ambiguities made possible the production of the artworks presented in this paper, which simultaneously evoke innocence and sexuality. These ambiguities also made possible the impassioned debates over images like Boldini's portrait of Giovinetta or Carroll's photographs of nude young girls in the 19th century, and they make possible the controversies surrounding the nude child portraits by artists Bill Henson, Polixeni Papapetrou, and Sally Mann in our own day. In scholarship there is often an impulse to "wash out" or explain away ambiguity.[63] Doing so, however, prevents us from seeing and appreciating the multiple meanings of artworks as well as the rich variability of the cultural contexts in which they were created.

The Sitter as Subject

The furor provoked by depictions of children in states of undress—both in the 19th century and today—reveals how much anxiety and fear collects around seeing children in any context that can be construed as sexual. One question that has not yet been explored here is: What is it about these images that sparks such controversy and heightened emotions? The widely publicized protests of child rights activists who liken the images to pornography may lead us to conclude that most people find the images disturbing because of concerns about child abuse: the images could be seen as indices of inappropriate, abusive relations between photographer (perpetrator) and child sitter (victim).

Seeing these portraits "through the prism of victim and abuser, rather than artist and subject"[64] casts the artist as active, as sole agent, and the child subject as passive object. Several writers have argued against viewing portraits in this way, for it overlooks the significant contribution of the sitter and the degree to which the process of creating a portrait is a collaboration between artist and sitter. Again referencing the neither-nor

ambiguity captured by the concept *neutre*, Mavor says that the girls who appear in Carroll's photographs "oscillate in a performative space: they are 'not artist,' yet they are 'not, not artist.'"[65] They are "neither subject nor object."[66]

Two artists who work frequently in the portrait genre have described the process of capturing a portrait and the end product—the portrait itself—in ways that are consistent with Mavor's "neither-nor" hypothesis. For example, in an interview published by the Australian Broadcasting Corporation, Polixeni Papapetrou described her experience of photographing children: "Often I just have to stand back and watch them, and then they will do something beautiful, they will do something unexpected. And it's that moment that I wait for."[67] Here, Papapetrou indicates that her work as portraitist entails sometimes taking on a passive role, "standing back," and allowing her subjects to act and exercise their agency, to be *subjects*, not merely objects. This does not mean that the role of photographer is entirely passive; there is certainly an element of artistic action in deciding when to "stand back" and in spotting those moments that are "waited for." Nevertheless, Papapetrou describes this process as a true collaboration between two subjects, a photographer and a sitter, each of who brings something unique to the table.

Speaking about the experience of photographing her daughter as a child, Papapetrou noted that the portrait sitter can even contribute something that is altogether foreign and surprising to the photographer:

> She [Olympia] has this mystery about her, and I think that's what's so disarming when I look at her through the lens, that she can look back at me and unnerve me sometimes. She has this very powerful, intense gaze that is profound. It comes from somewhere else. I don't have it, my son doesn't have it, my husband doesn't have it—but she does.[68]

Here, Papapetrou reveals that even when she photographs someone as close and intimately connected to her as her daughter, her subject can "disarm" and "unnerve" her by presenting an expression that the photographer herself could not have anticipated or planned.

Documentarian Ben Maddow made a similar point about the limits of the artist's role in creating a portrait and the degree to which photographic subjects shape their portraits. He stated: "It's the special naivete [*sic*] of the twentieth century to think that the artist alone determines the subject; in examining a succession of photographic portraits one is struck instantly by the will and the force of the sitter."[69] Doing that which Maddow recommends—looking at a succession of portraits to observe the force of the sitter—is effective even with the pictures included in this paper.

Observe the difference, for example, between Carroll's portrait of Beatrice Hatch (Fig. 7-5) and Papapetrou's *Olympia as Lewis Carroll's Beatrice Hatch Before White Cliffs* (Fig. 7-6). Though the latter is based on the former, Olympia's direct gaze—that gaze that Papapetrou said emerged spontaneously from her daughter—gives her picture a distinctly different feel from the dreamy quality of Beatrice's. Including Carroll's portrait of Evelyn Hatch (Fig. 7-4) in this comparison, we see that not all direct gazes are alike: both Olympia and Evelyn look directly into the camera, but the two looks have very different qualities and effects.

To whom, then, do we attribute the end products of portraits? To the artist? To the sitter? To neither? Or perhaps to both?

Nina Auerbach, professor of English and Victorian culture, takes a strong position on this issue, locating the sexuality that infuses Carroll's pictures not in the photographer but in the subject. She writes:

> Carroll as camera eye does perfect justice to the self-transforming mobility of this model. The eroticism, along with the passionate and seditious powers this had come to imply, belongs to the child; the artist merely understands it.[70]

Here Auerbach, like Papapetrou and Maddow, emphasizes the deterministic agency of the photographic subject. Unlike the others, however, Auerbach collapses the roles of photographer and camera and suggests that the two work in unison as a recording tool to capture a (presumably accurate) visual record of a subject at a given moment. While there is some truth to the idea that the photographer acts as recorder, or visual transcriber, I think Auerbach overstates the case and underestimates the artistic agency of the photographer, even the photographer working before the age of digital photography and editing. Nevertheless, Auerbach's comments about photographic portraiture, along with Papapetrou's and Maddow's, draw our attention to an important point: the children who appear in the photographs presented in this paper appear as *subjects*, that is, as persons with subjectivity rather than as mere objects. Whether their appearance as willful, forceful subjects is attributable to the real-life presence of the sitter or to the craft of the photographer may be impossible to tease apart, but that does not stop us today from recognizing that 19th-century photographers were interested in exploring and depicting the subjectivity, including the sexual subjectivity, of their child subjects.

Looking at paintings like Boldini's portrait of Giovinetta (Fig. 7-3) and even Millais' *Cherry Ripe* (Fig. 7-2), we can also recognize that painters of the 19th century were interested in exploring and depicting the

subjectivity of their child subjects. Though we cannot know whether Giovinetta really sat in front of Boldini with thigh exposed or whether she confronted him with the direct gaze we see in her portrait, part of the appeal and intrigue of the painting is that she comes across as a person with internal experiences, possibly even desire. Likewise with *Cherry Ripe*—whether or not Millais intended the sexual allusions that scholars like Reis see in the painting today, he created an image of a little girl whose features appear doll-like but whose gaze conveys a sense of interiority and intimacy that could only originate in a real person, not a doll. These paintings, like the photographs by Carroll, Cameron and Papapetrou, all depict children as subjects who feel, know, desire—depictions that can, to use Papapetrou's words, be "disarming" and "unnerving" to adult observers.[71]

Is it possible that the images studied here have been so disturbing to audiences, from the 19th century to the present, not only because they raise concerns about abuse, but also because they are depictions of that knowing, desire, and sensuality that can emerge spontaneously in childhood? That is, is it possible that adults respond negatively to these images out of discomfort with depictions of children as subjects, and particularly as sexual subjects? And would it have been possible for our Victorian counterparts, not yet familiar with Freud's "bombshell" theory, to see children as sexual subjects?

A passage from one of Carroll's letters suggests that Carroll, at least, could (and did) conceive of children as sexual subjects. In a letter to the mother of two of his favorite photographic subjects, two sisters aged 8 and 9, Carroll suggests that it may no longer be appropriate to photograph the girls in the nude. He writes:

> But, for the sake of their little brother,[72] I quite think you may find it desirable to bring such habits to an end after this summer. A boy's head soon imbibes precocious ideas, which might be a cause of unhappiness in future years.[73]

Written in 1880, Carroll's words here reveal a proto-Freudian attitude towards sexuality and childhood experience. First, he suggests that the girls' little brother may "imbibe" his own "precocious ideas" about his sisters' nudity, an acknowledgement of the spontaneous and endogenous nature of childhood sexual experiences. Second, he intimates that such ideas may cause later psychological difficulties. Here, Carroll's words seem to anticipate Freud's theory about the relationship between childhood sexuality and psychopathology.

Conclusion

Freud was not alone at the end of the 19th century in his interest in children and their experiences of sexuality. The images studied in this paper show that, in the decades leading up to Freud's works on this topic, much attention was paid to children and their bodies in the arts and culture of the West. 19th-century audiences, much like audiences today, recognized the eroticism and sexuality implied by images like Boldini's portrait of Giovinetta and Carroll's photographs of nude children. Also like audiences today, those 19th-century audiences responded to such images with anxiety and fear. This study helps us understand that the Victorian Era was not the "pre-Freudian" oasis it is sometimes made out to be, and Freud's ideas about childhood sexuality did not emerge from a culture with an entirely unified perspective on the sexual status of children. Instead, contradictory views on childhood—ranging from the view that children are sexually pure and naïve to the view that they are innately depraved—coexisted in some tension with each other, creating ambiguity around this issue and shaping the artistic, cultural, and intellectual discourse of the time.

Notes

[1] These shifting ideas about childhood have become the subject of a field of study unto itself: the history of childhood. Major works in this field include Philippe Ariès, *Centuries of Childhood: A Social History of Family Life*, trans. Robert Baldick (New York: Vintage Books, 1962); George Boas, *The Cult of Childhood* (London: Warburg Institute, 1966); and Hugh Cunningham, *The Invention of Childhood* (London: BBC Books, 2006).

[2] Paul Robinson, *Freud and His Critics* (Berkeley: University of California Press, 1993), 115.

[3] Anne Higonnet, *Pictures of Innocence: The History and Crisis of Ideal Childhood* (New York: Thames and Hudson, 1998), 8. See also Julie-Marie Strange, "Fairy Tales of Fertility: Bodies, Sex, and the Life Cycle, *c.* 1750-2000," in *The Routledge History of Sex and the Body, 1500 to the Present*, eds. Sarah Toulalan and Kate Fisher (New York: Routledge, 2013), 297-298.

[4] Higonnet, *Pictures of Innocence*, 8; Strange, "Fairy Tales of Fertility," 297.

[5] Robinson, *Freud and His Critics*, 115.

[6] Sigmund Freud, "Heredity and the Aetiology of the Neuroses," in *The Standard Edition of the Complete Psychological Works of Sigmund Freud, Volume III (1893-1899): Early Psycho-Analytic Publications*, trans. James Strachey (London: Hogarth, 1964), 141-156; Sigmund Freud, "The Aetiology of Hysteria," in *The Standard Edition of the Complete Psychological Works of Sigmund Freud, Volume III (1893-1899): Early Psycho-Analytic Publications*, trans. James Strachey (London: Hogarth, 1964), 191-221. For an overview of Freud's early writing on

childhood sexuality, see Emanuel E. Garcia, "Freud's Seduction Theory," *The Psychoanalytic Study of the Child* 42 (1987): 443-468.

[7] Jeffrey Moussaieff Masson, *The Assault on Truth: Freud's Suppression of the Seduction Theory* (Untreed Reads Publishing, 2012).

[8] Masson, *Assault on Truth*, chap. 2; Robinson, *Freud and His Critics*, 114.

[9] Masson, *Assault on Truth*, chap. 2.

[10] Strange, "Fairy Tales of Fertility," 298.

[11] David Lubin, *Picturing a Nation: Art and Social Change in Nineteenth-Century America* (New Haven: Yale University Press, 1994), 215.

[12] Sigmund Freud, "Infantile Sexuality," in *Three Essays on the Theory of Sexuality* (New York: Basic Books, 2000).

[13] George Makari, *Revolution in Mind: The Creation of Psychoanalysis* (New York: Harper Perennial, 2009), 110, 116.

[14] Makari, *Revolution in Mind*, 114.

[15] Henri Ellenberger, *The Discovery of the Unconscious: The History and Evolution of Dynamic Psychiatry* (New York, Basic Books, 1970), 295.

[16] Ellenberger, *Discovery of the Unconscious*, 296.

[17] Ellenberger, *Discovery of the Unconscious*, 504.

[18] Carol Duncan, "Happy Mothers and Other New Ideas in Eighteenth-Century French Art," in *Feminism and Art History: Questioning the Litany*, eds. Norma Broude and Mary D. Garrard (New York: Harper & Row, 1982), 200.

[19] Duncan, "Happy Mothers," 215.

[20] Higonnet, *Pictures of Innocence*, 40-42.

[21] Higonnet, *Pictures of Innocence*, 57.

[22] Eunice D. Howe, "Luke, St," *Grove Art Online*, *Oxford Art Online* (Oxford University Press, accessed http://www.oxfordartonline.com.proxy.libraries.rutgers.edu/subscriber/article/grove/art/T052395).

[23] Laurel Bradley, "From Eden to Empire: John Everett Millais's *Cherry Ripe*," *Victorian Studies* 34.2 (1991): 187.

[24] Bradley, "From Eden to Empire," 179.

[25] Higonnet, *Pictures of Innocence*, 125; Bradley, "From Eden to Empire," 179.

[26] Bradley, "From Eden to Empire," 179.

[27] Pamela Tamarkin Reis, "Victorian Centerfold Another Look at Millais' 'Cherry Ripe,'" *Victorian Studies* 35.2 (1992): 201.

[28] Reis, "Victorian Centerfold," 201.

[29] Reis, "Victorian Centerfold," 203.

[30] Laurel Bradley, "Reply to Pamela Tamarkin Reis," *Victorian Studies* 35.2 (1992): 206; Higonnet, *Pictures of Innocence*, 125.

[31] Steven Gundle, "Mapping the Origins of Glamour: Giovanni Boldini, Paris and the Belle Epoque," *Journal of European Studies* 29.115 (1999): 269-295.

[32] Christie's, *15 paintings by Giovanni Boldini Collected by the Late Baron Maurice de Rothschild* (New York, Christie's, 1995), 42.

[33] Alexandra Murphy, "Giovanni Boldini, Portrait of Giovinetta Errazuriz, Lot 75," *19-Century European Art, 04 November 2010, New York* (Sotheby's, accessed

http://www.sothebys.com/en/auctions/ecatalogue/2010/19th-century-european-art-n08673/lot.75.html).

[34] Quoted in Christie's, *15 paintings by Giovanni Boldini*, 60.

[35] Piero and Francesca Dini, *Giovanni Boldini, 1842-1931: Catalogo Ragionato* (Torino, U. Allemandi, 2002), 197.

[36] Lubin, *Picturing a Nation*, 210.

[37] This painting is not pictured here but can be viewed on the website of the Philadelphia Museum of Art where it is held today. See http://www.philamuseum.org/collections/permanent/102969.html?mulR=1632330743|1.

[38] Lubin, *Picturing a Nation*, 223.

[39] Helmut Gernsheim, *Lewis Carroll, Photographer* (New York: Dover, 1969); Morton N. Cohen, *Lewis Carroll, Photographer of Children: Four Nude Studies* (Philadelphia: Rosenbach Foundation, 1979).

[40] Carol Mavor, *Pleasures Taken: Performances of Sexuality and Loss in Victorian Photographs* (Durham, NC: Duke University Press, 2012), Kindle Edition, Kindle Locations 398-399.

[41] Mavor, *Pleasures Taken*, Kindle Locations 389-390; Patricia Meyer Spacks, "Hidden Meanings," *The Hudson Review* 33.2 (1980): 274-276.

[42] Spacks, "Hidden Meanings," 274.

[43] Mavor, *Pleasures Taken*, Kindle Location 440.

[44] Michael Pelly, "'No charges' against Bill Henson, NSW prosecutors decide," *The Australian*, June 6, 2008, accessed http://www.theaustralian.com.au/archive/news/no-charges-against-henson/story-e6frg6o6-1111116554237.

[45] Suzanne Ost, *Child Pornography and Sexual Grooming: Legal and Societal Responses* (New York: Cambridge University Press, 2009); Australian Associated Press (AAP), "Don't use children in art/porn debate, says Kevin Rudd," *Herald Sun*, July 8, 2008, accessed http://www.heraldsun.com.au/news/artporn-debate-no-place-for-kids/story-e6frf7jo-1111116854524; "Don't use kids in art/porn debate: Rudd," *Sydney Morning Herald*, July 8, 2008, accessed http://news.smh.com.au/national/dont-use-kids-in-artporn-debate-rudd-20080708-38ln.html.

[46] AAP, "Don't use children"; "Don't use kids."

[47] Maurice O'Riordan, "Editorial: To dream a child," *Art Monthly* 211 (2008), accessed http://www.artmonthly.org.au/artnotes.asp?aID=37&issueNumber=211; Denise Ferris and Martyn Jolly, "Collateral Damage," *Art Monthly* 211 (2008), accessed http://martynjolly.com/2013/05/10/collateral-damage-denise-ferris-and-martyn-jolly/.

[48] O'Riordan, "Editorial"; Richard B. Woodward, "The Disturbing Photography of Sally Mann," *New York Times*, September 27, 1992, accessed http://www.nytimes.com/1992/09/27/magazine/the-disturbing-photography-of-sally-mann.html.

[49] Ferris and Jolly, "Collateral Damage."

[50] Higonnet, *Pictures of Innocence*, 133.

---

[51] Spacks, "Hidden Meanings," 274.
[52] Carroll's photographs were all originally black-and-white, and any color images we have today are the result of hand painting after the photos had already been developed and printed. This is why some of his photographs have a painterly quality. Carroll did not paint the photographs himself; he sent his photos out to have them professionally painted.
[53] Cohen, *Lewis Carroll*, 13.
[54] Cohen, *Lewis Carroll*, 27. Carroll kept one set of prints of the nude portraits for himself and offered the remaining ones to the families of the girls pictured in the photographs. He destroyed the prints that the family did not take.
[55] Cohen, *Lewis Carroll*, 27.
[56] See notes 49 and 50 above.
[57] Joanne Lukitsh, "Cameron, Julia Margaret," *Grove Art Online*, *Oxford Art Online*, Oxford University Press, accessed http://www.oxfordartonline.com.proxy.libraries.rutgers.edu/subscriber/article/grove/art/T013434.
[58] Mavor, *Pleasures Taken*, Kindle Locations 620-621; Carol Armstrong, "Cupid's Pencil of Light: Julia Margaret Cameron and the Maternalization of Photography," *October* 76 (1996), 114.
[59] Mavor, *Pleasures Taken*, Kindle Locations 604-607; Armstrong, "Cupid's Pencil," 114-141.
[60] Armstrong, "Cupid's Pencil," 114.
[61] Mavor, *Pleasures Taken,* Kindle Location 581.
[62] Mavor, *Pleasures Taken,* Kindle Locations 590, 578, 581.
[63] Mavor, *Pleasures Taken*, Kindle Location 394.
[64] Ferris and Jolly, "Collateral Damage."
[65] Mavor, *Pleasures Taken*, Kindle Locations 687-688.
[66] Mavor, *Pleasures Taken*, Kindle Locations 578-579.
[67] "Turning the Gaze—Transcript," *Australian Broadcasting Corporation*, September 23, 2013, accessed http://www.abc.net.au/austory/content/2012/s3854540.htm.
[68] "Turning the Gaze."
[69] Quoted in Mavor, *Pleasures Taken*, Kindle Locations 684-686.
[70] Quoted in Mavor, *Pleasures Taken*, Kindle Locations 458-460.
[71] "Turning the Gaze."
[72] Since the two girls were 8 and 9 years old at the time Carroll wrote this letter, their little brother must have been 7 or younger.
[73] Quoted in Cohen, *Lewis Carroll, Photographer of Children*, 21-22.

References

Ariès, Philippe. *Centuries of Childhood: A Social History of Family Life*. Translated by Robert Baldick. New York: Vintage Books, 1962.

Armstrong, Carol. "Cupid's Pencil of Light: Julia Margaret Cameron and the Maternalization of Photography." *October* 76 (1996): 114-141.

Australian Associated Press. "Don't use children in art/porn debate, says Kevin Rudd." *Herald Sun*, July 8, 2008. Accessed http://www.heraldsun.com.au/news/artporn-debate-no-place-for-kids/story-e6frf7jo-1111116854524.

Boas, George. *The Cult of Childhood*. London: Warburg Institute, 1966.

Bradley, Laurel. "From Eden to Empire: John Everett Millais's *Cherry Ripe*." *Victorian Studies* 34.2 (1991): 179-203.

Bradley, Laurel. "Reply to Pamela Tamarkin Reis." *Victorian Studies* 35.2 (1992): 206.

Christie's. *15 paintings by Giovanni Boldini Collected by the Late Baron Maurice de Rothschild*. New York: Christie's, 1995.

Cohen, Morton N. *Lewis Carroll, Photographer of Children: Four Nude Studies*. Philadelphia: Rosenbach Foundation, 1979.

Cunningham, Hugh. *The Invention of Childhood.* London: BBC Books, 2006.

Dini, Piero and Francesca. *Giovanni Boldini, 1842-1931: Catalogo Ragionato*. Torino: U. Allemandi, 2002.

"Don't use kids in art/porn debate: Rudd." *Sydney Morning Herald*, July 8, 2008. Accessed http://news.smh.com.au/national/dont-use-kids-in-artporn-debate-rudd-20080708-38ln.html.

Duncan, Carol. "Happy Mothers and Other New Ideas in Eighteenth-Century French Art." In *Feminism and Art History: Questioning the Litany*, edited by Norma Broude and Mary D. Garrard, 200-219. New York: Harper & Row, 1982.

Ellenberger, Henri. *The Discovery of the Unconscious: The History and Evolution of Dynamic Psychiatry*. New York: Basic Books, 1970.

Ferris, Denise, and Martyn Jolly. "Collateral Damage." *Art Monthly* 211 (2008). Accessed http://martynjolly.com/2013/05/10/collateral-damage-denise-ferris-and-martyn-jolly/.

Freud, Sigmund. "Heredity and the Aetiology of the Neuroses." In *The Standard Edition of the Complete Psychological Works of Sigmund Freud, Volume III (1893-1899): Early Psycho-Analytic Publications*. Translated by James Strachey, 141-156. London: Hogarth, 1964.

Freud, Sigmund. "The Aetiology of Hysteria." In *The Standard Edition of the Complete Psychological Works of Sigmund Freud, Volume III*

(1893-1899): Early Psycho-Analytic Publications. Translated by James Strachey, 191-221. London: Hogarth, 1964.

Freud, Sigmund. "Infantile Sexuality." *Three Essays on the Theory of Sexuality*. New York: Basic Books, 2000.

Garcia, Emanuel E. "Freud's Seduction Theory." *The Psychoanalytic Study of the Child* 42 (1987): 443-468.

Gernsheim, Helmut. *Lewis Carroll, Photographer*. New York: Dover, 1969.

Gundle, Steven. "Mapping the origins of glamour: Giovanni Boldini, Paris and the Belle Epoque." *Journal of European Studies* 29.115 (1999): 269-295.

Higonnet, Anne. *Pictures of Innocence: The History and Crisis of Ideal Childhood*. New York: Thames and Hudson, 1998.

Howe, Eunice D. "Luke, St." *Grove Art Online. Oxford Art Online*. Oxford University Press, accessed http://www.oxfordartonline.com.proxy.libraries.rutgers.edu/subscriber/article/grove/art/T052395.

Lubin, David. *Picturing a Nation: Art and Social Change in Nineteenth-Century America*. New Haven: Yale University Press, 1994.

Lukitsh, Joanne. "Cameron, Julia Margaret." *Grove Art Online. Oxford Art Online*. Oxford University Press, accessed http://www.oxfordartonline.com.proxy.libraries.rutgers.edu/subscriber/article/grove/art/T013434.

Makari, George. *Revolution in Mind: The Creation of Psychoanalysis*. New York: Harper Perennial, 2009.

Masson, Jeffrey Moussaieff. *The Assault on Truth: Freud's Suppression of the Seduction Theory*. Untreed Reads Publishing, 1998.

Mavor, Carol. *Pleasures Taken: Performances of Sexuality and Loss in Victorian Photographs*. Durham, NC: Duke University Press, 2012. Kindle Edition.

Murphy, Alexandra. "Giovanni Boldini, Portrait of Giovinetta Errazuriz, Lot 75." *19-Century European Art, 04 November 2010, New York*. Sotheby's, accessed http://www.sothebys.com/en/auctions/ecatalogue/2010/19th-century-european-art-n08673/lot.75.html.

Maurice O'Riordan. "Editorial: To dream a child." *Art Monthly* 211 (2008). Accessed http://www.artmonthly.org.au/artnotes.asp?aID=37&issueNumber=211

Ost, Suzanne. *Child Pornography and Sexual Grooming: Legal and Societal Responses.* New York: Cambridge University Press, 2009.

Pelly, Michael. "'No charges' against Bill Henson, NSW prosecutors decide." *The Australian*, June 6, 2008. Accessed http://www.theaustralian.com.au/archive/news/no-charges-against-henson/story-e6frg6o6-1111116554237.

Reis, Pamela Tamarkin. "Victorian Centerfold: Another Look at Millais' 'Cherry Ripe.'" *Victorian Studies* 35.2 (1992): 201-205.

Robinson, Paul. *Freud and His Critics*. Berkeley: University of California Press, 1993.

Spacks, Patricia Meyer. "Hidden Meanings." *The Hudson Review* 33.2 (1980): 271-278.

Strange, Julie-Marie. "Fairy Tales of Fertility: Bodies, Sex, and the Life Cycle, *c.* 1750-2000," in *The Routledge History of Sex and the Body, 1500 to the Present*, edited by Sarah Toulalan and Kate Fisher, 296-310. New York: Routledge, 2013.

"Turning the Gaze-Transcript." *Australian Broadcasting Corporation*. September 23, 2013. Accessed http://www.abc.net.au/austory/content/2012/s3854540.htm.

Woodward, Richard B. "The Disturbing Photography of Sally Mann." *New York Times*, September 27, 1992. Accessed http://www.nytimes.com/1992/09/27/magazine/the-disturbing-photography-of-sally-mann.html.

Chapter Eight

Dimensionality and Adhesiveness in Jonathan Glazer's *Under the Skin*

Carla Ambrósio Garcia

I

Under the Skin (Jonathan Glazer, 2013) begins with silence over black. Moments later, an abrasive sound of strings fades in, and a spot of light appears in the centre of the image. The spot of light suddenly changes into a bright irradiating star, emitting circles of light, which brings to mind the image of the iris of an eye. This star is then seen behind a series of objects aligned in the surrounding darkness, slowly coming together, resembling astral bodies or lens flare. The star behind, and a black sphere in front, they cover two orifices of a larger white sphere that is hollow, its outer limits and orifices defined by circles of light that resemble the earlier ones. These two-dimensional circular shapes seem to enclose a surface that becomes concave on one side, convex on the other, thus separating an inside from an outside space. Over the increasingly turbulent, swirling violins, a female voice begins to utter monosyllabic sounds from which words can gradually be distinguished: "feel, field, film, filmed, films, foil, fail, film… fall, falls, fold… pool… cell". The inanimate shapes become an eye that is alive, covered with a protective, yet sensitive, crystalline membrane. In this prologue to *Under the Skin*, a link between eye and film is established: both can be seen as a kind of skin, sentient, impressionable, and on the border between different spaces.

The eye and the voice in this initial sequence belong to an alien (Scarlett Johansson), created in the form of a young woman, who is coming to Earth in order to substitute her no longer functional counterpart (Lynsey Mackay). Her mission is overseen by other aliens who take the outer appearance of male motorcyclists clad in thick leather suits. In the homonymous novel on which the film is based, written by Michel Faber, the purpose of these creatures is made clear: the alien seductress drives

around different parts of Scotland in a van, picking up male hitch-hikers, capturing them for their flesh that the aliens consume.[1] But in Glazer's film, what the aliens want from the humans is more open to interpretation; the film often slips into abstraction, both at the level of material spaces, objects and substances, and at the level of the characters' thoughts and feelings, their history and perceptions: in other words, their inner world. While the novel takes interest in the ruminations of the protagonist and her human prey, even when they remain mostly unspoken, the film makes very little use of dialogue. The first observation that the film critic Jonathan Romney makes in his interview with the director is precisely about the fact that the adaptation "radically pares down the original book".[2] To my mind, this process of paring down is accompanied by one of flattening, or thinning, so to speak. This two-dimensional quality of the film (and, as I shall discuss, the stickiness or adhesiveness of its surfaces), as well as its depiction of changes in dimensionality (of which the opening sequence is an example), are the focus of my reading of this film, which draws on the work of the psychoanalysts Esther Bick and Donald Meltzer.

When asked about the logic behind his approach to the adaptation, Glazer replied that his interest in the book was the alien's point of view – "*her*, the lens".[3] It is indeed a fascinating aspect of this film that the inhabited or deserted urban spaces and natural landscapes of Scotland, in their most mundane and magnificent detail, become unfamiliar and strange when seen through her perspective; paradoxically, what contributes to this strangeness is their very realness, as some of the scenes capture the image, and at times also the speech, of subjects unaware of the hidden cameras in use. These hidden surveying eyes reveal a wish to get at what is "under the skin" – one of the meanings of the idiom being "in reality, as opposed to superficial appearances".[4] In that respect the film becomes more of a scientific experiment than a science fiction. It wants to discover people's real reactions to probing questions in controlled situations. Those situations juxtapose the "alien" and the "human" so that their behaviour can be dissected; then distinctions become blurred, in that we perceive the strangeness in the "human" and the familiar in the "alien"; and, what also emerges from this experiment, as the alien's last moments before her death at the end of the film epitomize, is that a perceived reality is as much hiding from sight as plainly visible, as much under the skin as on its surface. Before proceeding with the analysis of the film, some theoretical considerations are necessary.

II

In recent scholarship concerned with the topic of skin and engaging with psychoanalysis, the work of Didier Anzieu is the main if not the only psychoanalytical reference.[5] In this piece I follow a different line by turning to the work of Bick and Meltzer, which in fact has been (and the British school of object relations more widely) highly influential in the development of Anzieu's ideas. Especially useful for my purpose of exploring how thinking is being represented and realised in *Under the Skin* are the specific concepts of the skin-container function, adhesive identification, and the dimensionality of life-space that were formulated by Bick and Meltzer. Much of their pioneering work in this area of primary containment was developed in collaboration, also with other colleagues.

Within film studies, this piece stands as part of a movement that advocates a renewed interest in psychoanalysis, after it having been deemed an exhausted field for film theory that could not contribute to the debates on the significance of the body and embodied experience that emerged in the early 1990s.[6] Recent psychoanalytic approaches to film demonstrate not only that such a claim is unfair, but that, as Agnieszka Piotrowska notes, "embodied and material existence can, and perhaps ought to, also allow for the unconscious".[7] The psychoanalytic theories that I am examining here foreground the sensual and bodily aspects of the problem of containment, as well as of the experience of time and space.

Bick first presented her thesis on the primal function of the skin in her seminal 1968 paper "The Experience of the Skin in Early Object Relations". She observed that the skin has a holding or containing function for parts of the self that in the early stages of life are felt to have no binding force to hold together.[8] But the experience of being held together, which for Bick has a passive quality, is dependent on the introjection of an external object that is perceived as being capable of holding. In favourable circumstances, that object is "the nipple in the mouth, together with the holding and talking and familiar smelling mother".[9] Only then can integration and organization begin, along with the establishment of a concept of space – space within the self, space inside objects, three-dimensional space.

If this containing function is disturbed, situations of catastrophic anxiety produced by the unintegrated state can manifest themselves in the frantic search for, and adhesion to, an external object. The eyes can stick to an image, or the ears to the sound of a voice. In a later article that further develops her findings, Bick gives an account of a separation ritual in the analysis of a six-year-old girl, which conveys this sense of adhesiveness:

> The sink with the water [...] could be seen to represent her mother's lap and nipple. Her last move at the end of each session was to go to the sink. There she lay on the sink, put her mouth round the tap and filled her mouth with water. She held the water until her mother came into sight as she approached the waiting-room, whereupon she swallowed the water and held on to the mother with her eyes. The number of mouthfuls she took was proportioned to the duration of separation before weekends and holidays.[10]

The action of filling the mouth with water but not swallowing seems to be an attempt to fill the gap of separation by sealing an orifice of her body. The child is clinging to her mother, first with her mouth, and then with her eyes, leaning up against the sink as if it was the mother's lap. This child would also lean against walls, while walking over the furniture and not touching the floor, which suggests adhesiveness to two-dimensional surfaces rather than an experience of space in which things are solid, with an inside and outside, and subject to gravity.

Holding water in the mouth in this way reveals a difficulty with introjection, with using internal spaces for identification. It can also be seen as tensing the muscles of a container so that it does not spill out. Bick refers to several cases in which the feeling of liquefying, of having one's life spill out or drain away is dealt with by what she calls "second-skin formations":[11] overdeveloped muscular activity either reflected in continuous movement, or clenching and frozen tension; and a kind of verbal muscularity, i.e. an early development of verbalization as a means to hold the self together.[12] Inadequate first-skin formation can manifest itself in unintegrated posture and motility, in the need for clothes and shoes tightly fastened. Corresponding states of mental unintegration can be discerned when words do not seem to be listened to, when they seem to go right through the body, or in instances of mimicry of another person's speech.

During the 1960s Bick was supervising infant observation and the treatment of psychosis in children and adults, while Meltzer's work involved the therapy of autistic children. Meltzer recounts that Bick described her experience with her analysands by sticking her hands together and saying "they're sticky, they stick"; he explains:

> She also thought that these people had some sort of difficulty about introjection and that they could not use projective identification very much, that their conception of their relationships was a very external one, that their values were very external and not generated by internal relationships, not based on internal principles, not based on observation of themselves, their own reactions but as it were looking in the mirror of other people's eyes all the time.[13]

Meltzer began to connect the phenomena Bick encountered with some of the material he was observing, such as autistic children's pronounced intolerance to separation. They also began to think about dimensionality:

> What gradually emerged for us, as we talked and talked about it, was that these children, outside the area of their autism, in what we came to think of as their post-autism, their post-autistic psychosis, functioned as if there really were no spaces, there were only surfaces, two dimensions. Things were not solid, only surfaces that they might lean up against, or that they might feel, smell, touch, so on, get a sensation from.[14]

Characteristic of this surface relationship to objects is the preclusion of projective and introjective identification, and attendant development, because there are no spaces to get into or take something into. It is then that Meltzer and Bick conceive of a distinct type of narcissistic identification, which they term "adhesive identification", seeing a relation with mimicry, and with the shallowness and external quality of values that Bick had observed in her analysands' personalities.[15] Once discovered, patches of this kind of shallowness became visible to them in everyone's lives, their own and other people's, in which "emotionality was very attenuated, not in a sense of flatness but in the sense of a kind of thinness".[16] It is important to note how these theories exceed the clinical setting.

In her 1968 paper Bick points out that the state of unintegration in infants that she is referring to pertains to a time before the operation of splitting-and-idealization, as Melanie Klein described it.[17] Drawing on the work of Bick, Meltzer and Frances Tustin, Thomas Ogden proposed to name this dimension of experience that is prior to the paranoid-schizoid position, the "autistic-contiguous position", which, following Klein's own concept of "position", he sees as "a developing and ongoing mode of generating experience as opposed to a phase of development".[18] Thus, adhesive processes related to primitive anxieties of unintegration and separation are configurations that occur throughout life.

Meltzer conceptualized in detail the evolution of the dimensionality of time and space, as he became aware of differences in how the world could be structured in the "geography of phantasy" of the organism. He divided this geography into four compartments: "inside the self; outside the self; inside internal objects; inside external objects; and to these may sometimes, perhaps always, be added […] the 'nowhere' of the delusional system".[19] Concomitant with the development of spatial dimensionality is the development of the dimension of time; the manner in which they develop is described by Meltzer, and I will weave these descriptions into my analysis of the film. I conclude this section with a last image that Bick

wonderfully evokes with the following statement: "When the baby is born he is in the position of an astronaut who has been shot into outer space without a spacesuit".[20]

III

The sequence that follows the creation of the eye continues to play with the perception of scale and dimensionality, and begins to convey a sense of adhesiveness. At night, just before dawn, we see a cascade of water running between frozen hills. Then, the distant headlight of a motorbike moving fast along a road that cuts through the mountains. The darkness contributes to the flatness of the landscape, while the spot of light resembles the one in the opening sequence, so that our perception of this image may shift to that of an object moving in the immensity of outer space, like the light that was eventually reflected on the iris of the eye. This becomes more obvious when a spot of light vibrates in the round black helmet of the motorcyclist framed in a close-up, the turbulence of the speed at which he moves controlled by his firm grip on the handlebar, while the lights of the passing traffic resemble comets leaving trails of coloured dust. This male alien (Jeremy McWilliams) is on his way to retrieve the lifeless female whom the protagonist is going to replace; he finds her body in an area of rough grass next to a road where a white van is parked, and puts it in the back of the van. The back space of this vehicle is a completely featureless, luminous white background, against which the protagonist, naked, begins to remove the other woman's clothes and to put them on. The sound here emphasizes the tightness of the clothes, as we hear the pulling of fabrics against the skin, the unzipping of the jacket and fastening of buckles on the high-heeled shoes. There is a hole in the dead alien's tights, and when her clothes are completely removed, a tear falls from one of her eyes. This suggests an interior space that is barely contained in her, which links to the cascade and the thawing ice, and will link to the last image of the film, as will be seen later. In retrospect, it could be said that the tear is a delayed emotional reaction to a previous experience, if we believe that her replacement is about to embark on a similar journey of gradual emotional involvement in this world.[21]

Wearing the other alien's clothes, she goes to a shopping centre to buy her own pair of tight jeans, a close-fitting pink top, a fur jacket, black suede boots and an orange red lipstick. If this outfit already appears to be a second skin, the motorcyclist's suit seems to function as an exoskeleton, barely holding the alien's body together and upright, at once allowing and constraining his movements. His actions are limited to ensuring that the

female fulfils her task; when she ceases to do so, he is seen riding his motorbike as a small point moving extremely fast in the distance, along the lines of the roads, towards the object that has strayed. The landscapes across which he moves look curiously flat, as the only movement registered on them is along the road, the uniformity of light and colour contributing further to the lack of depth. In this, his world appears to be one-dimensional – according to Meltzer:

> Freud's original systematic theory as expressed in the "Project", the VIIth chapter of the "Traumdeutung" or the "Three Essays" is essentially a description of one-dimensionality: source, aim and object of neurophysiologically and genetically determined drive patterns. A linear relationship of time-distance between self and object would give rise to a "world" which had a fixed centre in the self and a system of radiating lines having direction and distance to objects which were conceived as potentially attractive or repellent. [...] Time would be indistinguishable from distance, a compound of distance and velocity, one might say, closure-time. It is not a world conducive to emotionality except of the simplest polarized sort.[22]

Later in the film, when the female escapes from her presumably imposed routine, letting a man escape too, the alien motorcyclist efficiently captures the man first, and is subsequently joined by others who relentlessly search for her. Initially riding as a group, they split in different directions at a roundabout, as if breaking a centripetal force with a fixed centre from which only a distance, or a matter of time, separates it from the object. Another image evokes this centre with a system of radiating lines, of the alien male at the top of a snow-covered mountain, still looking for her: in a composition reminiscent of a famous painting by Caspar David Friedrich, *The Wanderer Above the Sea of Fog* (c. 1818), he stands with his back towards us, then slowly turns, scanning the landscape all around him.

In a different way, the female seems to stick to the strange world around her as an image, as a flat surface largely unknown and with limited functions, seen from behind the windows of the protective carapace of her vehicle. The tone of the sparse dialogues that typically take place inside the van with the men she picks up from the streets after asking them for directions, reveals the thinness of the emotionality – "Do you think I am pretty?"; "I think you are gorgeous". The men also seem to stick to her as image, drawn to the sensuousness of her surface qualities. This kind of tropism is also suggested by the violin motif composed of three notes growing higher in pitch, that is heard repeatedly as she lures them. When they enter her house – which is each time a different house, yet always derelict – they disappear into its dark interior only to emerge from it in a

space that is completely black, with no defined limits except for its highly reflective floor surface. Their eyes and ears are fixed on her image and voice, as they follow her oblivious to anything else, dropping their clothes on the floor, their penises erect, while their perfect upside-down reflection joins adhesively at the point of contact with the black surface. She continues to lead them inside, stripping her clothes as well, and the men follow her a few metres behind unaware that they begin to sink, as the floor turns to a viscous black substance; they become immersed in it, suspended, and they can only glimpse her diminishing figure still walking on the surface above.

This surreal and abstract space conveys precisely the idea of two-dimensionality, of paper-thinness: everything in it is given as reflection, image, two-dimensional surface; as a precarious membrane to which bodies adhere, and through which bodies fall into a void; as a flimsy skin through which bodies spill out.[23] In one of the most striking images of the film, one of the men trapped in the pool for some time suddenly implodes in his own empty skin, as if his flesh had been suctioned, and only the black substance filled it. We then see a long narrow tray full of fleshy and liquid matter being sucked into a bright red thin opening, again surrounded by blackness. What exactly is distilled from this matter that looks like waste is not known, but it becomes a thin pulsating red light, then a bright red star with a white core, then a white star with a spot of black in the middle. Meltzer writes:

> By speaking of two-dimensionality […] we appear to be making no statement referrable to consciousness, interest or attention at all, but purely with regard to the organization of perceptual processes concerning self and objects, the 'world'. By 'shallowness', for instance, I do not mean to refer in particular to the thinness of the emotionality but rather to imply that this same thinness is a necessary consequence of the surface to surface relation to objects.[24]

Perhaps not a great deal of consciousness, but certainly interest and attention, can be harnessed in this black space, generated thinly by a surface relation. At times, what we also see inside this space is the alien without her skin: a flayed, eyeless creature that appears to be made of the same black substance, though as solid as flesh and bones. This could suggest that the black space is her internal world, a void in which only remnants of objects exist. Regarding the self-living in a two-dimensional world, Meltzer notes that

> Its experiences could not result in the introjection of objects or introjective modification of its existing objects. It could not therefore conduct in thought experiments in regression or progression from which the memory

> of past events could be reconstructed more or less accurately, and future possibilities adumbrated with some degree of conviction. Its relationship to time would be essentially circular, since it would be unable to conceive of enduring change, and therefore of development – or cessation. Circumstances which threaten this changelessness would tend to be experienced as break-down of the surfaces – cracking, tearing, suppuration, dissolution […].[25]

The circularity of her time gives the first half of the film a circular structure, a sense reinforced each time she retraces her steps as soon as her victim is trapped, collecting her clothes from the floor and putting them back on.

However, this situation begins to change as the film unfolds, indeed when surfaces begin to break down. Seated inside the van with windows closed, she notices a baby crying in a vehicle next to hers, perhaps triggering a vague memory of a baby that she had left earlier on a shore, crying after its parents had drowned in the sea under her impassive gaze. In a later scene, she opens the window of her van to receive a rose that another driver, in the slow-moving traffic, has bought for her, and which is stained with blood from the seller's hand. The tearing of these surfaces produces exchange: the opening of the window, the seller's hand bleeding, her hand touching the rose and the blood with unfamiliarity. Changes to her two-dimensional world are also apparent when she trips while walking on the street, falling to the ground. We see her face close to the pavement, her hair delimiting an almost intimate space from which only the muffled voices of the passers-by who help her stand up again can be heard (real passers-by, as this scene was shot with hidden cameras).

During one of her nocturnal excursions, she picks up a man whose head is covered by a hood. Inside the van, he shyly removes it, revealing his face disfigured by neurofibromatosis. She takes his hand up to her cheek and her neck so he can feel her soft skin. Then, we see her leading him up a staircase, and after into the pool, while he looks behind sometimes, until the black substance covers him only up to his waist. We see her coming down to the bottom of the staircase, stopping in front of a mirror and observing her eyes attentively, as if her eyes and the mirror were a surface that is about to give way to a vertiginous fall into unknown space. The fragility of this membrane is echoed by the peeling paint on the walls and the dripping sounds. She lets the man out of the house, and gets into the van; she drives fast, no longer wearing her fur jacket, no longer with her usual poise.

In the countryside, a very thick fog prevents her progress on the road. She comes out of the vehicle into the surrounding whiteness, in which

only faint stretches of asphalt and grass in her immediate proximity are visible. Unsteady point of view shots suggest a subdued feeling of wonder and disorientation; but soon, in an extreme long shot, we see her walking away from the cloud of mist.

It is shortly after this scene that she encounters a kind man who lends her his jacket, takes her into his house, prepares dinner for both of them, and lets her sleep in a separate room. Intriguing reversals occur with this encounter. Before wishing her good night, he takes an electric heater stored in the wardrobe of the room and switches it on. In the dimness, the glowing red filament of the heater bears an uncanny resemblance to the thin red opening that was seen earlier in the film drawing the flesh of her victims. She looks at it for some time from a corner of the room; then, we see the warm red light enveloping her as she looks at herself naked in a tall mirror, touching her skin, twisting her body, examining it.

The next day while they walk in the woods they find a pool of rainwater as wide as their path. Noticing her hesitation, he takes her in his arms and walks right through it, the water reaching just above his ankles. In the distance can be seen the ruins of a castle. Inside the castle, they stand at the top of steep and narrow spiralling steps, hardly visible in the darkness. She looks anxiously behind her, and only slowly comes down the steps, holding on to a rope and to his hands, and to his reassuring words – "It's OK", he repeats, leading the way. Her method of capturing humans surely comes to her mind in these situations, and his ability to hold her through them must contribute to a growing sense of integration, containment, and trust in him. Her speechlessness throughout the time with this man also hints at a change in her.

When they are back from their walk, they kiss, but she discovers that it is physically impossible for her to be sexually penetrated. This calls to mind an earlier scene, just before her meeting him, in which she tries to eat a slice of chocolate cake – probably her first attempt at eating human food – and immediately spits out the first bite.[26] These are humorous moments, but they are also tinged with a certain sadness, because the increasing awareness of her body brings with it a sense of inadequacy and isolation. And yet, following Meltzer, this could mean that a transition has been made:

> Once the object has been experienced as resisting penetration, so that the emotional problems no longer seem merely ones of being on one side or the other of a paper-thin object (front-side and back-side for instance), the stage is set […] for the conception to arise of orifices in object and self. The struggle can then commence concerning the guarding or closing of these orifices, which are conceived as natural rather than forced or torn.

> With the inception of this new struggle the entire view-of-the-world rises to a new level of complexity, the three-dimensional one, of objects, and, by identification, the self, as containing potential spaces.[27]

Her alien body cannot swallow food and have sexual intercourse, at least in ways that are common to humans, but at these points in the film she seems to have formed a conception of orifices in her body, which means that she feels there is a space inside her that can contain thoughts, memories, desires. The geography of her life-space appears to have become three-dimensional, as her self is now experienced as having a potentially containing internal space.

Subsequent to her discovery that she cannot be penetrated, which disturbs her, we see her walking into a forest, by herself. It has started to rain lightly and she appears to be wet and cold. A tree logger approaches and asks her if she is alone, to which she distractedly assents. They continue on their separate ways, and later she finds a hut where she takes shelter. Inside the hut there is a fireplace, and when she looks at its blackness she zips up her jacket, before dragging herself into a corner, and then falling asleep. Her gesture of zipping up the jacket when she sees the blackness of the fireplace suggests her remembering the black space in which life spills out and drains away: she reacts with a gesture of closing or tightening a second skin. Meltzer states that "projective identification is the mechanism par excellence of narcissistic identification in a three-dimensional world"[28] and he makes the following comments on the consequences of this regarding the experience of time:

> Insofar as the inside of an object also persists in having the meaning of a prior state of mind, for the feeling of being adequately contained is a precondition for the experience of being a continent container, the movements in phantasy of getting into and out of an object necessarily have a significance with regard to the conception of time. Time […] now begins to take on a directional tendency of its own, a relentless movement from inside to outside the object. But the continued operation of omnipotence fashions the phantasy of projective identification. By this means not only is there asserted the reversibility of differentiation of self from object but also, as a corollary, a claim is put forward concerning the reversibility of the direction of time. Oscillatory time thus arises in the mind's conceptions of "the world" and must wait upon the painful, and never fully completed, movement of relinquishment of projective identification in order to become one-directional.[29]

Through the operation of projective identification the differentiation between self and object can be reversed, and thus time reverses too: from

being inside the object to outside the object, and back inside again, time oscillates. Her seeing the fireplace seems to have transported her to a prior state of mind, to an identification with the object in which her differentiation from it threatens to break down. In the quotation above, Meltzer is conceiving of projective identification as an omnipotent, invasive mechanism. It is perhaps worth noting that he will later continue to make distinctions according to the motive or use of the identification process, and propose to reserve the term "projective identification" for Wilfred Bion's understanding of it "as a primitive and largely unconscious mode of communication central to learning from experience."[30] What occurs in the film does not so much have this communicative aspect but rather an intrusive one, an identification with an internal object, which is also apparent in the image that follows: an image of her sleeping curled up dissolving into the centre of an image of the forest, as if she was protected inside it in her dream. However, her sleep is brought to an end by the logger touching her thigh; startled, she runs outside. He follows her and tries to restrain her, but there is a moment in which she stops her resistance, and this seems to be when she sees that snow has started to fall. It is during his violent tearing of her clothes, that he tears her skin. He looks at his hands stained with the black substance; dumbstruck, but unafraid, the man stops for an instant and suddenly runs off. She stumbles ahead with one hand in front of her as if she could no longer see, the other holding the back of her head. A deep cut extends from the back of her neck to the top of her skull; falling down to her knees, slowly, she pulls the skin from her head, then from the top of her shoulders, so that the eyeless black creature underneath is now holding the skin of her face with her eyes, alive, looking back at her. This extraordinary, poetic moment could be seen as one of introjection:

> It is only once the struggle against narcissism has been mounted and the omnipotence with which intrusion and control is imposed upon good objects in the inner and outer worlds has diminished, that the realization of a four-dimensional world can commence. [...] And this new hope inspires the process of a new type of identification, which Freud discovered and described in "The Ego and the Id". But introjective identification is a very different affair from the narcissistic ones. Relinquishment is its precondition, time is its friend and hope is its hallmark. [...] Introjective identification would then be seen as coming into play to raise the mental life out of the sphere of narcissism in specific connection with four-dimensionality.[31]

Indeed, it is not a perfect image of her unknown self that she sees, as the pool would return to her in narcissistic contemplation: it is a moment in

which she sees her own interior and recognizes it as such, she sees her self "under the skin". Here her interior is at once given to visibility and made of the most mysterious opacity; and her skin appears as sentient, impressionable, intelligent, capable of emotion. In my view, this moment is not the introjection of an external object, nor the introjective modification of her existing objects, but the introjective modification of her self. This encounter with the self "under the skin" requires relinquishment of omnipotent control over internal and external objects. From a primitive conception of time as distance to the object, through circularity, then oscillation, finally a conception of time in a four-dimensional world becomes one-directional, it frames the life-time of the individual, moving linearly from conception to death.[32]

She does not seem to realise that the man has returned and stands behind her, with a container of petrol, until she feels the liquid splashed on to her back, upon which she rises to her feet and begins to stagger. He sets fire to the petrol spilled on the ground and the flames quickly engulf her. Burning, she runs towards an open field covered in snow, and collapses. In the last shot of the film, the column of black ash rising from her burning body combines with white snow falling: as the camera tilts up, this grey icy substance falls on its lens, and thaws, continues to fall, accumulates. This is a very tactile image in that its surface becomes a kind of skin, sentient, impressionable, affecting the surface of our skin and our eyes. Earlier, her seeing this dispersal into wide open space seemed to comfort her, as if she had recognized in it traces of an emotion that was now in continuous expansion like a cascade of water collecting melted snow on its way. *Under the Skin* centres around these primal anxieties of falling apart, dispersing or liquefying, while inviting us to think about our need to be passively held or contained by another, before a capacity for emotionality can emerge. In its real, fictionalized and phantasized depiction of an alien's increasingly emotional response to the world and its people, it shows how this development is intimately connected to a bodily, physical experience that also becomes increasingly complex, unfolding and expanding into different dimensions of space and time.

Notes

---

[1] Michel Faber, *Under the Skin* (Edinburgh: Canongate, 2000), 157.
[2] Jonathan Romney, "Unearthly Stranger," *Sight and Sound* 24, no. 4 (2014): 26.
[3] Jonathan Glazer quoted in Romney, 26.
[4] "skin, *n.* and *v.*; phrases 'under the skin'." *Oxford English Dictionary*. 3rd ed. (Oxford: Oxford University Press, 2010).

[5] Studies of film include Berton (2005), Laine (2006), Scholz and Surma (2008), Pile (2009), Diena (2009), Haylett Bryan (2013) and, of broader scope, Segal (2009). Within the fields of cultural, gender and feminist studies see Prosser (1998), Ahmed and Stacey (2001), Benthien (2002), Connor (2004) and Cavanagh, Failler and Hurst (2013). For two exceptions to this general rule, the last mentioned volume contains one chapter by Failler in which she investigates the issue of self-harm and a video piece by artist Hope Peterson, while drawing on the work of Esther Bick; Harrang (2012) has written on Pedro Almodóvar's *The Skin I Live In*, also engaging with the work of Bick.

[6] I am referring to the phenomenological interventions of Sobchack (1992), Marks (1999) and Barker (2009) in particular for their interest in skin, touch and the experience of the "lived body".

[7] Agnieszka Piotrowska, ed., *Embodied Encounters: New Approaches to Psychoanalysis and Cinema* (East Sussex: Routledge, 2015), 1. Among the recent psychoanalytic studies of film that I am drawing attention to are the articles collected in Piotrowska's book and those mentioned above in note 3; see also Ince (2011).

[8] Esther Bick, "The Experience of the Skin in Early Object Relations," in *Surviving Space: Papers on Infant Observation*, ed. Andrew Briggs (London: Karnac, 2002), 55.

[9] Bick, "The Experience of the Skin in Early Object Relations," 56.

[10] Esther Bick, "Further Considerations on the Function of the Skin in Early Object Relations," *British Journal of Psychotherapy* 2 (1986): 294.

[11] Bick, "Further Considerations," 298.

[12] Bick, "The Experience of the Skin in Early Object Relations," 59.

[13] Donald Meltzer, "Adhesive Identification," *Contemporary Psychoanalysis* 11 (1975): 297.

[14] Meltzer, "Adhesive Identification," 299.

[15] Ibid., 301.

[16] Ibid., 303.

[17] Bick, "The Experience of the Skin in Early Object Relations," 56.

[18] Thomas H. Ogden, "On the Concept of an Autistic-Contiguous Position," *International Journal of Psychoanalysis* 70 (1989): 127. Ogden writes that "the autistic-contiguous organization is associated with a specific mode of attributing meaning to experience in which raw sensory data are ordered by means of forming pre-symbolic connexions between sensory impressions that come to constitute bounded surfaces. It is on these surfaces that experience of self has its origins" (128).

[19] Donald Meltzer et al., *Explorations in Autism: A Psycho-Analytical Study* (Strath Tay: Clunie, 1975), 223.

[20] Bick, "Further Considerations," 296.

[21] John Marmysz (2014, 39) writes that "In *Under the Skin*, the streets of Glasgow could be anywhere that people are difficult to understand and the territory is unfamiliar. This could be Boston or Bangkok; Moscow or Madrid. What is evoked is not uniquely Scottish, but a universal sense of displacement, or what Heidegger terms 'homelessness' […]. When the action in *Under the Skin* moves to the Scottish countryside, the backdrop becomes even more nondescript". On the contrary, I believe the setting of this film is very much a part of its context and

narrative, its atmosphere and affect: the Scottish and foreign accents that we hear in the English language juxtaposed with the English accent that Johansson learns and puts on, the haar rolling from the North Sea typical of the coastal areas of Scotland, in the thickness of which the alien leaves the van behind, are only two examples of important, specific aspects of the place where the film is set.

[22] Meltzer et al., *Explorations in Autism*, 224.

[23] This space is all the more remarkable for its difference to the one that is described in Faber's novel. In the novel, it is an underground space that is like an animal pen with separate cages, where men whose tongues and testicles have been surgically removed are being fattened up.

[24] Meltzer et al., *Explorations in Autism*, 238.

[25] Ibid., 225.

[26] An underlying narrative structure can be recognized in that some of her experiences can be successively attributed to each of the five senses: hearing (the sound of the baby crying), smelling (the rose episode), seeing (a sequence to which I do not refer in my analysis, beginning with an extreme close-up of her eye, then images of busy streets becoming increasingly superimposed, turning into a golden hue, her face dissolving into the image), touching (exchange with disfigured man inside the van), tasting (the Black Forest gateau episode). It is noteworthy that all of these experiences are in their own way excessive, for example the blood on the rose wrapping.

[27] Meltzer et al., *Explorations in Autism*, 226.

[28] Ibid., 228.

[29] Ibid., 226-7.

[30] Donald Meltzer, *Studies in Extended Metapsychology: Clinical Applications of Bion's Ideas* (Perthshire: Clunie Press, 1986), 67.

[31] Meltzer et al., *Explorations in Autism*, 227-8.

[32] Ibid., 223.

References

Ahmed, Sarah, and Jackie Stacey, eds. *Thinking Through the Skin*. London: Routledge, 2001.

Barker, Jennifer. *The Tactile Eye: Touch and the Cinematic Experience*. Berkeley, CA: University of California Press, 2009.

Benthien, Claudia. *Skin: On the Cultural Border Between Self and the World*. Translated by Thomas Dunlap. New York: Columbia University Press, 2002.

Berton, Mireille. "Le origini ecotattili dell'immagine cinematografica." *Bianco e nero. Rivista quadrimestrale del centro sperimentale di cinematografia* 551 (2005): 233-45.

Bick, Esther. "The Experience of the Skin in Early Object Relations." In *Surviving Space: Papers on Infant Observation*, edited by Andrew Briggs, 55-59. London: Karnac, 2002. Originally published in *International Journal of Psychoanalysis* 49 (1968): 484-86.

—. "Further Considerations on the Function of the Skin in Early Object Relations." *British Journal of Psychotherapy* 2 (1986): 292-99.

Cavanagh, Sheila L., and Angela Failler, Rachel A. J. Hurst, eds. *Skin, Culture and Psychoanalysis*. New York: Palgrave Macmillan, 2013.

Connor, Steven. *The Book of Skin*. London: Reaktion, 2004.

Diena, Simonetta. "The skin house: A psychoanalytic reading of *3-Iron*." *International Journal of Psychoanalysis* 90 (2009): 647-60.

Faber, Michel. *Under the Skin*. Edinburgh: Canongate, 2000.

Harrang, Caron. "Psychic Skin and Narcissistic Rage: Reflections on Almodóvar's *The Skin I Live In*." *International Journal of Psychoanalysis* 93 (2012): 1301-8.

Haylett Bryan, Alice. "A Mother's Touch: *Regarde la mer* (Ozon, 1997) and the Skin Ego." Paper presented at the Psychoanalysis, Culture and Society Conference, Middlesex University, June 15, 2013.

Ince, Kate. "Bringing Bodies Back In: For a Phenomenological and Psychoanalytic Film Criticism of Embodied Cultural Identity." *Film-Philosophy* 15, no. 1 (2011): 1-12.

Laine, Tarja. "Cinema as Second Skin: Under the Membrane of Horror Film." *New Review of Film and Television Studies* 4, no. 2 (2006): 93-106.

Marks, Laura. *The Skin of the Film: Intercultural Cinema, Embodiment, and the Senses*. Durham, NC: Duke University Press, 1999.

Marmysz, John. "The Myth of Scotland as Nowhere in Particular." *International Journal of Scottish Theatre and Screen* 7, no. 1 (2014): 28-44.

Meltzer, Donald. "Adhesive Identification." *Contemporary Psychoanalysis* 11 (1975): 289-310.

—. *Studies in Extended Metapsychology: Clinical Applications of Bion's Ideas*. Perthshire: Clunie Press, 1986.

Meltzer, Donald, and John Bremner, Shirley Hoxter, Doreen Weddell, Isca Wittenberg. *Explorations in Autism: A Psycho-Analytical Study*. Strath Tay: Clunie, 1975.

Ogden, Thomas H. "On the Concept of an Autistic-Contiguous Position." *International Journal of Psychoanalysis* 70 (1989): 127-40.

Oxford English Dictionary. 3rd ed. Oxford: Oxford University Press, 2010.

Pile, Steve. "Topographies of the body-and-mind: Skin Ego, Body Ego, and the film *Memento*." *Subjectivity* 27, no. 1 (2009): 134-54.

Piotrowska, Agnieszka, ed. *Embodied Encounters: New Approaches to Psychoanalysis and Cinema*. East Sussex: Routledge, 2015.

Prosser, Jay. *Second Skins: The Body Narratives of Transsexuality*. New York: Columbia University Press, 1998.

Romney, Jonathan. "Unearthly Stranger." *Sight and Sound* 24, no. 4 (2014): 22-27.

Scholz, Sebastian, and Hanna Surma. "Exceeding the Limits of Representation: Screen and/as Skin in Claire Denis's *Trouble Every Day* (2001)." *Studies in French Cinema* 8, no. 1 (2008): 5-16.

Segal, Naomi. *Consensuality: Didier Anzieu, Gender and the Sense of Touch*. Amsterdam: Rodopi, 2009.

Sobchack, Vivian. *The Address of the Eye: A Phenomenology of Film Experience*. Princeton, NJ: Princeton University Press, 1992.

CHAPTER NINE

"SUFFERING FROM REMINISCENCES": MEMORY AND TRAUMA IN ELIZABETH BOWEN'S SHORT FICTION

OLENA LYTOVKA

Introduction

Memory has found a prominent place in the works of twentieth-century writers and especially modernist fiction. It has been conceptualized as a "storehouse", a "container", intrinsically linked to identity and viewed as a temporal phenomenon.[1] In this chapter I will approach Bowen's short fiction in relation to memory and trauma. I will try to explore how traumatic experiences of the past are connected with the characters' perception of domestic space and how the crisis of their selves is projected onto the house.

The importance memory assumes in Bowen's fiction is connected with the placement of trauma in the centre of her concerns and projecting the personal crisis onto domestic space. Bowen seems to be extremely conscious of location and of the power of the house within the landscape but the particularity of her style relies on locating the house simultaneously in the present and the past, blurring the borders between now and then and, most of all, on making the house the reflection of her characters' identity disintegration.

The house is a focal point in many of Elizabeth Bowen's works and very nearly constitutes "the basis of her methodology".[2] She demonstrates an almost obsessive preoccupation with the house in her fiction, treating it as "the core of the world".[3] For Bowen, houses are the foundational element with and around which she structures much of her fictional writing. However, instead of standing for a site of comfort, safety and stability, the house, in Bowen, appears to be antagonistic to its inhabitants and makes them feel threatened and uncertain of their identity.

The atmosphere in Bowen's novels and short stories is often uncanny. Characters experience the presence of something disturbing and frightening in the house, perceive the domestic space as strange, sinister and feel entrapped there. Shafquat Towheed claims:

> "Bowen's overcharged concern with place, her repeated, insistent and enforced returns in her fiction to the place of an earlier event to reinscribe the validity of a narrated event (…) often through the character's interaction with material objects, verges on the obsessive and the Unheimlich".[4]

Her fictional characters are haunted not just by material things or chronological events, but by spaces, "whether occupied, emptied, displaced or imagined; the 'enforced return' (...) of so many of her protagonists, invariably re-engages with a previous spatial experience".[5]

Like many other modernist novelists, Bowen attempts to reimagine death and to reconsider losses that it inevitably yields. In her fiction, there is a recognition of both the need and impossibility of understanding the past, the longing and the failure to assimilate its painful experiences. The protagonists of Bowen's novels and short stories are distressed and disoriented individuals attacked by their own memory. The traumatic experiences of the past shatter the construction of their identity and plunge them into a state of existential crisis with the sense of uncanniness persisting. Therefore, psychoanalysis seems to be the most appropriate instrument for exploration of trauma and Freud's theories to be crucial to the reconceptualisation of death and loss in Bowen's work.

The Uncanny

The term "uncanny" came into wider use mainly thanks to the eponymous essay by Freud (1919). According to the psychoanalyst, the uncanny is defined as something that can be familiar, yet foreign at the same time, resulting in a feeling of it being uncomfortably strange or uncomfortably familiar; a feeling of not-being-at-home.[6] Freud asserts that it is undoubtedly related to what is frightening, to what arouses dread and horror.[7] The uncanny must have an element of danger in it; it may be something domestic but at the same time unfriendly, dangerous, something that sets the sense of insecurity within the four walls of one's house.

According to Freud, the uncanny is related to knowledge one would rather forget, it has undergone repression and returned in a transformed shape.[8] The uncanny is psychologically conditioned and represents anxieties and traumas, which manifest themselves through strange and terrifying images. The repetition or the return of these past images is

mandatory within the uncanny and signals mental fixation on the trauma. This fixation produces identity crisis and causes disintegration of time and space perceived by the subject.

Cathy Caruth claims that "to be traumatized is precisely to be possessed by an image or event".[9] It usually involves time disruption with the past surfacing in the present, especially the past which has not been worked through: the memory traces are revised and interweave with fresh experiences producing the uncanny effect. Time becomes fragmentary and kaleidoscopic, non-linear and circular, whereas space acquires features producing fear and strange uncertainty, making the subject insecure in his or her own abode.

Consequently, the source of the fear appears to be within the self, not coming from the outer world. In *Beyond the Pleasure Principle,* Freud explains that mental processes are regulated by "the pleasure principle": in their lives, people strive for avoidance of pain or production of pleasure.[10] That is why the traumatic episodes are forced to be forgotten, ousted from the conscious mind and appear in a disguised form. Thus, the original event is distorted to the unconscious mind and is inaccessible to reflection.

According to Dylan Trigg, "the subject that survives trauma does so less through the fortitude of subjectivity and more as the uncanny aftereffect of an event".[11] The deferment of the trauma's work upon the subject establishes a radical split in time and opens a portal between the past and the present. The result of its opening is becoming possessed by the past impossible to be reconstructed in a conventional narrative: "Instead, the place of trauma vibrates with an indirect language, blocked from interpretation and displacing the certainty of self, memory, and place".[12]

Psychoanalytic theory has provided the most rigorous account of the uncanny as "an unhomely subjective position by evocatively connecting imagery of home to the description of the subject".[13] It offers a number of views on the house in relation to the people that occupy it. For instance, according to Freud,[14] the house symbolically represents the female genitals or the female body in general. Freud interprets the fears connected with the house as a transformation of unsatisfied libido. In addition to that, Trigg claims that the orientation and experience of place are fundamentally affective and the totality of experience of place begins and ends with the body of the subject.[15]

However, Gaston Bachelard's concept of the house appears to be more appropriate in the interpretation of Bowen's texts. Bachelard regards the house as the representation of both body *and* soul (italics mine – O.L.). He claims that the house stands for the inner, intimate world of a person.[16]

The mental image of the house repeats or echoes the inside world of the subject and the image of the house is the imprint of his or her mental state.

The concept of the uncanny, derived from Freud and developed by twentieth century psychologists, philosophers and critics, provides a more insightful reading of modernist fiction and gives a clearer comprehension of its various themes and ideas than other approaches. The uncanny proves to be a key to understanding modernism as the latter is centred on interiority, oriented at subjectivization of time and space and externalization of consciousness. The modernist aesthetics of simultaneity, which attempts to retrieve the lost identity through the work of memory, combined with the recurring representation of alienation of the subject, makes the uncanny a master category of modernism.

In this chapter I would like to discuss the short stories where the tragic events of the past, seemingly buried and forgotten, haunt the houses but primarily the people who live there. Bowen's characters are what Freud called "suffering from reminiscences"[17]: they are possessed by the past, and the uncanniness they feel is the result of their painful memories.

Damned by the Past

Bowen's short story "The Apple Tree" opens when Simon Wing's weekend party are coming back to his house after a concert. The guests do not seem very willing to be back home because of its queer atmosphere and "oppressive" comfort.[18] All the way to the Wings' house, Simon's friends Lancelot and Mrs. Bettersley feel alerted because of what is waiting for them inside, so that even the outside environment seems sinister to them: the combination of wind and moonlight is "nerve-racking"[19], the sky is "eerie cold" and "pale" and the trees are "windshaken".[20]

Remarkably, the first word with which the story begins is "frightened"[21]; it is repeated many times throughout the text, sometimes being replaced by a more intense "horrified".[22] Surprisingly, the source of the fear appears to be Mr. Wing's young wife; in spite of her innocent looks, she is the one to be scared of. Although Myra Wing is hardly nineteen and is often referred to as "the child", it is her presence in the house that makes it queer and frightening: "'You think she *is* what's the matter?' 'Obviously there's nothing funny about the *house*'".[23] The "mannerless, sexless child, the dim something between a mouse and an Undine, this wraith (…), this cold little shadow across a hearth"[24], Mrs. Wing seems to be only half human and even her physical presence in the house is questioned by some of the characters.

Almost jokingly, she is compared to a werewolf at the beginning of the story, but as it turns out later she bears much more similarity to the monstrous creature than it might seem at first. By Brian J. Frost's definition, "a werewolf is a man or woman who, either voluntarily or involuntarily, is supernaturally transformed into the shape of a wolf".[25] The transformation, temporary or permanent, traditionally occurs under the influence of the full moon. However, with the appearance of Jungian theory of "a beast within us all", the phenomenon of werewolf has been viewed also from the standpoint of the role of the personality in dissociation.[26]

After having witnessed the suicide of her classmate Doria, who had hanged herself on an apple tree in the school garden, Myra's nerves were ruined, in part by the horror of what had happened and in part by the feeling of guilt. She started sleepwalking, and every time she was in this half-conscious state, she stood looking fixedly up and pointing at something above her head. This metamorphosis was bloodcurdling and turned the room where she was into a trap, "a cul-de-sac", making even her husband, "a man with the humility of a beast", become helpless and ill.[27] Neither Lancelot, nor Mrs. Bettersley could hide their shock on seeing Mrs. Wing in her transformed state: "horrified, horrifying – of something high up that from the not quite fixity of her gaze seemed unfixed, pendent, perhaps swaying a little".[28]

The way Myra Wing skips the concert in the village hall points at her unwillingness to leave the house after dark. And although she seems to be unaware of when this metamorphosis occurs or what brings it about, the insistent repetition of the images of moon and moonlight in the text and the fact that Doria killed herself on a moonlit night suggest that the moon is one of the factors that trigger this horrible change in Mrs. Wing.

Mrs. Wing's night transformations may be the result of dissociation of her personality, revealing the Other within her self. According to Charlotte F. Otten, the Other is identified as "the kind of person who has never been socially assimilated, who feels rejected by the community and even by the family".[29] Myra, like Doria, was not pretty as a child; an orphan and an outcast at school, she was rejected by other children. So, as soon as she had a chance to make friends with "more successful" children, she left Doria thus subjecting her to loneliness and suffering.

The haunting is more persistent when the secret is known to a group of people and yet they do not talk about it, treating it as unspeakable. Then, the trauma resides as much in secrecy as in the event itself, the burden of not telling creates a network of wounds that may even exceed the event itself.[30] The tragic event of the girl's death was carefully concealed from

the public and especially from the other girls; it was treated as if it had never actually happened. The ill-fated tree had been cut down, the school had been closed, but Myra never managed to forget the sight of branches and the dead girl's legs swaying from side to side against the moonlit sky and the sound of apples falling on the ground. Her fixation on the event is to a great extent connected with her feeling guilty of Doria's death, making her come back to the uncanny moment again and again.

However, finally, she gets liberated from her past, in part thanks to talking about it for the first time: "when it's once out it won't hurt any more".[31] An understanding of psychological trauma begins with rediscovery of the past: the past, which keeps surfacing in the present, has to be worked through, relived and reconsidered. Thus, recovery becomes possible through "cathartic reliving of the traumatic memories".[32]

In the short story "Home for Christmas", Tom Brosset brings his bride Millie to his family home for Christmas. The Brossets' house seems quite hospitable: the silence is enjoyable, Tom's family are kind and smiling. However, from the very first meeting, there arises a weird impression of the whole scene having been rehearsed: everybody seems to play their roles, even Tom. At breakfast, Tom's family keep glancing at each other and carefully picking up words as if trying to hide and to hint at something at the same time. The increasing tension can be felt, although "there seem[s] no physical reason to feel fear".[33] Soon, it appears obvious that the last time Tom was at home at Christmas something awful happened that made the family feel awkward and ashamed. The same events may have become the cause of Tom's "queernesses", "to which their honeymoon [had] accustomed her [Millie]"[34] and which aggravated with their arrival in the house.

Tom's agitation and nervousness noticeable on the day of arrival (brisk movements, swerves and mad veering of the car lights on crossing the house gate) increase the next morning when he sees snow outside. While Millie is glad to have a White Christmas, it seems to be disturbing for Tom, who looks out of the window "in a queer, rather caged way".[35] This is not the only reference to the house being a cage, for the text is abundant with claustrophobic images: the house is full of passages, cut-off rooms, "perplexing number of doors", some of which are sound-proof, and "the piercing light let in by skylights and windows".[36] Although the house is called "homey", its inhabitants walk there "with rather ironly happy steps".[37]

When the Brossets talk about anything, they always finish by mentioning the last Christmas with Tom; merely mentioning, as they never really talk about it, only exchange abrupt phrases and send brisk remarks

across. Their speech is fragmentary and allusive, and unease is present in all the conversations. Unable to bear the strain, one of Tom's sisters, Wendy, betrays the tragic story of the last Christmas to Millie. It turns out that a few years ago Tom brought a girl, his fiancée, home for Christmas. It was also snowing on that day and they were enjoying themselves playing hide-and-seek in the dark, but the girl got shut up in a chest in the old schoolroom which made her go mad and die. However, Wendy, unlike Olivia, who had let the girl out, was not aware of the fact that it was Tom who had put her in the box because she had changed her mind about marrying him.

The girl's madness and death were such a shock for the family and especially for Tom that he could not get over it. Since then, the rooms in the house have seemed to be "damned by the past"[38], full of memories unbearable for him. That is why when Millie urges Tom to show her all the remote corners of the house including the old schoolroom, she nearly gets shut in the same box herself.

> "School books and juvenile books in the bookcase gave out, in spite of the heating, a dead smell. Under one window stood a strong deal chest, hasped with iron: it stood the height of a table and was about five foot long. This room had not been decorated for Christmas; you could see that nobody came in here – and from here the snowy landscapes outside the windows looked metallic and threatening. The room seemed to stand in a frightened trance from the light".[39]

In fact, it is Millie who gets frightened, almost horrified by the room and its atmosphere of death, by Tom's curious smile and the way he kicks the chest offering her to look inside. With the painful memories having been brought up, he loses touch with reality and feels the compulsion to repeat the event of the past, which becomes more real for him than the present.

From the very beginning, the present in the house seems unreal: when Millie wakes up from "a deep, plausible dream", she finds herself in "the unreality of this unknown spare room silently glared into by the snow".[40] Also, Tom tends to escape from reality by cocooning himself in an enclosed world of his marriage, where "nobody knows". While sleeping, he is lying like "a papoose", rolled in the bed, and, at one of his "queer" fits, he wraps himself into *Millie's* eiderdown (italics mine – O.L.) unconsciously searching for the feeling of comfort and safety imitating a position in the mother's womb.

Throughout the text, the characters are overwhelmed with a feeling of being watched, followed by something or somebody that does not belong

to the real world. Even the snow seems to be a curse: "'I could swear *she* sent the snow'", says Tom.[41] The snow is a reminder of the last Christmas Tom spent in the old house; with its bright whiteness it stands in contrast to the darkness of the shut chest and the closed nature of the family secret. The snow "glare[s]", "glimmer[s]" and "glitter[s]" in the sun[42] and the light it reflects pierces the house. The whiteness of the snow, of the doors, of the mantlepiece and of the ends of the beds intensifies the white reflection frozen on Tom's face. On the whole, the white colour is used in the story to express the fear of the house or rather of the past that is connected with it (e. g. when Millie comes down from the schoolroom, she looks unnaturally white with horror).

By bringing Millie home, Tom is unconsciously trying to repeat the same scenario as with his first fiancée, hoping that this time it will have a happy ending; he expects that it may help liberate him from his painful memories. And although the story ending does not give the reader an explicit answer whether he succeeds or not, as in the previous story, speaking about the past does not only bring relief but often releases the character from its permanent burden.

In Bowen's short story "The Needlecase", a child born out of wedlock is placed in the centre of an intriguing plot. The story tells about a Miss Fox, a bleak ageless woman with an "expressionless" face and a "secretive" mouth coming to an upper-middle class family to sew for a week.[43] One of the sons of the family, Frank, arrives home at the same time. Another one, the eldest and the most loved by everyone, Arthur, is expected to come soon with his new girlfriend. The two daughters, Angela and Toddy stay home, bored with its routine and waiting for something to happen.

The house Miss Fox arrives at does not look cheery at all:

> "The front of the house loomed over them, massive and dark and cold: it was the kind of house that easily looks shut up, and, when shut up, looks derelict. (…) As it was, it was like a disheartened edition of Mansfield Park. The country around it was far too empty and flat".[44]

Its darkness is compared to the darkness of a well, and the house itself assumes the features of a living creature: "They saved light everywhere, you had to grope up the stairs, for this well of a house drank money".[45] To crown it all, the house is "horribly cold", "like ice"[46], and the stove is either unlit or "a thin fire rather uncertainly flap[s]".[47]

Miss Fox is received at the house both as a rescue (the ladies' clothes must be mended before the opening of the season), as a curiosity (there is not much going on around), but also as a disturbing presence (her look

inspires sublime fear and she is compared to a witch). Her arrival seems to bring more darkness and cold to the already gloomy estate. The way she looks at Toddy is very odd, she looks "as though she were a ghost, as though it were terror and pleasure to see her face".[48] That is why Toddy feels frightened to be alone with Miss Fox, "at the top of this dark, echoing house".[49] Gradually, the atmosphere in it is becoming more and more intense, the clouds grow blacker and the whole landscape looks "anxious and taut".[50] The whistling sound of the wind outside, the house creaking and straining like a ship[51] or growing silent like a tomb[52] create the atmosphere of an impending disaster.

Finally, it is revealed that Miss Fox's "odd, reminiscent look"[53] she casts on Toddy is accounted for by Toddy's startling similarity to her brother Arthur, who turns out to be the father of Miss Fox's illegitimate son. When Frank and Angela peep into the sewing-woman's needlecase, they suddenly see an image that makes them feel shocked and uncanny: "She and Frank both stared at the photograph of the child. They saw, as Toddy had seen, its curls and its collar. Like Arthur's collar and curls in old photographs downstairs. And between the collar and curls, Arthur's face stared back at the uncle and aunt".[54] The story Miss Fox tells Angela about a dummy damaged by Arthur when he was fooling around with his friends at the house Miss Fox used to work at is actually the story of the damage perpetrated to Miss Fox herself, making her social status, as an unmarried mother, forever low and embarrassing.

The ambiguous situation Miss Fox finds herself in working in the house of her illegitimate son's father produces an uncanny effect and turns the house into a sinister tomb-like abode. Surrounded by numerous reminders of her "fall" (Arthur's photos hanging on the walls, his brother and sisters looking so like him), Miss Fox experiences a crisis that makes her look like an "immobile shadow", a "sculpture" or a "jointed image".[55] Nicholas Royle calls this state "the crisis of the proper", when one's sense of oneself ("personality", "sexuality", etc.) seems strangely questionable.[56] Royle believes the connection between uncanniness and identity uncertainty is undeniable. The traumatic experience of a person's past contributes to their identity disintegration and makes them see the world and themselves differently, feel the danger and unfriendliness of the environment and be haunted by the memories of the past.

Another of Bowen's stories, "The Cassowary", is set in a remote and half-empty mansion called Crecy Lodge. The gates of the house are rusty, covered with dust and "open reluctantly"[57], which indicates that Crecy Lodge is not very popular with visitors. The Lampeters, new tenants of the

house, lead a reclusive life and their residence, standing off the road and obscured by the lime trees, seems to be a perfect place of exile.

The house has a peculiar form: it is over-large and asymmetrical, with a minaret in the Gothic style and pointed windows on one side and a long room with a rounded end on the other. The house thus looks a little like a cassowary, a big bird with a long neck and a round body. Cassowaries are known for their hostility to people, and so is Crecy Lodge. It stands gloomily and bleakly inspiring fear to the people in the neighbourhood, with its "darkly cavernous or lividly-shuttered windows"[58], which had a "black stare"[59], and "total blackness down the slippery drive".[60] The darkness and emptiness invade the inside of the house as well, for instance the drawing-room is "blackly dominated by a mantlepiece like a cenotaph"[61], other rooms are "bare" and even the inhabitants of the house have "a slight air of vacuity".[62]

The comparison of Crecy Lodge to a cenotaph is especially significant, as it reveals the main point about the house being an "empty tomb", a place of mourning for a man whose fate is obscure. The man is Paul Melland, a medical missionary who went to Central Africa and got missing two years ago. As nobody had heard from him since that time, he was considered dead by most people, but not by the Lampeters. Paul Melland was supposed to marry one of Mrs. Lampeter's daughters, although, at first, it is difficult to tell which one, since Paul has been engaged to Phyllis Lampeter for more than four years, but before he got missing he had changed his mind in favour of Nathalie Lampeter.

The story about the missing missionary might be amusing to their neighbours (Robert Bonner has made his family laugh till they cry by reciting a limerick "I wish I were a cassowary / On the plains of Timbuctoo, / I should eat a Missionary, / Coat and hat and hymn-book too"[63]), but, in Crecy Lodge, the anguish caused by Paul's disappearance seem to be all-absorbing. The uncertainty as to whether he is alive or not or whether he will marry Phyllis or not, has made their life unsettled. The two years of waiting added distress to the family and increased alienation between them. Mr. Melland, "taboo but intently vital", was present in every room and in every conversation[64] and his shadowy presence haunted the lives of both the young girls and their mother.

Without doubt, the Lampeters' house is ghostly; it is full of memories of the past, painful reminiscences haunting its inhabitants. It is positioned in a semi-real world where objects seem to be animated while the people play the passive role of dolls. This uncanny transformation becomes possible due the personal crises the characters undergo, the crises which

make them feel not at home with themselves, make them sealed inside a time-capsule.

In Bowen's story "The Shadowy Third", the main character and the owner of the house is oppressed by the feeling of déjà-vu wherever he goes or whatever he or his new wife do about the house. His wife's ideas concerning the house, the objects around and even the smells remind him of his first wife who died. The baby they are going to have and the furnishing of the nursery make him constantly think of the child from his first marriage who died. He tries to escape from his memories and get rid of the things his first wife may have liked or used (he takes the clock off the wall, he confiscates his new wife's thimble case which looks the same as the one belonging to his first wife, he wants to buy a new sofa instead of the one *She* used to sit on so often, etc.), but instead of forgetting his life with her, he keenly feels the absence of the objects she bought for the house. For instance, he keeps putting out his hand to sweep aside the portière as he passes through the archway, although the portière was removed a long time ago: "Funny how he could never accustom himself to the changes; the house as it *had* been was always in his mind, more present than the house as it *was*".[65]

However, his obsession with the past of the house is not only caused by the feeling of loss, but also by his pervasive guilt at his first wife's death. As it is gradually uncovered in the text of the story, Martin did not love his first wife, and his indifference may have killed her. In the recalled episodes of their life together, it cannot be unnoticed that he was always annoyed, irritated or angry with her. He never came home by the early train as he does now and often slipped home pretending he had not seen her waiting at the station. The only way his first wife is referred to is "*She*" or *"Anybody",* whereas Martin's second wife is called "little woman" or "Pussy". But despite the fact that his second marriage is happier than the first one, neither Martin nor his new wife feels safe in the house, they are frightened by the idea they took somebody else's happiness, somebody else's life.

The representation of the house is the correlative of the inhabitants' psychological condition, it is clear that the threat felt is not objective reality but a manifestation of the characters' disturbed mental state caused by their memories of the past. They are vulnerable to the ambiance and forced to confront the surrounding world, which seems different from what it actually is, but, in the effect, the perception of otherness is directed inwards.

In Bowen's short stories, there is an "indiscernible extra", to use Luke Thurston's terms, that intrudes on the relations between self and other.[66] The ghostly presence of the Other in Bowen's fiction is linked with the

characters' traumatic experiences of the past. The unconscious representations of the trauma are encoded and stored in their memory, and these unconscious memories appear in the form of intrusive images and hallucinatory vision. Although forgetting seems to be necessary in order to survive, the inability to completely forget or adequately remember the painful events of the past provoke a dangerous split in the characters' psyche and result in the haunting presence of the Other that they feel.

Conclusion

By addressing Bowen's work this study sought to extend the discussion of the symbolic role of the house in Bowen's fiction, to examine how traumatic experiences of the past are connected with the characters' perception of domestic space and how the crisis of their selves can be projected onto the house. It was found that Bowen's short fiction is centred on the house as the representation of human psyche and constitutes the focal point of her short fiction. The house in Bowen's short stories is not a place of confidence and continuity but a site of uncertainty and dissolution. The concept of home as a natural, organic place of comfort is challenged and its stability is upset.

The readings of Bowen's short stories revealed that the uncanniness of domestic space is the result of characters' misplacement of repressed wishes and fears from their internal world to the external environment and that the uncanny house in Bowen stands for her characters' traumatic experience of loss. Once they are traumatized, Bowen's characters keep returning to the painful event in their thoughts and often feel the presence of the Other within themselves.

The study of Bowen's short stories helped to examine the role memory plays in the disintegration of domestic space in Bowen's short fiction. It revealed that Bowen's short story characters suffer from reminiscences, they are haunted by memories that become a heavy burden and an awful curse in their lives, whereas the house in Bowen becomes a site of personal trauma.

Notes

[1] Paul Antze and Michael Lambek, eds., *Tense Past: Cultural Essays in Trauma and Memory* (New York, London: Routledge, 1996), xi.

[2] Bethany Chafin, *Created Spaces: Domestic Myth-making in the Novels of Elizabeth Bowen* (Winston-Salem: Wake Forest University Graduate School of Arts and Sciences, 2011), iii, vi.

[33] Elizabeth Bowen, *People, Places, Things*, ed. Allan Hepburn. (Edinburgh University Press, 2008), 39.

[4] Shafquat Towheed, "Territory, space, modernity: Elizabeth Bowen's *The Demon Lover and Other Stories* and Wartime London," in *Elizabeth Bowen: New Critical Perspectives,* ed. Susan Osborn (Cork University Press, 2009), 113.

[5] Ibid., 131.

[6] Sigmund Freud, "The 'Uncanny'," in *The Standard Edition of the Complete Psychological Works of Sigmund Freud,* trans. by James Strachey, with Anna Freud, Alix Strachey, and Alan Tyson. *Volume XVII (1917-1919): An Infantile Neurosis and Other Works (*London: Hogarth Press and the Institute of Psycho-Analysis, 1986), 245.

[7] Ibid., 219.

[8] Ibid., 241.

[9] Cathy Caruth, "Trauma and Experience: Introduction," in *Trauma: Explorations in Memory*, ed. Cathy Caruth (Baltimore: John Hopkins University Press, 1995), 4-5.

[10] Sigmund Freud, *Beyond the Pleasure Principle*, ed. Todd Dufresne, transl. Gregory C. Richter (Toronto: Broadview Editions, 2011), 51.

[11] Dylan Trigg, *The Memory of Place: A Phenomenology of the Uncanny* (Athens: Ohio University Press, 2012), 237.

[12] Ibid., 276.

[13] Daisy Connon, *Subjects Not-at-home: Forms of the Uncanny in the Contemporary French Novel* (Amsterdam, New York: Rodopi, 2010), 53.

[14] Sigmund Freud, *A General Introduction to Psychoanalysis* (1920) (New York: Boni and Liveright, Bartleby.com, 2010), accessed January 4, 2013, www.bartleby.com/283/.

[15] Trigg, *The Memory of Place*, 10.

[16] Gaston Bachelard, *The Poetics of Space (*Boston: Beacon Press, 1994), 7.

[17] Sigmund Freud, *Selected Writings,* ed Robert Coles, trans. James Strachey (New York: Book-of-the-Month Club, 1997), 88.

[18] Elizabeth Bowen, *The Collected Stories of Elizabeth Bowen (*New York: Vintage Books, 1982), 463.

[19] Ibid., 461

[20] Ibid., 462

[21] Ibid., 461

[22] Ibid., 465

[23] Ibid., 462

[24] Ibid., 463

[25] Brian J. Frost, *The Essential Guide to Werewolf Literature* (Madison, London: Popular Press, 2003), 6.

[26] Charlotte F. Otten, ed., *The Literary Werewolf: An Anthology* (New York: Syracuse University Press, 2002), xxvii.

[27] Bowen, *The Collected Stories,* 464.

[28] Ibid., 465

[29] Otten, *The Literary Werewolf,* xxviii.

[30] Paulina Palmer, *The Queer Uncanny* (Cardiff: University of Wales Press, 2012), 118.

[31] Bowen, *The Collected Stories,* 467.
[32] Judith Herman,*Trauma and Recovery* (New York: Basic Books, 1992), 25.
[33] Elizabeth Bowen, *The Bazaar and Other Stories,* ed. Allan Hepburn (Edinburgh University Press, 2008), 315.
[34] Ibid., 310, 318.
[35] Ibid., 310.
[36] Ibid., 315.
[37] Ibid., 312.
[38] Ibid., 318.
[39] Ibid., 315.
[40] Ibid., 309.
[41] Ibid., 312.
[42] Ibid., 309, 312.
[43] Bowen, *The Collected Stories,* 455.
[44] Ibid., 454-455.
[45] Ibid., 456.
[46] Ibid., 457.
[47] Ibid., 455.
[48] Ibid., 456.
[49] Ibid.
[50] Ibid., 458.
[51] Ibid.
[52] Ibid., 459.
[53] Ibid., 456.
[54] Ibid., 460
[55] Ibid., 455, 458, 453.
[56] Nicholas Royle, *The Uncanny* (Manchester University Press, 2003), 1-2.
[57] Bowen, *The Collected Stories,* 314.
[58] Ibid.
[59] Ibid., 320
[60] Ibid., 318
[61] Ibid., 315
[62] Ibid., 314
[63] Ibid., 318
[64] Ibid., 319
[65] Ibid., 78
[66] Luke Thurston, "Double-crossing: Elizabeth Bowen's ghostly short fiction," *Textual Practice* 27.1 (2013):11.

References

Antze, Paul, and Michael Lambek, eds. *Tense Past: Cultural Essays in Trauma and Memory*. New York, London: Routledge, 1996.

Bachelard, Gaston. *The Poetics of Space*. Boston: Beacon Press, 1994.

Bowen, Elizabeth. *The Collected Stories of Elizabeth Bowen*. New York: Vintage Books, 1982.

—. *The Bazaar and Other Stories*. Edited by Allan Hepburn. Edinburgh University Press, 2008.

—. *People, Places, Things*. Edited by Allan Hepburn. Edinburgh University Press, 2008.

Caruth, Cathy. "Trauma and Experience: Introduction." In *Trauma: Explorations in Memory,* edited by Cathy Caruth, 3-12. Baltimore: Johns Hopkins University Press, 1995.

Chafin, Bethany. *Created Spaces: Domestic Myth-making in the Novels of Elizabeth Bowen*. Winston-Salem: Wake Forest University Graduate School of Arts and Sciences, 2011.

Connon, Daisy. *Subjects Not-at-home: Forms of the Uncanny in the Contemporary French Novel*. Amsterdam, New York: Rodopi, 2010.

Freud, Sigmund. "The 'Uncanny'." In *The Standard Edition of the Complete Psychological Works of Sigmund Freud,* translated by James Strachey, with Anna Freud, Alix Strachey, and Alan Tyson. *Volume XVII (1917-1919): An Infantile Neurosis and Other Works,* 217-56. London: Hogarth Press and the Institute of Psycho-Analysis, 1986.

—. *A General Introduction to Psychoanalysis* (1920). New York: Boni and Liveright, Bartleby.com, 2010. Accessed January 4, 2013. www.bartleby.com/283/.

—. *Selected Writings*. Edited by Robert Coles. Translated by James Strachey. New York: Book-of-the-Month Club, 1997.

Frost, Brian J. *The Essential Guide to Werewolf Literature*. Madison, London: Popular Press, 2003.

Herman, Judith. *Trauma and Recovery*. New York: Basic Books, 1992.

Otten, Charlotte F., ed. *The Literary Werewolf: An Anthology*. New York: Syracuse University Press, 2002.

Palmer, Paulina. *The Queer Uncanny*. Cardiff: University of Wales Press, 2012.

Royle, Nicholas. *The Uncanny*. Manchester University Press, 2003.

Thurston, Luke. "Double-crossing: Elizabeth Bowen's ghostly short fiction." *Textual Practice* 27.1 (2013): 7-28.

Towheed, Shafquat. "Territory, space, modernity: Elizabeth Bowen's *The Demon Lover and Other Stories* and Wartime London." In *Elizabeth*

Bowen: New Critical Perspectives, edited by Susan Osborn, 113-31. Cork University Press, 2009.

Trigg, Dylan. *The Memory of Place: A Phenomenology of the Uncanny.* Athens: Ohio University Press, 2012.

Chapter Ten

Extracting the Extract: From Clinical Practice to Literature and Back, Utilizing a Signifier

Amir Klugman[1]

The signifier has therapeutic power – so I want to argue. A specific signifier can be a vector, a vehicle between psychic states, a Hermes within language. One such signifier, contingent but nevertheless critical, has been useful to me in illustrating how psychoanalysis and literature can balance one another and create a space of practical use. I want to show that with an analytic ear one can jump between clinical work and literature, hearing the two fields in proximity, as if in free association, and thus clarify ambiguous aspects of the clinic. By means of what I have encountered with patients and in clinical supervision, and in parallel, in a story by the Israeli writer David Grossman, I will propose a new concept that has been useful in my clinical practice: *the extract of jouissance*, a concept derived from the thought of Jacques Lacan. Additionally I will sketch a preliminary ethic for the analyst arising from this concept, by way of the movement of one signifier between a number of language games, and the implications of this movement. After all, this concerns a construct, a way of looking. But this construct does not stem only from the understanding of a renowned psychoanalyst (Lacan) or of a great writer (Grossman), but firstly, perhaps essentially, from what we can learn from our patients themselves, from the unique speech of each of them.

Getting Acquainted with the Extract

Clinical supervision is an ambiguous field. There is no formula or set menu. It is an unexpected encounter of two people, and preferably in a certain sense, of three: supervisor, supervised and psychoanalysis as a dimension of desire that the dyad can observe and investigate. It seems to

me that good supervision leads you to go on searching, talking and moving, as in analysis, but what hangs in the balance here is not your being in general, but a derivative of it - your stance as an analyst, to whom transference has been made, attributing knowledge to you.

In supervision in a public mental health clinic I shared with my supervisor a logic I had identified in the speech of a patient: as he saw it, to exist is to understand. Without understanding – he didn't exist. The supervisor did not react to the content itself, but reflected on a particular feature of my work. She paid attention, she told me, to the fact that I would "extract" from each patient's words some essential statement, a central motivating idea in the structure of their behaviour, and sometimes of their symptoms. She proposed an English verb that seemed to her appropriate, and perhaps closer to the mark than the Hebrew: *to extract.* It dawned on me just then that this was the beginning of an enquiry, that this signifier touches the body, so I felt. Although at this stage I still did not know what exactly spoke to me in the extract, I saw that I do indeed look for a kind of extract, a centre of gravity in my patients' words, and that this work of looking corresponds with ideas in Lacanian psychoanalysis that I have been exposed to in recent years.

The Stone and the Object

Jacques Alain Miller, one of Lacan's main successors, explains in the seminar *The Bone of Analysis*:

> When someone comes to analysis we receive him without prejudice, without knowledge, without memory, we receive him at the beginning of the path of his speech with us.
>
> But he comes because he has stumbled, because he feels there is a stone across his path. We invite him to speak, and what guides our hearing is that there is a stone in the path of his speech. We assume – perhaps it is the only prior assumption we allow ourselves – that his speech spirals around this stone, in a circling that gets progressively closer to it, until it sculpts it. This is the metaphor we find in Lacan's texts concerning a movement that restricts and delimits.
>
> Now we must pass from allegory to logic. One can say that in analysis there is an action of contraction, of reduction – an action that is without doubt quite familiar in the United States where they call analysts "shrinks". This is a phenomenal point of view, referring to the contraction that occurs in analysis, the contraction to a stone, to a bone. What is this contraction? How does it work? What are its mechanisms? What follows from this contraction? [2]

Working from a poem by the Brazilian poet Carlos Drummond de Andrade, Miller uses the metaphor of a stone on the path to formulate a basic principle of analysis; the path is the path of speech, and the "stone" is an essential part of the path, an immanent obstacle, appearing along with the path; analysis goes towards it, circles around it, but does not level or fragment it. In a spiral movement, but in a certain sense also asymptotically - it gets ever closer but never reaches it. Miller is interested in, and engages his listeners in, this stony focus that the movement of approach seeks out, and it is, as we saw above, an action belonging to an order of contraction and reduction and not to the order of expansive speech, what Miller calls "the expansion of the signifier"[3]. In other words, instead of saying "let's talk about it", where we interpret and understand, we gradually mark out a limit to speech, where meaning ceases to operate, and where all there is is a stone that won't be undermined or broken up. From a Lacanian perspective, this is a clinic directed towards the Real, at what won't yield to representation in language, "the impossible", in one of Lacan's formulations, that analysis converges on.

Here I am reminded of another stone, that of Ludwig Wittgenstein in his book *Philosophical Investigations*. See how the stone is used:

> Couldn't I imagine having frightful pains and, while they were going on, turning to stone. Indeed, how do I know, if I shut my eyes, whether I have not turned into a stone? - And if that has happened, in what sense will **the stone** have pains? In what sense will they be ascribable to a stone? Why indeed should the pain here have a bearer at all?!
>
> And can one say of the stone that it has a mind, and **that** is what has the pain? What has a mind, and what have pains, to do with a stone? [...]
>
> Look at a stone and imagine it having sensations.- One says to oneself: How could one so much as get the idea of ascribing a **sensation** to a **thing**? One might as well ascribe it to a number! - And now look at a wriggling fly and at once these difficulties vanish and pain seems able to get a **foothold** here, where before everything was, so to speak, too **smooth** for it. [4]

If in Kafka a man turns into an insect, Wittgenstein takes it further and turns him into a stone. This is to tell us that for a pain, first of all, a body is required; but not only a body, but also someone to speak or act out the pain. In Wittgenstein's argument the stone is an inanimate object, is not a significant object by itself. It is too "smooth" for the language of pain to get a foothold; however, as something that the pain, or the cause of pain, can get a foothold on, the stone turns into a significant object, helping to

mark the line between someone or something about whom it can be said that they are in pain and that about which one cannot say this.

On first glance, this seems far from Miller and from the stone/bone of analysis, but actually there is a connecting line. Miller's stone, that is in at least some senses an *object cause of desire* for the analysand (*objet petit a*) in Lacan's terminology – is in itself without sense or value, but is given particular significance for that speaking subject by the analysand's speech and its action of contraction in approaching the object. Speech binds the specific desire and pain of the analysand with that stone on the path. The stone is the inanimate and silent Real, because in it interpretations cease. That is the border of the language of pain. It is the place Wittgenstein was aiming for.

Extracting the Extract

Literature in my eyes sometimes gets closer to the bone than psychoanalysis itself, for one main reason: its existence does not depend on any agenda or guiding principle. Good literature does not call things by their names, but simply does things with words. There is no *objet petit a* for it, just the movement itself around it. We, as clinicians, come and extract from the movement the names of things, but at the same time we kill something in it. Freud suggested that an analytic cure works only obliquely, and warned against direct attempts at one[5]. So literature, in its existence free of analytic questions, reveals a true and polyvalent language relevant to them.

As part of my attempt to research the encounters between body and language in the stories of David Grossman, and in work towards a lecture on the subject, I came across Grossman's very first story, "Donkeys", published in a collection of his short stories from 1983, *Jogger*[6]. On another occasion I will develop my thoughts about this story as an early signpost to subjects Grossman would subsequently develop in his work, among them the body-language connection. On the matter in hand, I will say briefly that at the centre of the story is Roger, an American soldier who fled the Vietnam War for Austria, who has not found belonging or repose and is furthermore torn away from the Austrian woman he loves because he cannot marry her and find stable employment, being an illegal migrant. When agony and exhaustion overwhelm him, he goes to a familiar place, a forgotten motel, where he receives wordless love from the owner of the place and from a group of donkeys, that are happy with the white bread he brings them. At this inn Roger has a special ceremony, of drunkenness to the point of losing his senses, and a kind of rebirth, without

words, that allows him to carry on, although to where is not clear. His ceremony, for all that it is not part of an analysis, in a certain sense brings to mind that circling around the stone, an approach to an unavoidable obstacle, simply in order to continue and move. The ceremony is very effective for him, and despite its difficult and even humiliating nature, he maintains considerable love and some trace of hope.

Two parts of the story captured my attention, and in retrospect I can say that I chose these parts guided precisely by the compass of the extract, which I brought from supervision to my reading of the story. First: When the protagonist argues with his lover, Naomi, she cries for three hours, and, he relates, he is not allowed to stop her, even though he is beside himself because of her crying. "Her crying is a kind of special process that has to 'extract itself', so she specifically explained to me on one occasion. In fact, on many occasions"[7]. Subsequently, he calls this procedure "the extract of crying" [8], and here we already see the second meaning of the extract: to exhaust.

The second part that aroused my interest goes in the same direction. The protagonist describes his monthly meetings with American friends, partners in sorrow, renegades like him, who gather monthly in an American pub in Austria, to remember, complain and lament their bitter fate. The protagonist tells Martin, the innkeeper, about how meaningless he finds these meetings and moreover the pain they cause him. Martin, a character very much like an analyst in this story, keeps from responding, but eventually tells Roger not to stop going to the meetings, seeing that "despite everything, it is good for you" [9]. The "extract of crying" that constitutes an unfamiliar and excluded factor, when it was ascribed to his partner, metamorphoses and turns up in the protagonist's own life. Although he is unaware of it, there is in his life too an aspect of crying that must exhaust/extract itself. The innkeeper knows something about this, seeing in the protagonist what he himself does not notice.

These two parts, and particularly the protagonist's special purification ceremony, were for me a key to reading the story, and paved the way back to the clinic utilizing the signifier. There is great pain, mixed with the action of the drive, and as long as he has not reached the extraction, it is very difficult or impossible for the subject to move forward, and extricate himself. When this does happen, if only for an evasive moment, someone can all at once extract himself like Baron Munchausen pulling the rest of himself from the swamp by the hair.

The extract signifier, in its two senses, allows the extrication and the extracted essence to be bound together. The interpretive act in relation to Grossman's story is like the movement of response to a patient's words:

extracting a central idea, a centre of gravity of the discourse around which the rest of the material is organized, the motivating signifier. In this case, it is "the extract of crying", or "the extract of pain".

The Extract of Jouissance

The Merriam Webster dictionary gives two main meanings for the word "extract". The first: to extract or release/extricate. This meaning is particularly relevant to speech: to extract information or extract a confession. The second sense is "to squeeze". Here the emphasis is on the material aspect, as in the sentence "the machine extracts juice from apples"; making a concentrate, an essence, a distillation. The combination of spoken and material aspects is what gives a further level of meaning to the signifier, the *extraction of the subject*. What is sought after is the essence of a process, a certain element of speech, its extract, in coming close to its material aspect, to the "bone" or "stone", so as to "extract the subject", to produce him or her in speech. It is an action relating to the patient's speech as material, less in the familiar metaphorical sense, but as actual material, on which one can do the work of selection, separating the wheat from the chaff, so as to get to the essence.

The idea of staying with the painful situation, despite the suffering it causes, brings us to Freud's *Beyond the Pleasure Principle*[10] as Lacan reads it, with the concept of *jouissance*[11]. One can say that painful phenomena accompanying satisfaction at the level of the drive, as we find in Grossman, constitute instances of jouissance. This is pleasure bound up with suffering, pleasure derived *from* suffering, a kind of tie between the libido and the death drive. From a Lacanian perspective, in "difficult" cases too, like overt paranoia or melancholia, there is unconscious satisfaction at the level of the drive. Consequently, in Lacan's formulation, "the subject [of the unconscious, A.K.] is happy-go-lucky [*heureux*]"[12], by definition, in a structural sense, also when the individual is suffering.

Grossman's protagonist in "Donkeys" brings to mind, in fact, a question about jouissance: this repetition of taking the stance of suffering, of being a powerless offering - What does it mean? What brings it about? Faced by Naomi's jouissance he is astonished, but as we discover as the story progresses, it is an astonishment before his own jouissance. While his body brings him repeatedly to the meetings with his friends, his head continually asks: Why return to that place where suffering is sharpened, where "the wound is aggravated"? And aggravating the wound, as we know, can damage and give pleasure together, making it a good metaphor for jouissance. Roger has no rational explanation for the special ceremony

at Martin's inn, in a way that corresponds with the lack of rationality in Naomi's ceremony of crying, whose inexplicable process is not to be interfered with.

We see that jouissance here flows from many sources, but remains an unclear phenomenon, having an essential bodily aspect, unexplained, open to the reader's interpretation, and at the same time, necessary for the subject and ineradicable, and as such having to extract itself. With this Grossman gives us a living example of the action of jouissance, without recourse to the name reserved for it in the psychoanalytic language game; here literature is, as I said, much closer to the bone. The innkeeper wisely directs Roger to what his lover already knows: crying and pain have to extract themselves. As long as they are not extracted, and about such extractions only the subject himself can bear witness, it is difficult to extricate oneself and go forward. So the innkeeper tells Roger to continue with the meetings of the crying friends. This much he says and no more. At the level of the signifier, Grossman's story adds the aspect of "exhaustion" to the extract signifier, and now we can talk about "the extract of jouissance" or the "jouissant extract" and return to the clinic utilizing the signifier.

To Exist is Not to Understand

In outpatient contexts among others, it is not unusual for patients to come to us with chronic conditions, where, although they also come with motivation and interest in therapy, and make relatively stable transference relationships, their difficult symptoms tend to remain static, almost without alleviation. Attempts to invite them to thought and free association fall into familiar and repetitious complaining, along with minimal movement from the starting point. Even when analytic interventions "speak to them" (an expression it is important to put in quotation marks), they don't bring the patients to act, aren't assimilated by the body. From our point of view, we are talking about cases of expansive jouissance with a declining ability to invest libido in external objects and with the withdrawal of the libido into the self, as Freud describes in "On Narcissism"[13]. We see a repetitive concern with self-suffering, a strong need then to speak it and the inability to extricate oneself from it. It seems that broadening speech about suffering, "expanding the signifier" in Miller's terminology, works precisely against extricating oneself from suffering, contrary to the opinion of some conventional therapeutic orientations. This situation, beyond it being very irksome for analysands, is liable to be frustrating for and provoke despair in the analyst. In most

cases, analytic interventions do not promote action, and attempts to "push" patients towards a restriction or contraction of jouissance mostly amount to nothing. Like Wittgenstein's smooth stone, the feeling is that there is nothing to grasp, speech slides and expands, but in a certain sense lacks a body, is without a presence that would allow movement.

The idea of "extracting the extract", or "extracting the extract of jouissance", was born from my helplessness as an analyst in situations like these. In the Lacanian psychoanalytic clinic, where the countertransference is not used as a therapeutic tool – that is to say, the emotions and feelings of the analyst are not the key to understanding the patient and are not part of the dialogue in the therapy room (their place is in the analyst's own analysis) – there is a more urgent need to investigate what the stance of the analyst should be towards the patient's expressions of jouissance, so that the analyst's discomfort and frustration does not disturb the patient's work; so as to create a certain logic where it seems not to exist. In this case, using the insights of literature, along with the aimed arrow of the signifier, I could delineate a possible point of extrication.

I will demonstrate with some clinical vignettes, omitting identifying details for the sake of therapeutic confidentiality.

I have to express doubts at the start about this form of presentation and say that schematic descriptions and the use of accepted psychiatric definitions are designed, after all, to point to essentiality in precisely that which departs from familiar and universal schema.

> A patient suffering from melancholia and severe anxiety did not function during the day, spent hours in bed and found no reason to do anything at all. Although there was a background of complicated family relationships in the past and present, contributing to maintaining the situation, interpretations and discoveries along these lines did not lead to significant change in his condition. To complete the picture, the many medications, that were frequently changed, did not lead to any appreciable alleviation; but there was one interesting point, where the trace of a change appeared. During several weeks when I was not present at the clinic, this patient seldom came to the therapy groups organized for day patients, and also withdrew from his rehabilitation work. For a certain time, he related, he felt he had no frame, that he had "really reached rock bottom"; and then, in a moment, that for him too was not comprehensible, apart from the phrase "there's nowhere further to fall", he got out of bed, went to work, and decided to go back to rehabilitation with renewed interest. Beyond what has been said, he could not explain what had happened in that moment, and immediately went back to his routine complaints. What I did as an analyst was *not* to allow him to miss this moment, to mark it as different and unique, where something stopped and was replaced by something else. A

moment when his strengths, previously hidden, suddenly showed themselves. A moment of an act.

A patient suffering from post-trauma because of a serious road accident was consequently in intensive withdrawal for two years, with recurrent flashbacks of the accident. She remained mostly in her room, had difficulty spending any length of time even with her children, was fearful of sounds, and had difficulty sleeping, passing her nights staring at the television and in ceaseless thought. In one of the sessions she recounted that her husband had suggested they went/compelled her to go to a restaurant for her birthday. Earlier attempts at enjoyment had been unsuccessful, because she remained focused on her suffering; but this time, and don't ask why, she said that she enjoyed the restaurant, felt that suddenly she could breathe, and that she was coming back, surprisingly, to behaving in a way she knew from before the accident. She suddenly felt alive. For a moment she even managed to see her husband, from whom she had kept great distance for the preceding two years, with new eyes. One can see the momentariness and interchangeability of the situation in her account of how immediately on her return home, as if "putting her mourning suit back on", she went back to isolation and withdrawal; but there was the singular moment, where she had "succeeded in breathing", and my job was to be on guard, to jump from my chair and draw her attention to that moment: "here you succeeded in breathing... perhaps only for a moment... but you succeeded."

A patient suffering from severe anxiety, having taken medication for years without significant change in her condition, then developed great difficulty in leaving the house and doing everyday things. Her conduct was very meticulous, bound by restrictions and rules she imposed on herself. Previous therapies focused on her "illness" and her avoidance behaviour. Other activities and libidinal investments were neglected as less relevant in a therapeutic context. But in the framework of our sessions she mentioned her intense involvement with hearing and playing music, and I began to tune into to this living part of her life. This was an attempt to deviate a little from the scripted tendency to talk about her "disturbance" towards the pursuit of her particular solution. In one of the meetings she told me about a special interest she had in the *suspended* chord, that, she said, "is neither major nor minor, and so allows for free improvisation following one's desire, in open possibility". I decided to return to the word, repeating her signifier, "suspended", giving it special emphasis, and then finish our session as an act of punctuation. It was a moment, like those I have already described, albeit more subtle, where a new direction opens up, where something in the routine and deathly meticulousness got turned around. In my reading, it was a moment of "extracting the jouissance", a moment when something in language (in Lacan's terms, "the Symbolic"), in this case the "suspended", places bounds on jouissance, limiting it, allowing

> improvisation within inflexibility. And again, my role was to indicate and emphasize what was already demarcated, not to add to it.

Here it is important to stress: these clinical interventions don't go in the direction of augmenting the meaning of signifiers, of attempting to *understand* moments of change and what happens in them. One can point to an abundance of imaginary interpretations that, although allegedly explaining what occurred in these moments, are given without having an effect on these patients, and certainly don't bring about a contraction of the generally static jouissance bound up with their conditions. In this respect, there is importance in emphasizing and marking moments of the "extract of jouissance", when the analyst extracts such moments from the repetitious grey screen that sometimes constitutes the analysand's speech, when the analyst punctuates the chain of signifiers. The action of the extract requires only that a flag is raised over that component of speech constituting the *boundary of jouissance.*

If we go back for a moment to the patient from supervision, for whom to exist is to understand (and if he didn't understand – he wouldn't exist), we can say that the action of "extracting the extract" proposed another way of existing: *to exist is not to understand*, or even *to exist is to not understand.*

It is Spoken

Why is the action of extricating moments of the "extract of jouissance" important? Seemingly they are happenstance, without meaning, and the patient does not "understand" anything new about their occurrence. These marks, emphasizing these particular moments in the patient's speech, function as a kind of interpretation, not however on the plane of meaning, but more on the level of the drive, of setting a limit to jouissance. This is consonant with the last teaching of Lacan and with his attempt to get close to the order of the Real. In his lecture "Interpretation and drive" Miller says, paraphrasing Wittgenstein:

> One does not speak of what cannot be spoken of, and of what he desires [referring to unconscious desire, A.K.]. On the contrary: **it is spoken**. What cannot be spoken, one cannot be silent about, but says between the lines. It is impossible to say it except between the lines, by hinting. It is impossible to say it except obliquely [...] It is impossible except by pointing to it.[14]

Miller indicates that at a certain stage Lacan suggests "the raised finger of Leonardo's Yohanan the Holy" as a symbol of interpretation, and adds: "At

> the end of the day, we raise a finger when we do not have the ability to say".[15]

I relate to the position of the analyst in cases such as I have described, as one who "points and cuts" so that the analysand can gather. From out of a long and continuous outpouring of pictures, s/he identifies those it is good to cut out, to isolate, and keep in an album. If one listens well, there are always such pictures, here and there. Little by little, in the course of analysis, these pictures are gathered, where jouissance is restricted for a moment, and this collection has a cumulative effect on the patient. He begins to identify the wheat among the chaff, his moments of self-extraction. The analyst does not push, does not himself actually extract or provide solutions, but his job is essential and important - he is there to point and cut, point and cut, over and over, so that little by little the patient can himself point to, cut and gather by himself. For all that a psychiatric definition is a universal, the album of fragments is entirely particular, bearing the patient's first name.

* * *

“Crying is a process that has to extract itself"... – so we have learned from Grossman. And the crying finally, in a moment, although we don't know what that moment is, breaks through to something else that comes as a surprise. So from within the repetitive complaining, the static absorption in jouissance, at a certain moment, an impediment is liable to appear, a break in the routine flow. It is important that someone is there, someone who will identify, mark, impede, gather. What can be learned, additionally, from Grossman's story, is that jouissance has a certain trajectory, which cannot be accelerated or erased. The responsibility falls to us to patiently listen for its turning points.

To this end one needs an **ex-tract**ive listening, ("out of the zone") - a listening directed towards extracting those parts that are not on the "main route", shining exceptions to what is familiar and usual for that patient. It is an ethics whose compass is not empathy and understanding, but spotting the subjective needle in the haystack. There is a double meaning to the standpoint of the **ex-tract**: to persist in being outside the area that is known in advance, taken for granted, repetitive and static, a domain of ceaseless jouissance; and simultaneously outside the path of the push towards adaptation and cure – that is to say, spotting the "jouissant extracts" exposed in speech itself, and not imposing them on the patient.

In a certain sense, I suggest, literature is a kind of dam or boundary on our jouissance, as analysts immersed in professional discourse. Precisely

because unlike the discipline of psychoanalysis, literature has no pretension to a cure, at least not explicitly, it is sometimes wiser and more exact in its observations of psychic space. Freud already took a step in this direction. In a saying attributed to him he observes: "Everywhere I go I find a poet has been there before me".[16] One can say, and we would do well to make use of it, that **literature is the *ex-tract* of psychoanalysis**.

Notes

[1] I wish to thank Mark Joseph for the intelligent and devoted translation of this chapter. All the translations of citations, except those of Wittgenstein, were made by him. I also wish to thank Bina Bergman who was the first to extract the extract for me.
[2] Miller, 2001, p. 21, translated from Hebrew.
[3] ibid, pp. 21-2.
[4] Wittgenstein, 1953, §283-284, p. 284.
[5] For example, Freud, 1926.
[6] Grossman, 1983.
[7] ibid, p. 56, translated from Hebrew.
[8] ibid, p. 65.
[9] ibid, p. 68.
[10] Frued, 1920.
[11] Lacan, 1959-60; 1960; 1972-73.
[12] Lacan, 1974, p. 22.
[13] Freud, 1914.
[14] Miller, 2009, p. 43, translated from Hebrew.
[15] ibid, p.42.
[16] This is a caption on a wall in Freud Museum in Vienna.

References

Freud, S. (1914). On Narcissism. In: *The Standard Edition of the Complete Psychological Works of Sigmund Freud, Vol. XIV (1914-1916): On the History of the Psycho-Analytic Movement, Papers on Metapsychology and Other Works* (pp. 67-102). (trans. by J. Strachey). London: The Hogarth Press and The Institute of Psycho-analysis, 1957.

—. (1920). Beyond the Pleasure Principle. In: *The Standard Edition of the Complete Psychological Works of Sigmund Freud, Vol. XVIII (1920-1922): Beyond the Pleasure Principle, Group Psychology and Other Works* (pp. 7-23). (trans. by J. Strachey). London: The Hogarth Press and The Institute of Psycho-analysis, 1955.

—. (1926). The Question of Lay Analysis: Conversations with an Impartial Person. In: *The Standard Edition of the Complete Psychological Works of Sigmund Freud, Volume XX (1925-1926): An Autobiographical Study, Inhibitions, Symptoms and Anxiety, The Question of Lay Analysis and Other Works* (pp. 177-258). (trans. by J. Strachey). London: The Hogarth Press and The Institute of Psycho-analysis, 1959.

Grossman, D. (1983). Donkeys. In: *Jogger* (short stories) (pp. 49-74). Tel-Aviv, Israel: Hakibbutz Hameuchad/Siman Kriah. [in Hebrew: *Ratz*].

Lacan, J. (1959-1960). *The Seminar, Book VII: The Ethics of Psychoanalysis*. (trans. By D. Porter). London: Routledge, 1992.

—. (1960). The Subversion of the Subject and the Dialectic of Desire in the Freudian Unconscious. In: *Écrits* (pp. 671-702). (trans. by B. Fink). New York: W.W. Norton & Company, 2006.

—. (1972-73). *The Seminar, Book XX: Encore, On Feminine Sexuality, the Limits of Love and Knowledge*. (trans. by B. Fink). New York and London: W.W. Norton & Company.

—. (1974). Television. In: *Television; A Challenge to the Psychoanalytic Establishment.* (pp. 3-46). (trans. by D. Hollier, R. Krauss & A. Michelson). New York and London: W.W. Norton & Company, 1990.

Miller, J.-A. (2001). *The Bone of Analysis*. (trans. by E. Pichotka). Jerusalem, Israel: Keter. [in Hebrew: *Etsem Ha'analiza*].

—. (2009). Interpretation and Drive. [in Hebrew: Perush Vedachaf]. In: *The Lacanian Interpretation* (pp. 21-52). (trans. by S. Pichotka & E. Pichotka). Tel Aviv, Israel: Resling. [in Hebrew: *Haperush Ha'Lacaniani*].

Wittgenstein, L. (1953). *Philosophical Investigations, German and English, revised fourth edition*. (trans. by G. E. M. Anscombe, P. M. S. Hacker & J. Schulte). New Jersey: Wiley-Blackwell, 2009.

CHAPTER ELEVEN

ON MONEY AND PSYCHOANALYSIS: FROM THE FREUDIAN ANAL OBJECT TO LACAN'S SURPLUS-ENJOYMENT

MAURICIO RUGELES SCHOONEWOLFF

Introduction

Even though money is an important part of everyday life, this subject hasn't historically been given enough weight by psychoanalysts. This paper intends to address the following question: *how has Psychoanalysis thought and theorized money?* We take a theoretical and clinical perspective based upon Jacques Lacan's work and his reading of Freud. According to Pierre Martin[1], a Lacanian psychoanalyst, money has a double status: simultaneously sign and object. I would slightly change this formulation, not sign but signifier, a sign being univocal, a connection between word and referent, and a signifier equivocal, ambiguous. The signifier's slippage with regard to the signified allows it to participate in metaphors and metonymy. Thus, money would have two sides, being both a symbolic means of exchange and an object of the drive.

Freud: Money and Anal Erotism

According to Freud the concept of money stems from anal erotism. In his article "Character and Anal Erotism", Freud describes how young infants play with their faeces: they can either withhold or expel them, or even give them as a gift to their parents. Freud begins this text by describing the character of people who are orderly, obstinate, and parsimonious with a tendency to avarice. According to Freud, the explanation of these character traits can be found in a certain fixation of the anal drive. About this drive, Freud wrote:

> As infants, they seemed to have belonged to the class who refuse to empty their bowels when they are put on the pot because they derive a subsidiary pleasure from defecating; for they tell us that even in somewhat later years they enjoyed holding back their stool, and they remember-although more readily about their brothers and sisters than about themselves-doing all sorts of unseemly things with the faeces that had been passed.[2]

We must note that there are two types of enjoyment[3] involved in the process of defecation: the retention and the expulsion of faeces, and retention can be used to increase the enjoyment of defecation. As in Freud's "Fort-da" example, there is a coupling of signifiers that regulate enjoyment, and this enjoyment is found mostly in expulsion. Furthermore, children find their first anal object in the form of faeces, demanded by the other, and which can be given as a gift to the Other.

Once young children learn to be disgusted by their faeces, they have begun sublimating their relationship to this *ex-time* part of the body; they enter the symbolic dimension of gifts and presents. In this new dimension, one sees the relation between faeces and money, as it is illustrated in traditional stories such as those of the devil and of the *Dukatenscheisser*, "The Ducat Shitter". In the first tale, someone receives gold from the devil, through defecation; afterwards, when he goes to purchase with the gift, it sometimes returns to its original form.

> In reality, wherever archaic modes of thought have predominated or persists- in the ancient civilizations, in myths, fairy tales and superstitions, in unconscious thinking, in dreams and in neurosis- money is brought into the most intimate relationship with dirt. We know that the gold, which the devil gives his paramours, turns into excrement after his departure, and the devil is certainly nothing else than the personification of the repressed unconscious instinctual life. [...] Indeed, even according to ancient Babylonian doctrine gold is 'the faeces of Hell.'[4]

This process already exemplifies how the anal object is used in a series of metaphors: for example, Little Hans' "Lumf" is related to faeces, children, a gift between parents, the "little one" (the penis), the phallic signifier.

In another article written some years later, Freud continues to develop the link between faeces and money. The title of the article is "On transformations of Instinct[5] as Exemplified in Anal Erotism".[6] The interest of this text is double: first and foremost, he demonstrates how there is mixing of the partial drives, in this case genital and anal drives. He wrote: "As a starting point for this discussion, we may take the fact that it appears as if in the products of the unconscious- spontaneous ideas, fantasies and symptoms- the concepts *faeces* (money, gift), *baby* and *penis* are ill-

distinguished from one another and they are easily interchangeable".[7] This is Freud's main thesis in this article. In Lacanian terms, drives are structured in a network, and in relation to the phallic signifier as well. It is also important to note that Freud is introducing two very important objects in the economy of drives: gift and money.

The second interest of this article is how Freud goes deeper in the explanation of these last two objects. From the starting point of his analysis of women's relationship to the phallus and little Hans' to faeces and the phallus, he wrote:

> It is probable that the first meaning which a child's interest in faeces develops is that of 'gift' rather than 'gold' or 'money'. The child knows no money apart from what is given him- no money acquired and none inherited of his own. Since his faeces are his first gift, the child easily transfers his interest from that substance to the new one which he comes across the most valuable gift in life.[8]

Freud exposes thus how starting from excrements the subject begins to form a relationship with an Other, and how this object that is given will become for the subject, through metaphor, money. If, in the first article that we quoted, Freud exposes money more as an object, in this article the side of money as a symbol, as a signifier, is shown more clearly.

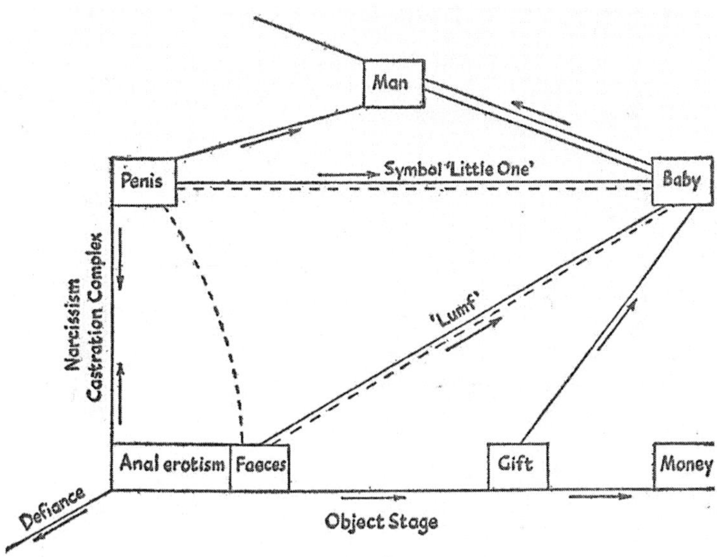

FIG. 2.

9

In this graph Freud expressed how - beginning from anal erotism -the anal object, the phallus, and the symbols of man are all linked. This graph should be read as a network of signifiers that are inked through metaphor, and that condense the enjoyment of the subject's drives. It's important to insist on how money is part of the economy of drives, and also on its double status as both object and signifier. As a signifier, money needs an Other so that it can be exchanged; yet when found as pure object, in the autoerotic enjoyment of the act of defecating, or of withholding; there is no need for an Other.

Among Freud's published cases, the one in which the relationship to money is most evident is the case of "Rat Man". Our commentary of the case will be reduced to two examples of how this obsessive neurotic related himself to money. For this patient, Freud explains how the word "rat" became a nodal point in his treatment. Firstly, sometimes, as he paid his session, he told Freud the expression "so many florins, so many rats". In the notes of the analysis, Freud wrote:

> If the rat is a worm, it is also a penis. I decided to tell him this. If so, his formula is simply a manifestation of a libidinal urge towards sexual intercourse- an urge characterized both by rage and by desire and expressed in archaic terms (going back to the infantile sexual theory of intercourse by the anus). […] After I told him that a rat was a penis, *via* worm, (at which point he interpolated 'a little penis')- rat's tail- tail, he had a flood of associations, not all of which belonged to the context and most of them coming from the wishful side of the structure. […] Thus, he came back to his delirium of 'so many florins, so many rats' i.e. 'so many florins, so many tails (copulations).'[10]

In this quote the link of money and the phallic signifier is clearly evident: the word "rat", used to order the psychic structure of this patient, is linked with sex, his father and mother, and money. Syphilis and children are also associated with rats for this patient. It is clear that he had prostitution phantasms as Freud also described in this article: this links sex and money more directly. It is also noteworthy that, for this patient, rats, money and copulations are all in the realm of that which is to be counted, of the numerical. In another part of the notes, and about the expression "so many florins, so many rats"; Freud remarks how the patient pronounces the German word *Ratten* (rats) the same way he pronounces the word *Raten* (rates, partial payments). In a certain way, he was paying Freud in rats.

These are not the only associations the Rat Man has to money; money is an important component in his "personal myth". His father was divided between marrying a rich woman, the Rat Man's mother, and the woman he loved; the patient found himself in a similar situation, repeating his

father's story. In the case it is difficult to grasp what relationship did his parents had to money; in other words, how money, among other signifiers, made a link between his parents where there is "no sexual relationship". This helps us grasp how the patient uses money in relationship to love, sex, desire and the opposite sex.

The patient remembers when, as a child, his father insisted that he take his mother's purse and to steal some coins from her. Here Freud finds an explanation for the Rat Man's avarice. He wrote:

> His miserliness is now explained. He was convinced, from a remark which his mother let fall to the effect that her connection with Rubensky was worth more than a dowry, that his father had married her and abandoned his love for his material advantage. This, together with his recollection of his father's financial embarrassment during his military service, made him detest the poverty that drives people into such crimes. In this way the low opinion of his mother found satisfaction. He economized, therefore, so as not to have to betray his love. For this reason, too, he hands over all of his money to his mother, because he does not want to have anything from her; it belongs to her and there is no blessing on it.[11]

Did the Rat Man's father desire his wife? It seems as if he only wanted her money, that he didn't love her. His father was lacking something - money, but also the phallus - that his mother had. It also seems as if she did love her husband, a "castrated" man. The patient wants to love, but he mistrusts desire, because what the opposite sex wants from him is money. And he denies his mother's castration by covering her lack by giving her all his money. Avarice, a trait of anal enjoyment, is a way for the patient to protect himself from desire. In his phantasm his parents are linked through money and not through lack; this explains his prostitution phantasm and fantasies. Also, he is paying a debt to her mother, his and his father's debt to her, keeping thus an ambiguous love to each of them.

In *Seminar XI*, Lacan made remarks about the anal drive and its relevant *objet a*:

> The anal level is the locus of metaphor- one object for another, give the faeces in place of the phallus. This shows you how the anal drive is the domain of oblativity, of the gift. Where one is caught short, where one cannot, as a result of the lack, give what is to be given, one can always give something else. That is why, in his morality, man is inscribed at the anal level. And this is especially true of the materialist.[12]

Thus, Lacan summarises Freud's position of the anal object; for Lacan the anal object is a metaphorical object, akin to phallus in its functioning on the lack, an object of gift and exchange. As in the speech of the classically

obsessive patient, “I need money so I can get girls.” Money would be, in its objectal side, an *ex-time* part of the body, not far from what Lacan here calls "the soul".[13] Therefore, there is no “normal” relationship to money, just as everybody has his own unique relationship to his object *a*, so it is with money. However, Lacan goes further than Freud, asking himself not only what money is for the subject, but also how it is produced? What is the subject's role in contemporary economic processes? For this, Lacan refers to Marx. According to Lacan, Marx is the inventor of the symptom, of "the sign of that which is not alright in the real".[14]

A Marxian interlude

Even in his early works, Marx realized that money plays a part as a signifier; that it has a metaphorical character. In his *Economic and Philosophical Manuscripts* Marx defined money through its capacity of reversal. He said:

> As this perverting power, money then appears as the enemy of man and social bonds that pretend to self-subsistence. It changes fidelity into infidelity, love into hate, hate into love, virtue into vice, vice into virtue, slave into master, master into slave, stupidity into intelligence and intelligence into stupidity.[15]

This quote is very telling: money has the power to force the exchange of signifiers, to generate metaphors, and to change a signifier to its opposite. Even the sexual relationship exists in the form of prostitution when money is involved! Marx's biggest contribution is to remark how the subject is an essential part of the functioning and production of money. In *Capital*, Marx's late masterpiece, though the definition of money is refined, the subject as motor of capital is always present.

The starting point in *Capital* is the posing of use-value and exchange-value. On one hand, use-value refers to the utility of the commodity, how it is used, and depends on its materiality. Use-value is measured qualitatively. On the other hand, exchange-value is how much of a commodity one can have if one exchanges one commodity with another commodity: its measurement is thus quantitative. Marx was intrigued because exchange-value seems arbitrary and relative. Nonetheless, according to Marx, the value of commodities is determined by the amount of labour measured in social time needed to produce these commodities. Thus, labour also becomes a commodity: different types of labour (the qualitative) are all measured by the average time a society needs to produce it, introducing the quantitative dimension.

Marx's example is a situation where there are only two commodities: 20 yards of linen and one coat, and the yards of linen can be exchanged by the one coat. The numerical exchange-value of the 20 yards represents the use-value of one coat. Thus, there is short-circuiting between the two forms of value, a quantitative one expressing a qualitative one. Then, if we take the equation 20 yards of linen=one coat, and multiply this mathematical equivalence by two, thus having 40 yards of linen=2 coats, both values become exchange values, numerical quantitative values.

(d) The Money Form

$$\left.\begin{array}{l} \text{20 yards of linen} \\ \text{1 coat} \\ \text{10 lb. of tea} \\ \text{40 lb. of coffee} \\ \text{1 quarter of corn} \\ \tfrac{1}{2}\text{ ton of iron} \\ x\text{ commodity A} \end{array}\right\} = \text{2 ounces of gold}$$

16

Now one can image a situation in which there are not only two, but many commodities in an economy. The new equation would be 20 yards of linen = 1 coat, or 10 lb. of tea, or 40 lb. of coffee, or 1 quarter of corn, or ½ ton of iron, or any amount x of commodity A, or 2 ounces of gold. Even if the value of all these commodities in this set is the same, and all commodities can be exchanged with each other, there is one that, because of what is more useful in a society, starts representing the exchange-value of all other commodities: the 2 ounces of gold. Here, the money-form begins to exist.

Now, one commodity can be exchanged for all of them, becoming the means of exchange in this set. From this moment onwards exchange passes from bartering to buying, and money exists to fix prices. Still, this form has a residue of use-value: gold (or silver) can have other uses other than money because of its material composition.

The Lacanian reading of this process than I'm proposing is the following: commodity can be understood as a Saussurean "sign", composed of its signifier and signified. Exchange-value would be the dimension of the signifier, S, and use-value would appertain to the dimension of the signified, s; use value would be the definition of the

commodity outside exchange. Marx also finds that there is a link between name, the signifier, and exchange-value. He wrote:

> The name of a thing is entirely external to its nature. I know nothing of a man if I merely now that his name is Jacob. In the same way, every trace of the money-relation disappears in the money-names pound, thaler, franc, ducat, etc. The confusion caused by attributing a hidden meaning to these cabalistic signs is made even greater by the fact that these money-names express both the values of commodities and, simultaneously, aliquot parts of a certain weight of the metal, namely the weight of the metal that serves as a standard of money. On the other hand it is necessary that value, as opposed to the multifarious objects of the world of commodities, should develop into this form, a material and non-mental one, but also a simple social form.[17]

This quote exemplifies how money has a strong dimension of the signifier, without giving much importance to the signified. Thus, the exchange of one signifier for another (S-S) constitutes a metaphor, and one that creates new meaning, new signified. Exchange is then a metaphorical operation. Money would then be a signifier with very little signified, that in neurotics can be linked to the phallic signifier, which has no signified. And money as a signifier would operate by permitting almost all other signifiers to be exchanged with it easily. So, in the case of Rat Man's subjectivity, money, the same as" rat", can occupy a wide variety of places and be linked to many different signifiers. This would be for Marx money in its signifier form.

Another concept that Lacan took from *Capital* to express a part of the psychoanalytical clinic is the concept of surplus-value. In logically analysing the origin of money through commodity exchange, Marx discovers the subject participates as labour-power, meaning as a commodity. The hidden detail in the logic of the origin of commodities is that human labour is needed to produce commodities. In the capitalist mode of production, human labour becomes a commodity, indeed one with its own exchange-value and use-value. According to Marx, the XIXth century saw the consolidation of contemporary capitalist industrial society with wage labour, its form of exploitation. The question Marx poses himself in his analysis of surplus-value is the following: if exchanges are composed of zero-sum equations, where does profit come from? Marx introduces the concept of surplus-value in the seventh chapter of *Capital,* where he analyses the production of value.[18] According to Marx, if the capitalist decides to produce cotton yarns, the total sum of the costs of raw materials and salaries should be equal to the total value of the finished product. In this case there would be no production of profit. But by

making workers work more and paying them less, profit is produced. Wage labour is measured in time units, in the average necessary worker hours needed to produce a commodity. Surplus-value would then be the objectal side of money. Still, this process being a structure of language[19], exploitation does not depend on the individual capitalist's will, but stems directly from capitalist's discourse.

This process generates surplus-value that feeds the productive machine of capitalist economy. According to Lacan, this is the core symptom in the real of economy:

> There is only one social symptom - every individual is really a proletarian in the real, in other words, has no discourse to make the social bond, also called semblance.[20]

The existence of surplus-value would be, in Lacan's reading of *Capital*, the symptom at the core of the real: the economy needs to augment the rate of surplus-value, but this rate of growth has a tendency to fall even as absolute value grows. Thus capitalism is always in crisis: it is capitalism's condition of existence that prevents and necessitates its limitless growth. Also, Marx wrote elsewhere in his works that the existence of capitalism is linked with the weakening of the patriarchy and the father's role; from this moment onwards the father cannot oppose this growth.

Lacan: Surplus-Value as Surplus-Enjoyment

Lacan, in *Seminars XV* and *XVI*, appropriates the Marxian concepts of use-value, exchange-value and surplus-value to form his concept of surplus-enjoyment. In *Seminar XVII*, Lacan rereads and criticizes Hegel's Lord and Bondsman (Master and Slave) dialectic *via* Marx and Kojève in order to create the concept of surplus-enjoyment. According to Lacan, it's not the master who enjoys, but rather the slave. The slave keeps knowledge, and it is knowledge which is intimately linked with enjoyment. The master, to be a master, renounces enjoyment, and thus creates surplus-enjoyment. Surplus-enjoyment is the paradoxical enjoyment produced by the renouncement of enjoyment. Lacan wrote:

> Surplus-*jouissance* is a function of the renouncement of *jouissance* under the influence of discourse. It's what gives object *a* its place. So long as the marketplace defines merchandise as any object made by human labour, this object carries in itself something of surplus-value.[21]

This process will form that which becomes, during *Seminar XVII*, the master's discourse, that is to say a structure of language. In this process there is a loss of jouissance, a lack-of-jouissance (Lacan plays with the French signifier *plus,* which means both surplus and lack depending on context and pronunciation) that, following his argument, becomes the surplus-value that the capitalist earns. That is why, for Lacan, surplus-enjoyment and surplus-value are the same thing. As we have seen, every subject is a proletarian in the real; every subject who enters language and thus the social bond must enter this dialectic.

Nonetheless, according to Lacan, it is not master's the discourse which governs the contemporary social bond, rather is has been substituted by the capitalist's discourse, albeit a variation of the master's discourse. This variation explains contemporary subjectivity and the subject's role in the contemporary economy. Then, in synthesis, Lacan explains capitalist production when he said that the proletarian's surplus-value is the capitalist's cause of desire:

> Because this cowrie shell, surplus-value, it is the cause of desire of an economy which makes it its principle: The principle of extensive production, thus insatiable, of the want-for-enjoyment. Firstly, the means of this production accumulate, swell in the name of capital. Secondly, it extends consumption, without which this production would be in vain, precisely because of its ineptitude to procure an enjoyment which could slow them.[22]

This quote evidences the link between political economy and clinical work, especially of a clinic that deals with addiction. If the capitalist renounces enjoyment, sexual enjoyment, of course he now lacks this enjoyment; he has the *manque-à-jouir*. This generates an intense production of commodities trying to fill in this enjoyment, an enjoyment that never accomplishes its goal as it never ends the capitalist's position of renunciation. And so, a circular process of consumption is created. It produces some enjoyment but no satisfaction, because the lack-of-enjoyment is still there. This is easily perceived in markets: a full range of commodities promise some satisfaction that will never happen, and even at the moment of consumption are already obsolete so that satisfaction remains ever in the future. This accelerates consumption, exploitation and production asymptotically to infinity. According to Lacan, the capitalist's discourse appears to substitute the master's discourse, though both of these discourses are very close to each other. Describing how the capitalist's discourse works, he said:

> It's not at all that I'm telling you the Capitalist' discourse is ugly, quite the contrary, it's something crazily cunning, isn't it? Crazily cunning but fated to blowout. At any rate, it's the most astute discourse one's made after all. That doesn't make it no less devoted to death. It's untenable in a thing I could explain to you… because the capitalist's discourse is there, you see… simply a very small inversion between the S_1 and the barred S which is the subject… this suffices for it to glide as if on skates, it can't work any better, but precisely it goes too fast, it consumes, it consumes so well, that it consumes itself.[23]

Lacan indicates that the capitalist's discourse arises from an inversion of the places of S_1, the master-signifier, and \$, the barred subject, giving the subject access to *objet a* as surplus-enjoyment, which had been limited in the master's discourse. This means that if in the master's discourse there is a renunciation of enjoyment, in the capitalist's discourse there is an effort to recuperate this lost enjoyment. In capitalism, subjects try to get back a primordially lost enjoyment through consumption of commodities, and because of this through money. The effects of the capitalist's discourse on the social bond are multiple: firstly, no master figure is needed to make individuals work. The master seems divided, or the divided subject appears to be the master; this means that because individuals work because of their "own will" and not because they are externally constrained, they are more efficient thus making the capitalist's discourse more efficient. But there is a limit, even in this seemly limitless discourse: the subject pays with the creation of new psychic symptoms, like addiction for instance, and socially we see the destruction of the social bond. Some psychoanalysts do not consider capitalist's discourse to even be a discourse, because it can't be reversed as the rest of Lacan's four discourses, and because if the principle of a discourse it to renounce enjoyment so that subjects are bonded through the symbolic, then a discourse who provokes enjoyment and breaks the social bond becomes the opposite of discourse.

Speaking about this phenomenon, of the sexuality of the subjects in relation to capitalist's discourse, Lacan said:

> What distinguishes capitalist's discourse is this - *Verwerfung* [foreclosure], the rejection from all fields of the symbolic, with the consequences that I have already explained, the rejection of what? Of castration. Every order, every discourse that is akin to capitalism leaves aside what we simply call the things of love, my good friends.[24]

Observing subjectivity and the capitalist's discourse, Lacan finds out that unlimited *jouissance* causes the foreclosure of castration. *Jouissance*,

in early Lacan, can kill desire (as explained at the end of *Seminar VI*), and in late Lacan it is opposed to the signs of love. This means that *jouissance* does not pass through the symbolic part of sexuality. A subject totally taken in by capitalist's discourse has little or no place for being in a love relation. *Jouissance* passes through money and commodities, and in them drugs, gadgets, and everything that can be consumed; this covers castration, and lack is filled by these various objects of enjoyment.

If the economy needs this movement of enjoyment to grow, society would have an "addictive style". The push to consumption and enjoyment is an essential part of the economy. As is the case for the language structure that produces surplus-value and surplus-enjoyment. Therefore, one of the means of capitalist society to produce the "foreclosure of castration" is money. It is of the utmost importance that psychoanalysts and other clinical specialists remain conscious that money plays a unique role for each subject in his singularity, especially in the rehabilitation of addictions.

To free oneself from this situation, Lacan proposes a formula in his "Television". He proposes being what he calls saints:

> The saint doesn't really see himself as righteous, which doesn't mean he has no ethics. The only problem for others is that you can't see where it leads him. […] The more saints, the more laughter; that's my principle, to wit, the way out of capitalist discourse – which will not constitute progress, if it happens only for some.[25]

The exit out of the capitalist system is thus through laughter, in the Freudian and Lacan sense of the word. This means that the structures of the unconscious are present and have a privileged place that the subject's speech is taken into consideration. Psychoanalysis is anti-capitalist insofar as its ethics of desire do not direct the subject to consume universal objects or their metaphor of money, but rather a search for the singular *objet a* of each, a search which concedes castration, not even all the consumer objects in the world would fulfil one.

The bet of psychoanalysis is that it will not only be for some.

Notes

[1] Pierre Martin, *Argent et psychanalyse* (Paris: Bibliothèque des Analytica, Navarin Éditeur, 1984), 14-17.

[2] Sigmund Freud, "Character and Anal Erotism", in *Complete Works*, Vol.9 (Toronto: Hogarth Press, 1959), 170.

[3] The term enjoyment is a translation of the French *jouissance*, that is a very important term in Lacanian psychoanalysis. Synthetically, it is pleasure that turns into pain as it goes beyond the pleasure principle.

[4] Freud, "Character and Anal Erotism", 174.

[5] Drive is undoubtedly a more appropriate translation of Freud's term, *Trieb* - "Über *Triebumsetzungen* und Analerotik".

[6] Sigmund Freud, "On Transformations of Instinct as Exemplified in Anal Erotism", in *Complete Works*, Vol.17 (Toronto: Hogarth Press, 1959).

[7] Freud, "On Transformations of Instinct as Exemplified in Anal Erotism", 128.

[8] Freud, "On Transformations of Instinct as Exemplified in Anal Erotism", 130-131.

[9] Freud, "On Transformations of Instinct as Exemplified in Anal Erotism", 132.

[10] Sigmund Freud, "The Rat Man: Original record of the case", in *Complete Works*, Vol.10 (Toronto: Hogarth Press, 1959), 311-313.

[11] Freud, "The Rat Man: Original record of the case", 297.

[12] Jacques Lacan, *Seminar XI: The Four Fundamental Concepts of Psychoanalysis* (Toronto: Norton, 1978), 104.

[13] Lacan, *Seminar XI: The Four Fundamental Concepts of Psychoanalysis*, 196.

[14] Jacques Lacan, "Séminaire XXII, R.S.I. ; leçon du 10 décembre 1974", published in *Ornicar ?*, Vol. 2 (Paris : Éditeur Le graphe, March 1975), P.96. Translation by Mauricio Rugeles Schoonewolff and David Hafner.

[15] Karl Marx, "Economic and Philosophical Manuscripts", in *Selected Writings* (Oxford: Oxford University Press, 2000), 119.

[16] Karl Marx, *Capital, Volume One* (London: Penguin books, 1990), 162.

[17] Marx, *Capital, Volume One,* 195.

[18] In the French translation, Marx introduces surplus-value in the VII chapter in the subsection, « Production de valeurs d'usage et production de la plus-value »; however, in the English translation, this subsection is entitled « The Labour Process and the Valorisation Process ».

[19] Jacques Lacan, *Le séminaire, livre XVII : L'envers de la psychanalyse* (Paris: Éditions du Seuil, 1991).

[20] Jacques Lacan, " La troisième", in *Lacan au miroir des sorcières : revue La Cause freudienne*, N°79 (Paris: Navarin éditeur, 2011), 18. Translation by Mauricio Rugeles Schoonewolff and David Hafner.
« Il n'y a qu'un symptôme social – chaque individu est réellement un prolétaire, c'est-à-dire n'a nul discours de quoi faire lien social, autrement dit semblant.»

[21] Jacques Lacan, *Le séminaire, livre XVI : D'un Autre à l'autre,* (Paris : Éditions du seuil, 2006), 19. Translation by Mauricio Rugeles Schoonewolff and David Hafner.
« Le plus-de-jouir est fonction de la renonciation à la jouissance sous l'effet du discours. C'est ce qui donne sa place à l'objet *a*. Pour autant que le marché définit comme marchandise quelque objet que ce soit du travail humain, cet objet porte en lui-même quelque chose de la plus-value ».

[22] Jacques Lacan, "Radiophonie", in *Autres écrits,* (Paris : Éditions du Seuil, 2001), 435. Translation by Mauricio Rugeles Schoonewolff and David Hafner.

[23] Jacques Lacan, “Du discours psychanalytique”, in *Lacan in Italia,*(Milan :La Salamandra, 1978). Translation by Mauricio Rugeles Schoonewolff and David Hafner. Minor editions by trans.

« C’est pas du tout que je vous dise que le discours du capitaliste ce soit moche, c’est au contraire quelque chose de follement astucieux, hein ? De follement astucieux, mais voué à la crevaison. Enfin, c’est après tout ce qu’on a fait de plus astucieux comme discours. Ça n’en est pas moins voué à la crevaison. C’est intenable dans un truc que je pourrais vous expliquer… parce que le discours capitaliste est là, vous le voyez… une toute petite inversion simplement entre le S_1 et le $ qui est le sujet… ca suffit pas à ce que ça marche comme sur des roulettes, ça ne peut pas marcher mieux, mais justement ça marche trop vite, ça se consomme, ça se consomme, si bien que ça se consume.

[24] Jacques Lacan, *Je parle aux murs,* (Paris: Éditions du seuil, 2011), 96. Translation by Mauricio Rugeles Schoonewolff and David Hafner.

« Ce qui distingue le discours du capitaliste est ceci- la *Verwerfung*, le rejet en dehors de tous les champs du symbolique, avec les conséquences que j’ai déjà dites, le rejet de quoi ? De la castration. Tout ordre, tout discours qui s’apparente du capitalisme laisse de côté ce que nous appelons simplement les choses de l’amour, mes bons amis.

[25] Jacques Lacan, *Television: a challenge to the establishment,*(New York: Norton & Company, 1990), 16.

References

Lacan, Jacques. "Radiophonie", in *Autres écrits.* Paris : Éditions du Seuil, 2001.

—. *Je parle aux murs.* Paris: Éditions du seuil, 2011.

—. "La troisième", in *Lacan au miroir des sorcières : revue La Cause freudienne*, N°79. Paris: Navarin éditeur, 2011.

—. "Du discours psychanalytique", in *Lacan in Italia,* Milan : La Salamandra, 1978.

—. *Le séminaire, livre XVI : D'un Autre à l'autre.* Paris : Éditions du seuil, 2006.

—. *Le séminaire, livre XVII : L'envers de la psychanalyse.* Paris: Éditions du Seuil, 1991.

—. *Le séminaire, livre XVIII :D'un discours que ne serait pas du semblant.* Paris: Éditions du Seuil, 2007.

—. *Le séminaire, livre XIX : ... ou pire.* Paris : Éditions du seuil, 2011.

—. *Le séminaire, livre XX : Encore.* Paris : Éditions du seuil, 1975.

—. "Séminaire XXII, R.S.I. ; leçon du 10 décembre 1974", published in *Ornicar ?*, Vol. 2. Paris : Éditeur Le graphe, March 1975.

—. *Seminar XI: The Four Fundamental Concepts of Psychoanalysis.* Toronto: Norton, 1978.

—. *Television: a challenge to the establishment.* New York: Norton & Company, 1990.

Marx, Karl. *Capital, Volume One*. London: Penguin books, 1990.

—. "Economic and Philosophical Manuscripts", in *Selected Writings.* Oxford: Oxford University Press, 2000.

Freud, Sigmund. "The Rat Man: Original record of the case", in *Complete Works*, Vol.10. Toronto: Hogarth Press, 1959.

—. "On Transformations of Instinct as Exemplified in Anal Erotism", in *Complete Works*, Vol.17. Toronto: Hogarth Press, 1959.

—. "Character and Anal Erotism", in *Complete Works*, Vol.9. Toronto: Hogarth Press, 1959.

Martin, Pierre. *Argent et psychanalyse.* Paris: Bibliothèque des Analytica, Navarin Éditeur, 1984.

Chapter Twelve

Representing the Inner World

Naftally Israeli

When we speak about the inner world, we are referring, first and foremost, to experiences and feelings. Experiences and feelings are the nursery of our psychological self. For us, experiences and feelings symbolize who we are, our status in the world, and the attitude of the world to us. For others, our experiences and feelings signal our mental state, and thus how we want others to relate to us. As such, feelings and experiences serve as mediators between our own inner world and the external world, the world out there that we share with others. Feelings and experiences therefore have a unique and confusing characteristic: they are separate from the external world but are also connected to it in various ways; they express our own subjectivity, but also serve us for interpersonal communication and can be interpreted by others[1].

The unique characteristics of experiences and feelings are the raw material of two disciplines that place special emphasis on changes in experience and feeling – psychoanalysis and children's literature for the very young. The aim of early childhood literature is to establish and validate the experiential and emotional world of the toddler and young child, who live in a world that is, for the most part, still unverbalized and still not representational. The purpose of psychoanalysis is to examine transference relations based on experiences and feelings established very early in life.

Both disciplines do not operate in a vacuum. The medium through which this work of building and changing takes place is communication through language. In order to share personal experiences and feelings, we must speak to one another, in other words, we must use general abstract formulas[2]. And therefore, these two disciplines assume the existence of feelings and experiences from which words are born. Both deal with birth: the birth of words from experiences, and the birth of experiences from words. This relationship between the medium and the material raises many

difficult questions, among them: How is it possible to speak about experiences and feelings that are still not verbalized? Does the very act of speaking establish certain experiences and feelings? How can language attest to the reality of an experience or feeling that existed before they were expressed in language?

The most common answer to these questions is that language functions as a means of transmitting thoughts and experiences between people, who maintain verbal communication between them. Speech is about thoughts and experiences, but it is not the thoughts and experiences themselves; the thoughts and experiences exist "in their own right," separate from speech about them.

In his groundbreaking article of 1979, Michael Reddy called this approach the "conduit metaphor"[3]. In his opinion, this is the main metaphor for describing verbal communication between people in the English language, and it limits our ability to think about other communication options. Using the terms introduced by linguist Roman Jakobson, the conduit metaphor marks the triumph of the cognitive function of language over all its other functions[4]. The cognitive function focuses on the message, and therefore assumes that there is a message – one that exists separate from the medium through which it is transmitted. The success of this function is the triumph of the message over all the other dimensions of language – the emotive, the connotative and the aesthetic, among others.

Is it possible to extricate ourselves from the problem indicated by Reddy? One way to solve the problem is to forgo the linguistic representation of experiences and feelings, in other words, to remain silent. This is Wittgenstein's well known conclusion at the end of the Tractatus: "Whereof one cannot speak, thereof one must be silent"[5]. The problem with this solution is that it rejects language as a medium of communication. If language does not transmit something from one person to another, then it only expresses the inner world of the person who is speaking. Therefore, if we decide not to be silent, in other words, we decide to **speak** about experiences and feelings, we are left with two options regarding the relationship between language and our inner world: either to choose language as a means of communication which transmits a message; or to choose language as a means of expression that establishes an experience. These two options – actual experience on the one hand and verbal communication on the other – are very far from one another, as Sigmund Freud noted in a comment in his article "The Unconscious":

> "To have heard something and to have experienced something are in their psychological nature two quite different things, even though the content of both is the same"[6].

Paradoxical Representation

In post-Freudian psychoanalysis, the one who related to this gap as a necessary and irresolvable paradox that must be accepted was Donald W. Winnicott. It was Winnicott who pointed out that words used for communication are not able to communicate experience, which is always and forever personal. The key to understanding this phenomenon lies in the concept that Winnicott calls the transitional object. In his article "Transitional Objects and Transitional Phenomena" he writes:

> "Of the transitional object it can be said that it is a matter of agreement between us and the baby that we will never ask the question 'Did you conceive of this or was it presented to you from without?' The important point is that no decision on this point is expected. The question is not to be formulated"[7].

And in a later article, "Communicating and Not Communicating Leading to a Study of Certain Opposites", Winnicott states explicitly that this is an irresolvable paradox:

> "In health the infant creates what is in fact lying around waiting to be found. But in health *the object is created, not found.* This fascinating aspect of normal object-relating has been studied by me in various papers, including the one on 'Transitional Objects and Transitional Phenomena'. A good object is no good to the infant unless created by the infant. Shall I say, created out of need? Yet the object must be found in order to be created. This has to be accepted as a paradox, and not solved by a restatement that, by its cleverness, seems to eliminate the paradox"[8].

Thus, the transitional object is paradoxical because it is an object that on the one hand exists because it is there and on the other hand does not exist because it is made up. In the conceptualization that I will propose below, I will say that such an object is a successful paradoxical representation because it fails in terms of its existence. In the introduction to his last book, "Playing and Reality," Winnicott writes that the ability to accept this particular paradox is his most important contribution:

> "It is now generally recognized, I believe, that what I am referring to in this part of my work is not the cloth or the teddy bear that the baby uses – not so much the object used as the use of the object. I am drawing attention

> to the *paradox* involved in the use by the infant of what I have called the transitional object. My contribution is to ask for a paradox to be accepted and tolerated and respected, and for it not to be resolved. By flight to split-off intellectual functioning it is possible to resolve the paradox, but the price of this is the loss of the value of the paradox itself"[9].

The book "Playing and Reality" ends by emphasizing the fact that accepting the paradox is essential for normal human development from the subjective domain to the real domain, and from dependence to independence:

> "I am proposing that there is a stage in the development of human beings that comes before objectivity and perceptibility. At the theoretical beginning a baby can be said to live in a subjective or conceptual world. The change from the primary state to one in which objective perception is possible is not only a matter of inherent or inherited growth process; it needs in addition an environmental minimum. It belongs to the whole vast theme of the individual travelling from dependence towards independence. This conception-perception gap provides rich material for study. I postulate an essential paradox, one that we must accept and that is not for resolution. This paradox, which is central to the concept, needs to be allowed and allowed for over a period of time in the care of each baby"[10].

In other words, the transitional object is not only a successful paradoxical representation in terms of existence but also in terms of separation – it is separate from the experience and therefore capable of creating it, but it is also not separate from it and therefore it is capable of transmitting it as it is. Thus, Winnicott emphasizes two aspects of the paradox – that of communication and that of separation – which connect experience and its representation in words.

In the philosophy of language two different traditions have developed that try to explain this relationship in another–non-paradoxical–way. The literal tradition assumes that every word has content. The literal meaning in the relationship between language and experience indicates that there is a correspondence theory of truth, in which each word refers to a specific experience, which is separate from the word.

The metaphorical tradition in the philosophy of language does not abide by this view. According to the metaphorical tradition, each word assumes its meaning only from its relationship to other words. That is, the word itself is **empty** of content. Each word is **not** what it signifies, and meaning is determined from context, use or life style as a whole. Metaphorical meaning in the relationship between language and experience means that language succeeds in transmitting to us not content

but relationships, a connection or interaction between experiences and feelings, without transmitting any of their **content**.

Traditionally, these two traditions did not deal with the relationship between language and the inner world – meaning experiences and feelings – but rather with the relationship between language and the world at large. My contention is that when we want to talk about representation of the inner world, that is, the relationship between language and experience, in contrast to the representation of the external world, we must connect and combine the underlying assumptions of both traditions. Connecting them creates a unique representation, which in a Winnicottian tradition I call a **paradoxical representation**.

This type of representation is characterized by three aspects. First, paradoxical representation simultaneously represents and does not represent the feeling and the experience – it symbolizes them in terms of content but it is not the content. In paradoxical representation, the word does not observe the rules of traditional logic, because it is both a symbol of something and a symbol of what that thing is not. If we represent a word or a sentence by p*, and its literal meaning by p, then the literal tradition assumes that p* means p, and the metaphorical tradition assumes that p* means (not p). These two assumptions–taken together–are paradoxical. This is one aspect of what Michael Parsons and Shahaf Bitan call "The logic of play", which according to Bitan *founds* the psychoanalytic relations[11].

Second, paradoxical representation also fails to represent, or its representation is faulty, because it is at one and the same time connected to the experience and the feeling but is also separate from them[12]. In the conceptualization proposed by Vered Bar-On, paradoxical representation is simultaneously metonymous and metaphorical[13]. And finally, paradoxical representation is situated somewhere between expression and communication, between what is completely original and what is controlled by rules, and can therefore serve as agreed upon symbols between people.

I can summarize as follows: A paradoxical representation of experience and feeling is a successful representation if it fails in three aspects: it fails in terms of existence – it is impossible to know with certainty whether it relates to the experience that also exists separately from what is spoken about it; it fails in terms of separateness – it is impossible to know with certainty whether it refers to the experience under discussion or whether it only represents it – in other words, it refers to something else that resembles it in certain ways but is different from it in other ways; and it fails in terms of communication – it is impossible to

know with certainty whether it is a personal tool being used for subjective expression or a public tool that is intended for interpersonal communication.

In the psychoanalytical literature, the one who best understood the paradoxical nature of the verbal representation of experiences and feelings was Hanna Segal, a student of Melanie Klein. In her short, six-and-a-half page article from 1957, "Notes on Symbol Formation," Segal attempted to change the psychoanalytical approach from its foundations[14]. Instead of the conscious-unconscious distinction, Segal proposed the identical-representational distinction. Her contention was that in the initial stage, the word is felt to be identical to the feeling or experiential situation; only in a more advanced stage is the word felt to be separate from this situation, but still connected to it in a certain way – as representation.

The roots of this conception can be found in Klein's criticism of Ernest Jones' conception of the unconscious. According to Jones, representation is connected to unconscious processes because it is a result of conflict between what is repressed and the forces that try to repress it: "Only what is repressed undergoes symbolization," Jones wrote; "Only what is repressed must become a symbol"[15]. When it is necessary to forgo and repress desire, it will express itself symbolically – through representation. On the other hand, representation is not necessary when unconscious desire undergoes sublimation – at least according to Jones.

Melanie Klein, who focused on the clinical treatment of children, disagreed with this approach. The main reason for her disagreement was that she viewed the play of children – which many, including Ernest Jones, considered to be sublimation– as a symbolic expression of anxieties and of wishes. Observing the play of children again and again, Klein saw it as sublimation but not as repressive activity, and as something that had the value of representation. This was not possible according to Jones' idea, and Klein wanted to clarify how her ideas differed from his.

Her main article on this subject–"The importance of symbol formation in the development of the ego"–was written in 1930. In this article Klein unfolds her contention, according to which symbolic development is connected to the development of object relations. When symbolic development is impaired, object relations are also affected, as are emotional ties with the mother and reality testing. In contrast, proper symbolic development encourages emotional relations with the environment and ensures proper reality testing.

For this reason Klein maintains that the ability to represent, that is, the basic ability 'to put two things together' – whether motivated by desire or by anxiety – is the basis for all sublimation and for every skill[16].

Continuing this line of thought, Hannah Segal proposes that object relations and representational ability develop together, from the beginning of life[17]. In Segal's approach, the term "paradoxical representation" which I propose here, is representation that is connected to continual movement between the paranoid-schizoid position, which uses symbolic equations, and the depressive position, which uses real representations. In the symbolic equation of the paranoid-schizoid position, the representation is the thing; in the depressive position, the representation differs from the thing, that is, it is not what the thing is. The movement between the positions is constant, because it is impossible to maintain representational equilibrium in either one. In the paranoid-schizoid position, representation is the thing, and therefore more and more representations must be created all the time[18]; in the depressive position, representation differs from the thing, and so there is constant suspiciousness towards it, inviting opportunities for regression to the paranoid-schizoid position. One way or the other, it is not possible to arrive at a state of equilibrium and the constant fluctuation between positions is the heart of paradoxical representation, in which a representation is simultaneously the thing and not the thing. This is a failure in terms of existence and of separateness: in symbolic equation, the word is the thing and not something separate from it; in actual representation, the word is not the thing and is separate from it. Thus paradoxical representation contains two self-contradictory aspects.

The Development of Paradoxical Representation

Children's books that are intended for the very young, which deal with establishing and validating the children's experiences, also deal with paradoxical representations. Thus, for example, A.A. Milne's well known story of Winnie the Pooh illustrates all possible failures of paradoxical representation. The books moves between two frames of reference. One frame is the "realistic" frame, in which words denote what there is – the adult who is telling the story, the child Christopher Robin, his games and his dolls. The second frame is the "imaginal" frame, in which the words denote what there is not, what will be told in the story – Winnie the Pooh and his friends, the relations between them and their connection to the "real" world of Christopher Robin and the story-teller. Milne moves between these two frames of reference without explaining anything, and in this unique way the story contains the paradox:

> "You can't be in London for long without going to the Zoo… the nicest people go straight to the animal they love the most, and stay there… I have written as far as this when Piglet looked up and said in his squeaky voice,

> "What about *Me*?" "My dear Piglet," I said, "the whole book is about you." … And now all the others are saying, "What about *Us*?" So perhaps the best thing to do is to stop writing Introductions and get on with the book"[19].

The containment of the paradox is expressed here by confusing the act of representation. For example, it is not clear if the words "the others" denote an actual or imaginal world. When the question "And what is said here about us?" is asked, the reader and hearer do not know if the question refers to them or to the heroes of the story.

Another example for this type of paradoxical writing is given at the end of the story, after a dialogue between Pooh and Piglet at the end of Pooh's party:

> "And what did happen?" asked Christopher Robin. "When?" "Next morning." "I don't know." "Could you think, and tell me and Pooh sometime?" "If you wanted it very much." "Pooh does," said Christopher Robin. He gave a deep sigh, picked his bear up by the leg and walked off to the door, trailing Winnie-the-Pooh behind him. At the door he turned and said, "Coming to see me have my bath?" "I might," I said. "Was Pooh's pencil case any better than mine?" "It was just the same," I said"[20].

Again, it is not clear where reality begins and where fantasy ends, and in this way the story presents a paradoxical representation, which focuses our attention not on the outer world but on the inner one – the world of experiences and feelings.

Another typical example from Milne's famous book can be found in Chapter Six, in which Eeyore has a birthday and gets two presents, Pooh is surprised to discover that Eeyore is sunk in sadness because he has a birthday that day and no one is paying any attention to it. He calls his friend Piglet and the two run to bring Eeyore presents. This is the important representation in the story – that of the present. What is the present that Pooh and Piglet choose? Pooh chooses a can of honey, and Piglet – a red balloon. Both presents contain a special tension between the inside and the outside, tension connected to the paradoxical representation – a tin with honey inside, and a balloon with air inside. The present is the inside, which cannot be seen; and the present supposedly does not exist without it. And here, on the way to Eeyore, Winnie gets tired and sits down and eats the honey in the tin, while Piglet trips and bursts the balloon. It would seem that without the content there is no present. Both Pooh and Piglet understand this:

> "And then, suddenly, he [Pooh] remembered. He had eaten Eeyore's birthday present! *'Bother!'* said Pooh. 'What *shall* I do? I must give him *something*'."[21]

> And Piglet: "'Oh, dear!' said Piglet. 'Oh, dear, oh, dearie, dearie dear! Well, it's too late now. I can't go back, and I haven't another balloon, and perhaps Eeyore doesn't *like* balloons so *very* much'."[22]

Pooh decides to go to Owl, and ask him to write a greeting to Eeyore on the tin, and we as readers discover that the content (which is written on the tin) is not identical with the original intention:

> "So Owl wrote… And this is what he wrote: HIPY PAPY BTHUTHDTH THUTHDA BTHUTHDY. Pooh looked on admiringly. 'I'm just saying 'A Happy Birthday',' said Owl carelessly. 'It's a nice long one,' said Pooh, very much impressed by it"[23].

In other words, the representation failed here in terms of existence – the greeting on the tin does not say "Happy Birthday," but this is what the writing **says**. A similar development occurs at the end of the story. Pooh and Piglet are broken by the time they reach Eeyore because they expect him to be very disappointed by the presents they brought. But Eeyore, who perhaps at first does not discern their original intention but only what he sees in front of him, is moved and excited by the very essence of the presents. Together with them, he succeeds in investigating his fantasy world (What colour was this balloon when it was a balloon? How big was it?) and is happy about it (My favourite colour, My favourite size), and the story ends with him playing with the balloon, putting it into the tin and taking it out – a metaphor for the ability to connect between inside and outside, in contrast to the depressive sinking into the inner world that characterized him at the beginning of the story.

What, then, is the function of the present, the most important representation in this story? The story is intended for toddlers, for the developmental stage in which the inner world of experience and feeling enters the world of words and is expressed by them. By means of the representation of the present, Milne successfully creates a paradoxical representation because it fails three times. First, in terms of existence – it is impossible to understand with certainty whether the gift exists or does not exist in the real world. Is the present the real content – in other words, the honey, or the balloon inflated with air? Or perhaps the present is the act of giving something? Milne of course does not venture an answer. Piglet's original intention, for example, was to bring Eeyore a balloon because, as Pooh says, "nobody can be uncheered with a balloon"[24]. At the

end of the day Piglet brings Eeyore "…a small piece of damp rag"[25] which in Eeyore's eyes is a very special balloon – a balloon that does not look like a balloon, that it is possible to do things with that cannot be done with any other balloon, and nevertheless is called a balloon.

Second, the paradoxical representation in the story is successful because it fails in terms of separateness – it is impossible to know with certainty whether the present is necessarily connected to the present givers (Pooh and Piglet) or whether the present receiver (Eeyore)is the one who determines that it is a present. In essence, the tension in the story is connected to this, because the original intention of Pooh and Piglet does not materialize, and only the cooperation of Eeyore allows what they bring him (an empty tin of honey and a wet rag) to be considered wonderful gifts. Finally, the paradoxical representation in the story is successful because it fails in terms of communication – the original intention of Pooh and Piglet meets the expectations of Eeyore, and the result is unexpected cooperation among the three and not only a personal representation of the personal inner world of one of them.

I want to present one final and amusing example from Lewis Carroll's "Alice in Wonderland", which is undoubtedly familiar. I cannot go into it at length but it is interesting because it illustrates the most mysterious paradoxical representation – the 'I'. When I am not I (failure in terms of existence), when one separates from itself and becomes something else (failure in terms of separateness), and at the same time expresses an inner world while trying to communicate in public (failure in terms of communication) – it is a successful paradoxical representation, but mysterious and not entirely understood:

> "'Who are *you*?' said the Caterpillar… Alice replied, rather shyly, 'I hardly know, sir, just at present – 'Explain yourself!' 'I can't explain *myself*, I'm afraid sir', said Alice, 'because I am not myself, you see.' '…when you have to turn into a chrysalis – … - and then after that into a butterfly, I should think you'll feel it a little queer, won't you?' 'Not a bit,' said the Caterpillar. 'Well, perhaps your feelings may be different,' said Alice; 'all I know is, it would feel very queer to *me*.' 'You!' said the Caterpillar contemptuously. 'Who are *you?*' Which brought them back again to the beginning of the conversation"[26].

Other Possibilities of Representing the Inner World

Paradoxical representation is one major "solution" to the problem of representing feelings and experiences. Besides this "solution", other possibilities of representing the inner world also exist. I will present two

important ones below. The first one is the acceptance of non-verbal experiences and feelings, which cannot be expressed by words. The second one is an attempt to create a shared language, which communicates experiences and feelings between two (or more) people. I will comment on these "solutions" briefly, giving a few examples from psychoanalysis and children's literature for the very young.

(1) The Non-Representational

If the inner world is taken to be primary to any attempt to represent it, there exists a different connection between it and language. This "solution" assumes that the inner world contains a part which in its very essence cannot be expressed in words. In contemporary psychoanalysis, Donnel Stern expresses this view time and time again. Stern thinks that we have to pay attention to that which is still not represented. In his article from 1983, "Unformulated experience", he writes:

> "Lack of formulation is lack of symbolization. Not to have a thought means not to translate unformulated experience into language. … Bergson and James conclude that language, although it formulates the formless and is therefore constitutive of experience, also seduces us into accepting a mythology of the world around us that is based—circularly—on the properties of language itself. In these ways, language and culture set the limits beyond which even creative disorder cannot spread"[27].

Thus, Stern thinks that we need to be aware of the magical way in which language not only reveals our experiences, but also creates them in its own image. For this reason Stern emphasizes the importance of the unformulated, unrepresentational experience.

John McDowell presented a paradox, which he called "The Myth of the Given", which is connected to this view[28]. This paradox is a mixture of two contradicting views. According to the first view, what is given to us by our senses is known immediately. According to the second view, what we feel is not given, but conceptualized by us, and only then becomes known. Stern contends that Freud was driven by the first view. Freud thought, according to Stern, that what is given by our senses is known immediately, and only then is it distorted by various defense mechanisms[29]. But Stern thinks that this view does not take into account the fact that language constitutes experiences:

> "Today, partially because of data and theory which have accrued since Freud wrote, it has become clear that experience, even at its most basic levels, is not

> a given: It is made, or constructed, and its construction proceeds in levels of progressive articulation"[30].

For this reason Stern thinks that in order to know experience we have to step out of the boundaries of language, and find it in non-representational ways. This view is rooted in a central critique about the concept of the unconscious, which emerged in the 1970's and from then on was supported by empirical and conceptual research. Jean Schimek's 1975 article, 'A critical re-examination of Freud's concept of unconscious mental representation' clearly expresses this view.

The concept of unconscious mental representation–mental content that is kept in the unconscious and expresses itself in a disguised form in consciousness–is one of the basic concepts in the psychoanalytic literature[31]. One of Freud's basic assumptions was that thought is driven by (conscious and unconscious) representations, and these representations determine each and every action. Schimek criticizes this view by suggesting that not all actions are driven by representations; some have not yet gained the status of mental content. Thus, according to Schimek, Freud's unconscious representation can be thought about as prerepresentational:

> The general concept of prerepresentational unconscious organizers of action… has the same methodological status as Freud's concept of unconscious mental representation[32].

Donnel Stern's view is a continuation of this critic. Stern suggests an alternative that uses the concept of the unconscious, but does not necessitate that it needs to have content or representation. The philosopher and psychologist Eugene Gendlin supported this view in many of his writings. In his article from 1964, "A Theory of Personality change", for example, he attacks the idea that we should always think about ideas as something 'hidden', which is already 'there' and only given external clothing by using words. Gendlin writes:

> Meaning depends on a *relationship* between experience and symbols. Hence, we would expect that experienced meaning is something different when symbolized than it was "before" it was symbolized. We can only speak of an experienced meaning as already "symbolized" in *some* way[33].

Another psychoanalytic writer who emphasizes this way of thinking is Thomas Ogden. In his writings, Ogden tries to integrate Winnicottian ideas and the theory of object relations. A basic tenet in Ogden's writing is that psychological meaning is always given in a pre-verbal realm – in

unverbalized feelings and emotions. The peak of this way of thought is Ogden's suggestion of a third position, in addition to two prior positions suggested by Melanie Klein – the depressive and the paranoid-schizoid positions. Ogden's third position – the autistic-contiguous position – is suggested in his book, "The primitive edge of experience". In this book Ogden suggests that the most ancient and primitive form of our experience is non-verbal:

> "The history of the development of British object relations theory in the last twenty years can be viewed as containing the beginnings of an exploration of an area of experience lying outside of the experiential states addressed by Klein's concepts of the paranoid-schizoid and depressive positions; by Fairbairn's conception of the internal object world; by Bion's conception of projective identification as a primitive form of defense, communication and containment; or by Winnicott's conception of the evolution of the mother-infant relationship and the elaboration of the transitional phenomena.
>
> The clinical and theoretical work of Esther Bick, Donald Meltzer and Francis Tustin, developed in the context of their clinical work with autistic children, has served to define a heretofore insufficiently understood dimension of all human experience (more primitive than the paranoid-schizoid position) that I refer to as the autistic-contiguous position"[34].

The autistic-contiguous experience is the most primitive experience possible, according to Ogden. It is the basis for all experiences to follow, and in normal development it comes first. The autistic-contiguous form of experience is sensory-controlled. It is as pre-symbolic form of experience and meaning, and one of the major contributions of Ogden to contemporary psychoanalysis. As mentioned above, it integrates many different ways of thinking which emerged in the last decade. All these ways of thinking emphasize the non-verbal dimension as the most basic non-representational mode of experience, which words – which always come after it – get their meaning from.

(2) "Private" dialogical language

Another "solution" to the problem of representing the inner world of experiences and emotions is an attempt to create a common "private" language between two (or more) people trying to understand one another. This possibility assumes that meaning lies in the uniqueness of language itself, and in the fact that only few (usually two) people understand it[35].

Children's books are full of examples for this type of "solution", which usually involves an attempt to describe a new experience. For example, in the book "Winnie the Pooh", Pooh heads an expotition to the north pole. This word–"expotition"–is Pooh's private invention, and it is used more and more times as the story unfolds. In the beginning of the story Christopher Robin tells Pooh, to bring provisions. "Bring what?", asks Pooh. "Things to eat." "Oh!" said Pooh happily. "I thought you said Provisions"[36]. Thus, sometimes using a new word makes way for a "private" dialogical language (like the word "expotition"), and sometimes it is used to teach the child the reference of a new word – a word that already exists in language but the child does not know it yet.

In another story from this book Pooh and Piglet try to catch a Heffalump, after this dialogue between them and Christopher Robin:

> "I saw a Heffalump to-day, Piglet." "What was it doing?" asked Piglet. "Just jumping along," said Christopher Robin. "I don't think it saw *me*." "I saw one once," said Piglet. "At least, I think I did," he said. "Only perhaps it wasn't." "So did I," said Pooh, wondering what a Heffalump was like"[37].

The experiences Pooh and Piglet have are those having to do with trying to catch the Heffalump. In the end of the story they found out that they haven't found any Heffalumps; but their experiences as expressed in their "private" language exist. In this way, a "private" dialogical language is a solution to the paradox: it organizes emotions and experiences around a fictional or abstract word–i.e, a word that has a meaning but has no reference–and in this way builds an inner realm, which does not have any reference to an outer, physical or realistic world.

This type of "solution" can also be found in psychoanalytic case studies, like Winnicott's famous case study – "The Piggle"[38]. In this clinical case Gabrielle ("The Piggle") talks with Dr. Winnicott in a way that is very different from everyday speech. She invents a "private" dialogue that allows both of them to feel understood. An example of this special dialogue can be found even in their first meeting. Winnicott says: "You feel frightened; do you have frightening dreams?", and Gabrielle (the Piggle) answers: "About the babacar." "This is the name her mother had already given me," Winnicott writes, "in connection with the baby, the Sush Baby" (Gabrielle's little sister)[39]. Gabrielle's private word ("babacar") is used by her in order to communicate various emotions and experiences, that are not known to Winnicott; but the use of this special word allows her to create an apparent feeling of understanding and communication, in a situation of great anxiety and tension which is characteristic of a first analytic meeting,

Another way of keeping this word as "private" is to disguise it when speaking to other people. Gabrielle's mother writes to Winnicott after the first session:

> "She seemed very pleased that you will see her. Sometimes when in difficulty talks about asking Dr. Winnicott. Still plays: 'You are the Piggle, I am the mummy, I'll take you to Dr. Winnicott, say no!' – 'Why?' – 'To tell him about the babacandle (instead of babacar, with a little furtive smile, as if disguising babacar)"[40].

Another concept that the Piggle uses in order to communicate feelings and experiences is the concept of the "black mummy". "Presumably the 'black mummy' is a relice of her subjective preconceived notion about the mother", writes Winnicott[41].

In the sessions to come, both Winnicott and Gabrielle use these words again and again – the "babacar" and the "black mummy" – and by doing so create their own special language, because its **uses** are known only to them. For example, Gabrielle says: "The black mummy is now Winnicott, and he is going to send the Piggle away."[42], or asks: "If the black mummy and the babacar caught you would they eat you?"[43]; or when Winnicott says: "I would be frightened of the black mummy and the babacar"[44]. At the end of the third consultation Winnicott asks Gabrielle: "All right, but have we understood about the black mummy and the babacar?"[45] and he writes:

> "She looked at all the toys, ... as if she were saying the babacar has to do with bryyyyyh and wee-wee belonging to the black mummy who is black because she is hated since daddy gave her a baby"[46].

This interpretation is written in Winnicott's words, and was not said literally. But using the "private" concepts (the babycar, the black mummy) again and again allowed Winnicott to understand that Gabrielle, when saying "the babycar is in its place", **as if** said the same thing. This is the power of a "private" dialogical language, which creates an illusional feeling of connection between private emotions and experiences and between a language which is understood by everyone.

Summary

In this chapter I introduced the concept of **paradoxical representation** as a "solution" to the problem of representing experiences and emotions in language. In the philosophy of language, the concept of paradoxical representation is a fusion between two assumptions of two different traditions – the literal and the metaphorical traditions. Alongside this "solution", I focused on two other "solutions": preferring the non-representational (upon the representational, which can be expressed in language); and an attempt to create a "private" common language between two (or more) people. I have shown how psychoanalysis and children's literature use these "solutions" in order to deal with representation of what is called "the inner world" – the space of human feeling and experience.

When using **paradoxical representation**, the way in which this space is represented is unique. I proposed that the relationship between language, experience and feeling, which psychoanalysis and children's literature wish to reveal, is truly paradoxical in nature, and presents two different and contradictory manners of representation–one in which the word symbolizes–and does not symbolize –the experience; one that is separate–and not separate–from it; and one that serves as subjective expression and public communication. This unique manner of representation is one in which successful representation, which symbolizes the thing, is a representation that fails, and therefore does not symbolize it. This manner is unique to children's literature and psychoanalysis, both of which–through words–seek to speak about that which is beyond words and at the same time is not what it is without them – human experience and feeling.

Notes

[1] Stein 1991.
[2] James 1902.
[3] Reddy 1979.
[4] Jakobson 1960.
[5] Wittgenstein 1949.
[6] Freud 1915, p. 176.
[7] Winnicott 1953, p. 95.
[8] Winnicott 1963, p. 181.
[9] Winnicott 1971, p. xi-xii.
[10] Winnicott 1971, p. 151.
[11] See Parsons 1999, Bitan 2012. In the beginning of his paper, Bitan writes: "The present paper has affinity with Parson's article, 'The logic of play in psychoanalysis'

(1999), that offers a thorough examination of the concept of play and its logical foundation in paradox… Nonetheless… through consideration of Winnicott's playfulness, I emphasize the work of play within the clinical situation and its role in *founding* the psychoanalytic relations". (Bitan 2012, p. 29, footnote #2)

[12] Therefore it is not a sufficient condition for knowledge – and for this reason we do not have knowledge of the inner world as we have knowledge about the outside world.

[13] Bar-On 2014.

[14] Segal 1957.

[15] Jones 1918, p. 210.

[16] Klein wrote: "Some years ago… I drew the conclusion that symbolism is the foundation of all sublimation and of every talent, since it is by way of **symbolic equation** that things, activities and interests become the subject of libidinal phantasies." (Klein 1930, p. 25, my emphasis)

[17] Segal 1957, p. 393.

[18] In her paper from 1930, Klein wrote: "Since the child desires to destroy the organs (penis, vagina, breast) which stand for the objects, he conceives a dread of the latter. This anxiety contributes to make him equate the organs in question with other things; owing to this equation these in their turn become objects of anxiety, and so he is impelled constantly to make other and new equations, which form the basis of his interest in the new objects and of symbolism." (Klein 1930, p. 26)

[19] Milne 1971, pp. 13-14.

[20] Milne 1971, p. 220.

[21] Milne 1971, p. 110.

[22] Milne 1971, p. 116.

[23] Milne 1971, p. 112.

[24] Milne 1971, p. 108.

[25] Milne 1971, p. 116.

[26] Heath 1947, p. 47.

[27] Stern 1983, p. 91.

[28] McDowell 1996.

[29] Stern 1983, p. 72.

[30] Stern 1983, p. 73.

[31] Schimek 1975, p. 171.

[32] Schimek 1975, p. 183.

[33] Gendlin 1964, p. 125.

[34] Ogden 1989, pp. 47-48.

[35] This can also be a source of pathology, as is the case of sects, fanatic groups or religious fundamentalism. See for example Stein 2006.

[36] Milne 1971, p. 160.

[37] Milne 1971, p. 76.

[38] Winnicott 1977.

[39] Winnicott 1977, p. 11.

[40] Winnicott 1971, p. 22.

[41] Winnicott 1971, pp. 16-17.

[42] Winnicott 1971, p. 61.
[43] Winnicott 1971, p. 45.
[44] Winnicott 1971, p. 46.
[45] Winnicott 1971, p. 47.
[46] Ibid.

References

Bar-On, V. (2014). "It cuts both ways: An analysis of the psychological discourse on self-injury from a linguistic point of view". *Psychoanalytic Review, 101(5),* 701-734.

Bitan, S. (2012). "Winnicott and Derrida: Development of logic-of-play". *International Journal of Psychoanalysis, 93,* 29-51.

Freud, S. (1915). "The Unconscious." *The Standard Edition of the Complete Psychological Works of Sigmund Freud, Volume XIV (1914-1916): On the History of the Psycho-Analytic Movement, Papers on Metapsychology and Other Works,* 159-215.

Gendlin, E. T. (1964). "A theory of personality change." In: *Personality Change,* ed. P. Worchel and D. Byrne. New York: John Wiley, 100-148.

Heath, P. (1974). *The Philosopher's Alice*. Academy Editions: London.

Jakobson, R. (1960). Concluding statement: Linguistics and poetics. In: Thomas A. Sebeok (ed.), *Style in language.* Wiley: New York, 350-377.

James, W. (1902). The varieties of religious experience: A study in human nature. London: Longmans, Green.

Jones, E. (1918). "The Theory of Symbolism".*The British Journal of Psychology, 9 (2)*, 181-229.

Klein, M. (1930).The importance of symbol-formation in the development of the ego.*International Journal of Psycho-Analysis, 11*, 24-39.

McDowell, J. H. (1996). *Mind and world.* Cambridge: Harvard University Press.

Milne, A. A. (1971). *Winnie the Pooh*. London: Methuen.

Odgen, T. (1989).*The primitive edge of experience.*Northvale, N. J. : J. Aronson.

Parsons, M. (1999)."The logic of play in psychoanalysis".*International Journal of Psychoanalysis, 80,* 871-84.

Reddy, M. J. (1979). "The conduit metaphor: A case of frame conflict in our language about language", in: Ortony, A. (ed.) (1998). *Metaphor and thought.* Cambridge: Cambridge University Press, 248-310.

Schimek, J. G. (1975). "A critical re-examination of Freud's concept of unconscious mental representation."*International Review of Psycho-Analysis, 2,* 171-187.

Segal, H. (1957). "Notes on symbol formation", *International Journal of Psychoanalysis, 38*, 391-397.

Stein, R. (2006). "Fundamentalism, Father and Son, and Vertical Desire."*Psychoanalytic Review, 93,* 201-229.

Stein, R. (1991). *Psychoanalytic theories of affect.* London: Praeger Publishers.

Stern, D. B. (1983)."Unformulated experience – from familiar chaos to creative disorder."*Contemporary Psychoanalysis, 19,* 71-99.

Winnicott, D. W. (1977). *The Piggle: An account of the psychoanalytic treatment of a little girl.* Madison: International Universities Press.

—. (1971). Playing and Reality. London: Tavistock Publications.

—. (1963). "Communicating and Not Communicating Leading to a Study of Certain Opposites", in: Winnicott, D. W. (1965), *The Maturational Processes and the Facilitating Environment.* International Psycho-Analytic Library, 64, London: The Hogarth Press and the Institute of Psycho-Analysis, 179-192.

—. (1953). "Transitional Objects and Transitional Phenomena—A Study of the First Not-Me Possession".*International Journal of Psycho-Analysis, 34*, 89-97.

Wittgenstein, L. (1949). Tractatus logico-philosophicus. London: Routledge & Kegan Paul.

Chapter Thirteen

Biological Complexity and Subjective Singularity in the Clinic of Autism

Thomas Harding

Recent advances in the life sciences have contributed to a dramatic shift in the representation of autism put forward by biopsychiatry. Once perceived to be a relatively uniform and straightforwardly heritable disorder, autism has been redefined as a highly complex constellation of different symptoms, each one resting on a heterogeneous neurological and genetic foundation. As François Ansermet and Ariane Giacobino have recently observed, this new representation of autism recognises that no two diagnosed individuals are exactly alike in respect of their biological profiles: "More than governing over the repetition of the same, genetic determinism encounters the question of the production of difference."[1] The consequences of this shift are profound. If the aim of biomedical (and especially of genetic) research was to identify a consistent set of biomarkers for autism, then it must be admitted to have failed. Researchers now largely agree that this is an impossible project, in light of the fact that there are simply too many genes with some possible role to play, which are not necessarily shared by significant subsets of diagnosed individuals, acting across delicate networks of causal interactions far too complex to predict in their entirety. In short, it seems that there is no blueprint for autism awaiting discovery in our genetic code. Yet the hypothesis that autism is a highly heritable disorder with a significant genetic component continues to dominate the research agenda, absorbing substantial portions of available funding, and promoting the conceptualisation of autism as a complex "genetic disease."[2]

This is as much an ethical and political issue as it is a scientific one, because it concerns the place of the subject in our contemporary society. Biomedical science increasingly provides the framework through which we articulate distinctions between health and illness, normality and pathology, life and death.[3] As the domain of biomedicine continues to

encompass ever more of our lives, the subject becomes internally displaced, "rejected by science" as an unpredictable and unmeasurable variable.[4] This goes hand in hand with the growing intolerance for the subject's (always singular) mode of suffering, and any practices which situate him or her beyond the norm. The function that such practices may have for a subject is totally disregarded in favour of their reduction to a minimum through behavioural therapy and pharmaceutical treatment. We see this clearly in relation to autism, where the search for its causes is sustained by the hope that their discovery will lead to earlier and more effective interventions. Yet it is far from clear that all members of the autistic community subscribe to this position. I would like to include here a quote from Ari Ne'eman, who co-founded the Autistic Self Advocacy Network (ASAN),

> "For many of us, the prospect of cure and normalization denies essential aspects of our identity. The autism spectrum is defined as 'pervasive' for a reason; while it does not represent the totality of what makes us who we are, it is indeed a significant part of us, and to pursue normalization instead of quality of life forces us into a struggle against ourselves."[5]

Psychoanalysis opposes the pathologisation of autism and its portrayal as a disease in need of a cure. It supports the view that autism is a distinct subjective position which, as such, cannot be straightforwardly reduced to any set of linear causes, biological or otherwise. This position is often misinterpreted as an assertion of psychogenesis (the notion that autism is caused by psychological factors) against somatogenesis (the notion that autism is caused by biological factors), which is not at all the case. In his seminar on the psychoses, Lacan explicitly distanced psychoanalysis from a psychological model of causality: "[T]he great secret of psychoanalysis is that there is no psychogenesis."[6] Psychoanalysis is more interested in the contingent encounter between language and the body which functions as an exception to any causal chain. Neither the laws of biology nor those of psychology can fully account for this encounter or its consequences for the subject, because the encounter is itself "without law."[7] Consequently, psychoanalysis does not need to oppose the possibility of some biological component in the aetiology of autism, because there will always also be a subject. Éric Laurent makes this clear when he argues that the involvement of a biological factor "in no way excludes the specificity of the space in which the subject is constituted as a speaking being."[8]

What we may well be critical of, though, is the far stronger claim that biological knowledge may one day serve to totally explain—or to explain away—the presence of autism and the function of autistic symptoms. Such

a claim risks the evacuation of the subject and the reduction of autistic subjectivity to the level of an organic disorder. Behaviours and practices labelled as autistic would then be reduced to a kind of automatism; mere epiphenomenal manifestations of underlying biological disturbances. Autistic activist Amanda Baggs describes this as being turned into an "unperson," which is to be represented as "a hollow shell, a body without a soul, a changeling child, or a vegetable."[9] Equally, we might propose a critique of the assumption that locating the supposed genetic foundations of autism should be a priority for research, or that such research will lead to a set of clinically useful and ethically desirable outcomes. Ari Ne'eman has criticised the continued attention of researchers on finding the causes of autism, "with little to no practical implications for the lives of autistic people."[10]

In this chapter, I would like to challenge some of the assumptions that underlie contemporary biomedical autism research, and suggest a revised approach—taken from psychoanalysis—which might allow us to hold together any eventual biological knowledge about the causes of autism with an insistence on the dignity and activity of the subject. Specifically, I would like to make the following points. First, the hypothesis that autism is *essentially* a genetic disorder (that genetic factors are the most important in the aetiology of autism and have the greatest explanatory power when it comes to describing its features) has not been sufficiently demonstrated by current research. We must therefore remain uncertain about the potential contribution that genetic factors might make to the aetiology of autism. Equal uncertainty surrounds the question of how genes might exercise an influence over the eventual clinical picture. Second, representing autism as a genetic disorder tends to narrow research perspectives and channels unjustifiable portions of available funding towards biomedical research, rather than service provision or support initiatives. It also contributes to a reductionist interpretation of autism and reinforces an equally questionable drive for more effective treatments or cures. Third, that psychoanalysis can provide us with a critical framework through which the contributions of biological research can be set alongside an insistence on the subject and a reflexive approach to clinical work.

Research in Autism Genetics

Twin studies provided the first substantial evidence that autism might have a significant genetic component. Though the hypothesis that autism was caused by "innate" or "inborn" factors had an illustrious heritage, it lacked evidentiary support.[11] Strict diagnostic criteria and an initial lack of

awareness about autism made it difficult to recruit research subjects, so the genetic hypothesis remained a possibility, but was not a focus of early research. This all changed with the publication of four landmark twin studies between 1977 and 1995.[12] The so-called "classical twin method" attempts to find out how heritable a given trait might be by comparing the frequency with which it occurs in both members of identical (monozygotic or MZ) twin pairs against fraternal (dizygotic or DZ) twin pairs. If a trait occurs in both members of a twin pair, they are said to be "concordant" for that trait. If the rates of concordance for MZ twins are much higher than the rates for DZ twins, then a heritable factor may be involved, because MZ twins share 100% of their genetic material (as opposed to 50% for DZ twins). A heritability estimate can be derived once the concordance rates for MZ and DZ twins have been found. This is usually expressed as a percentage, in order to show what percentage of the trait's appearance can be attributed to genetic factors. [13]

Susan Folstein and Michael Rutter published the first twin study in 1977. They assessed 21 twin pairs (11 MZ and 10 DZ) for both "strictly defined autism" and for a more broadly defined "cognitive disorder." For the strict phenotype, they reported concordance rates of 36% in MZ twins and 0% in DZ twins; for the broader phenotype, they reported increased rates of 82% in MZ twins and 10% in DZ twins. On the basis of these results, they concluded that there was autism was highly heritable, and that genetic factors were the most significant in its aetiology. But there were two complicating factors. First, the concordance rates in MZ twins were nowhere near 100%, as we might expect if autism were a Mendelian disorder like sickle-cell anaemia or cystic fibrosis. Second, even concordant pairs of MZ twins exhibited striking differences from one another in terms of their symptoms and clinical presentation. Folstein and Rutter took these problems as indicative of some underlying genetic heterogeneity, as if autism were an aggregate of genetically determined cognitive disabilities.[14] The majority of twin and family studies published since 1977—including the three other landmark studies leading up to 1995—either confirmed or increased the heritability estimates given by Folstein and Rutter, leading to a combined heritability estimate of over 90%.[15] One significant deviation from this trend is an extensive 2011 study (the largest carried out to date) which concluded that the role of genetic factors had been dramatically overstated in previous research.[16]

Twin studies are often referred to as having provided incontrovertible evidence of autism's genetic aetiology. Yet there are significant problems with the twin method. For example, the diagnostic criteria and practices used to assess research participants will have a substantial impact on how

concordance rates are established.[17] The researchers responsible for the 2011 study cited above were critical of the small sample sizes used in previous studies (a total of 36 MZ pairs and 30 DZ pairs) as well as the failure to consistently apply the best standards of diagnostic assessment; when they corrected these errors, the heritability estimate was just 38%, compared to an environmental component of 58%.[18] Another problematic feature of the twin method is known as the equal environment assumption (EEA). The EEA holds that the upbringing and relationship between identical twins is not significantly different to that of fraternal twins. Critics of the EEA observe that if it is not correct, then twin studies might be detecting "nothing other than the more similar environment and greater emotional bond experienced between MZ twins."[19] Research investigating the sustainability of the EEA has consistently demonstrated that identical twins do in fact "spend more time together," "are treated more similarly by parents," "share a closer emotional bond," and even "view themselves as being two halves of the same whole."[20] It is thus quite plausible that higher concordance rates in MZ twins could indicate something other than their shared genetic influences.

On the basis of the high heritability estimates provided by twin studies, autism quickly came to be regarded as one of the most heritable of the psychiatric disorders, and it was widely anticipated that molecular research would confirm this hypothesis. Early successes included the identification of the genes responsible for causing a number of syndromes associated with a higher risk of developing autism, such as Fragile X syndrome (FXS), tuberous sclerosis (TS), Rett syndrome (RS), and Angelman syndrome (AS). The likelihood that a genetic component was involved in autism seemed to increase if it appeared with greater frequency in cases of monogenic disorders. However, researchers have recently questioned the extent to which symptoms of syndromic autisms like FXS actually overlap with those of non-syndromic autism.[21] Even in cases of monogenic disorders like FXS or TS the presence of autism is not 100%, suggesting that when individuals with these disorders meet the diagnostic criteria for autism, there may well be complicating non-genetic factors involved.[22] Nonetheless, the observation that many individuals with a known genetic disorder meet the diagnostic criteria for autism has been a central pillar supporting the genetic hypothesis.

Attempts to identify candidate genes involved in nonsyndromic autism have not been as successful. One of the methods available to researchers is candidate gene analysis. This seeks to establish links between identifiable symptoms and genetic factors which might be involved in the biological processes relating to those symptoms. Though it would be impossible to

summarise all of the available candidate gene research in this chapter, a clear example can be found in the body of work examining the role of the serotonin transporter gene *SLC6A4* in autism. Serotonin was first associated with autism because autistic research subjects exhibited elevated levels of serotonin in blood samples and unusual patterns of serotonin synthesis in neuroimaging studies; experiments restricting the intake of dietary precursors of serotonin also reported an exacerbation of symptoms.[23] Molecular studies then set out to sequence *SLC6A4* in autistic individuals and compare this with the same gene in controls, in the hope of identifying relevant mutations or variations common amongst the autistic population. Whilst some results seemed to indicate significant links between *SLC6A4* and autism, researchers would probably now agree that a positive association has not been replicated across a significant number of studies. A review of candidate gene research concluded that the serotonin transporter gene was "unlikely to play an important role in the genetic aetiology of autism."[24]

Whole genome sequencing is an alternative approach to autism genetic research which makes use of relatively recent developments in genomic technology. Advancing in sequencing methods enable researchers to assess vast quantities of genetic material quickly and affordably in genome wide association studies (GWAS). These studies compare the genetic material of autistic and non-autistic populations in order to assess the frequency with which shared single-nucleotide polymorphisms (SNPs or "snips"), the most common form of genetic variation, occur across the sample. This has the distinct advantage of saving researchers the trouble of having to identify candidate genes in advance. A number of prominent autism GWAS have now been conducted. Perhaps the most famous of these is the Autism Genome Project (AGP), which sequenced the genetic material of 1558 subject families across one million SNPs.[25] One of the difficulties with GWAS is that they often result in the identification of a very large number of potentially significant variations, which are not always widely shared across the population of research subjects. The variations identified as potentially significant by one study may not be reflected in the results of another. In the case of AGP, researchers concluded that there was only "limited evidence that common alleles affect risk for autism," and that "findings appear to rule out a common allele increasing relative risk by 2-fold or more."[26]

Whole exome sequencing (WES) examines only those elements of the genome which code for proteins (known as the exome). Autism research using WES has shown the extent to which rare or *de novo* (occurring in the diagnosed individual but not in their parents) mutations appear in cases of

autism. Based on the results of four autism WES studies, Antonio Persico and Valerio Napolioni concluded that the genetic portrait of autism may well involve *de novo* mutations occurring across potentially hundreds of genes, none of which would by themselves be "sufficient to cause the disease."[27] The results of these studies have been interpreted as a sign of just how complex the genetic profile of autism is likely to be. They suggest that diagnosed individuals exhibit an almost innumerable set of potentially significant variations, each of which may only slightly increase the risk of developing autism, and many may be unique to the individual in question. This recent tendency in autism genetics has been highlighted by François Ansermet and Ariane Giacobino, who argue that genetics has moved away from a search for the "transmission of the identical," and towards a search for the "production of difference."[28] Far from exhibiting the repetition of a single set of genetic factors across the entire autistic population, research has shown that each diagnosed individual is "unique" at the biological level, just as they are at the clinical level.[29]

The Appeal to Complexity

Results taken from twin studies and the linking of monogenic disorders like FXS to autism appeared to provide strong evidence of genetic factors playing a predominant role in autism's aetiology. On this basis autism was redescribed as a "genetic disease" and research came to focus on finding its molecular basis.[30] However, molecular research has not successfully identified a set of genes which can be consistently linked to autism across a sufficient number of studies. Moreover, there appears to be good reason to doubt the methodological integrity of twin research and the link between syndromic and nonsyndromic autisms. If the objective of autism genetics was to provide clinicians with a reliable set of biomarkers, in order to facilitate earlier diagnosis or to work towards better treatments, then it can reasonably be regarded as having failed. Much of the most recent research indicates that the role ascribed to genetic factors may have been substantially overestimated, and that if genes do indeed have a role to play, which genes are involved and how influential they are may differ from person to person. Yet the hypothesis that autism is *essentially* a genetic disorder remains curiously beyond doubt, and genetics continues to dominate both the research agenda and media headlines. How might we begin to understand this contradiction?

A number of critics have suggested that this is partly achieved through a rhetorical appeal to the complexity of the phenomena under study. In a review of the literature surrounding the genetics of schizophrenia, Adam

Hedgecoe suggested that researchers used a "narrative of enlightened geneticization" to ensure that "schizophrenia can only be considered in terms of *some* necessary genetic aetiology (even if it is not sufficient)."[31] As Kristin Bumiller has observed, this narrative represents twin studies as having provided certain evidence of autism's genetic aetiology whilst at the same time reframing the failures of molecular research as "indicative of the complexity (and implicit value) of genetic knowledge about the causes of disease."[32] One clear example of this practice is the use of a "complex disease model" to frame the causes of autism. Complex disease models are designed to account for the interaction of multiple causal factors occurring at a number of different biological levels. Environmental factors are integrated hierarchically and are understood to act upon and through existing biological elements, including a substantial genetic predisposition.[33] Framing autism as a complex disease protects the assumption of some genetic component from doubt, in the absence of substantial confirmation from molecular research. To cite Hedgecoe once again,

> "[This] suggests that the variety of possible environmental factors should be seen against a 'genetic baseline' which is the only single necessary condition for causation."[34]

Similar observations have been made by Jay Joseph, who argues that the failures of molecular genetics in psychiatry are masked through an appeal to the inherent complexity of polygenic diseases, and an assertion of the discoveries that await in the future.[35] One example of this in relation to autism research is the current speculation about the possibility that there are epigenetic mechanisms involved in triggering autism. This speculation received a boost from the identification of epigenetic factors in both FXS and RS.[36] Researchers hope that epigenetics might provide an insight into some of the more intractable mysteries of autism, like the disparity in rates of diagnosis between males and females.[37] Whilst epigenetic mechanisms have not yet been implicated in the aetiology of nonsyndromic autism, epigenetic research acts as a conduit for the disappointed hopes and deferred expectations which were initially attached to genetic research. These hopes are sustained by the questionable assertion that the discovery of relevant epigenetic interactions may lead to the development of epigenetic therapies and new approaches to treatment.

One of the consequences of this appeal to complexity is that research priorities continue to focus on biomedical research, at the expense of alternative research approaches and the provision of services for those with a diagnosis of autism. Funding for biomedical projects has enjoyed

significant increases over the last two decades, consistently dwarfing the amounts spent in other fields of autism research.[38] Total spending on autism research in the UK between 2007 and 2011 was around £20.8 million, where total spending in the US was approximately eighty-nine times more.[39] During the same period, 56% of total UK spending on autism research went towards neurological and cognitive studies, 18% towards researching treatments and interventions, and 15% towards identifying the causes of autism; a comparatively tiny amount (just 5%) was spent on researching improvements to services and only 1% was spent on research into societal issues faced by people with autism.[40] This was in spite of a reported "high degree of consensus" amongst members of the autism community that areas of service provision and support were drastically underfunded.[41] Despite a growing body of literature documenting the frustrations of families and autistic individuals with the process of receiving a diagnosis or accessing services, the commitment to biomedical research continues. This perpetuates the current paucity (or inaccessibility) of available support and services for autistic people in the UK, without leading to the development of any relevant outcomes.

Another consequence of the relative popularity of genetic research is that it can lend support to the assumption that problems experienced by autistic people stem solely from their genetic endowment rather than from societal prejudices and expectations. According to this perspective, what counts as disabling for autistic people is something essential about their biological makeup, rather than the conflict between autistic and non-autistic ways of being in the world. Consequently, efforts to help autistic people are framed in terms of removing the biological impediments to full participation in society, obscuring the "disabling circumstances" in which autistic people are often expected to live.[42] Stereotypical representations of autistic people as isolated and lonely figures reflect a failure to appreciate that there may be other modes of sociality and communication which do not correspond to normal expectations. Autistic activist Jim Sinclair, who co-founded Autism Network International (ANI) in 1992, has written about the diverse modes of sociality available to autistic people and the kinds of spaces necessary to foster them.[43] Forcing autistic people to engage in activities which provoke their anxiety in the hope of rendering them non-autistic is the stated aim of many of the more aggressive behavioural therapies currently available for autism. Such authoritarian approaches to treatment often clothe themselves in the borrowed rhetoric of biomedicine, making the highly dubious claim that they can "rewire the brain" of their autistic patients.[44]

Genetic research has not delivered on its promise of improving either diagnosis or treatment. Yet these potential outcomes are themselves the subject of a great deal of controversy. One of the most frequently cited potential outcomes of biomedical research is a genetic screening test similar to that used to screen for Down's syndrome. In a 2005 article published on the CNBC news website, leading autism geneticist Joseph Buxbaum claimed that within the next ten years, a prenatal test for autism would have been developed.[45] Activists immediately posted a countdown timer online under the heading "The Autistic Genocide Clock," which recorded the time that had elapsed since the article's publication.[46] This rather striking example highlights the extent to which biotechnological interventions are subject to heated debate, even when they are framed as unambiguously progressive. Equally controversial is the prospect of gene therapies or pharmaceutical treatments designed to reverse or remove autism. Such interventions often view the autistic person as the victim of a somatic situation beyond their control, into which it is legitimate to intervene. However, Jim Sinclair argues that autism should not be thought of as a disease but as a "way of being" and that it "is not possible to separate the autism from the person."[47]If such interventions were carried out, Sinclair suggests, "the person you'd have left would not be the same person you started with."[48]

Reframing Autism Genetics

Lacanian psychoanalysis offers a way to critically reframe biological autism research. This enables us to take into account the possibility of some biological (or indeed environmental) component in the aetiology of autism, without evacuating subjectivity in the process. It is important to recall that the psychoanalytic approach to autism does not depend on there being nothing biological at play. Psychoanalysis works on a case by case basis, and as Éric Laurent observes, whatever biological knowledge may eventually exist will simply form part of the broader context of each case.[49] Though current research does not allow us to make any definitive conclusions, we can say that even if autism were shown to depend upon a substantial genetic predisposition, the space of the subject would be preserved. How is this possible? Biological approaches to autism examine the causal links between different elements in order to evaluate their impact on the eventual clinical picture. Autism is therefore understood to be the outcome of a series of aetiological events which can be linked together in a causal chain. Yet the encounter between language and the body cannot be reduced to this same order of linear causality, and it is

precisely this event which psychoanalysis situates at the heart of the clinic of autism.[50] Both this encounter and the subject's response to it are impossible to predict, and thus constitute an exception from the deterministic chain which governs the biological field.[51]

This is an essential consideration for clinical practice. It indicates that from a psychoanalytic perspective, there is always a subject working to invent solutions to the threatening jouissance which confronts them, regardless of how their situation might appear to an outside observer. We have reviewed some of the consequences of assuming that there is *not* a subject present in the previous section. This assumption leads to the idea that the autistic person is a passive victim of their body, in which they are trapped, and from which we are entitled to try to free them. It does not involve any attempt to ascertain what function a given behaviour might have for the particular subject in question. Autistic behaviour is thought to be incapable of serving a function because it is seen as the result of a deficit inscribed at the cognitive, neurological, or genetic level. If we take seriously the effect that the encounter with language has on the body, and the disjunction that it imposes between the speaking being and the organism, then we can begin to take a more productive approach to autism. This involves orientating clinical practice around the inventions which the subject makes themselves in order to protect against anxiety or to provide some limit to an otherwise chaotic and overwhelming jouissance. It means ascribing dignity to these inventions and working alongside the subject in their elaborations. This is the kind of work being done in the institutions of the RI^3, which orientate themselves according to the idea of "*pratique à plusiers*."[52]

The recognition that there is no universal solution available to the problem of language situates a respect for the subject's singularity at the heart of psychoanalytic practice. Each subject invents singular solutions which can serve to construct a liveable world for him or her. The clinic of autism can therefore have no other basis than to follow the inclinations of the subject as they attach themselves to certain objects or activities. To do otherwise would be to assume that it is the clinician who knows in advance about how things work for a particular subject. Of course, this is precisely the approach taken by the purely educative methods of autism therapy like Applied Behaviour Analysis (ABA), which seek to fill in a supposed deficit in the knowledge of the subject. As Jean-Claude Maleval has attested, "[t]hey do not set out from the inventions of the subject; they consider that it is above all a question of transmitting to him a knowledge which he lacks."[53] Autistic subjects themselves have argued against the application of ABA therapy to autism, as Ari Ne'eman writes,

> "Do we really want the normalcy, the 'indistinguishability from peers,' that Lovaas-style ABA promises? Or is this just a proxy for the more tangible things people desire, like the ability to communicate or the chance to hold a job and live in the community?"[54]

By supposing that the subject possesses no knowledge about their own situation, behavioural and biomedical approaches alike locate it elsewhere; for the former in the expertise of the therapist, for the latter in the real of the subject's own body. Psychoanalysis on the contrary asserts that "[n]one other than the subject himself could know how to teach clinicians about his functioning."[55]

With this in mind we can return to the question of how biological knowledge might be understood within a psychoanalytic framework. As François Ansermet has argued, the scientific enterprise belongs to the register of the symbolic, and thus sets itself the impossible task of covering over the real "without remainder."[56] This is not simply a question of knowledge, but also one of power, as scientific knowledge is "applied to phenomena not simply to get to know them but to dominate them and to operate on them."[57] It is in part through the exercise of these activities that science has historically had the function of providing some fixity to our sense of the real, as Jacques-Alain Miller has observed.[58] Yet it is also through this process that science destabilises our sense of the real, by producing a mass of semblants which seek to represent it but which are incommensurable with one another; science thus joins with the capitalist discourse in the "industrial production of semblants" that characterises our contemporary society.[59] It is through these semblants that science believes it has direct purchase on the real, mistaking its own activity for an unmediated *presentation* of the real as such. It does not recognise these semblants as artefacts of discourse, believing instead that it is simply the recipient of some knowledge already inscribed in the real, "written from the start […] waiting to be read."[60] The "semblant-notion" of the gene is one of the most successful of these "discoveries."[61]

To recognise that the notion of the gene as the bearer of a code which will express itself in the behaviour of the individual is a semblant is to acknowledge that science has less of a grip on the real than it might like to think. The body with which biology is concerned is a body divided up by the signifier into separate and separable components; a symbolic body rendered knowable and manipulable through language.[62] This symbolic body fragments the totality and unity of the "body image" taken from the mirror stage.[63] Insofar as it has been transposed into a body of knowledge it is also located at an ineliminable distance from the "living body [*corps vivant*]" as such, or "the body which is affected by jouissance [*affecté de*

la jouissance]."[64] Lacan described this dimension of the body in *Encore* by saying that "we don't know what it means to be alive except for the following fact, that a body is something that enjoys itself [*se jouit*]."[65] It is precisely the living body as a site of jouissance which biology does not and cannot grasp, even if the application of its knowledges and technologies have an (often unforeseen) effect on this jouissance. The psychoanalytic approach to autism attempts to discern how a subject—always in a singular way—can come to construct a solution to this jouissance, which has not been ordered and regulated by the symbolic, and which therefore remains unmediated and chaotic. Consequently, though biological knowledge may form part of the broader context of each case, it cannot tell us much about the subject's singular mode of functioning, nor can it be used to formulate a universal approach to clinical work.

Conclusion

The question of what causes autism remains one of the most controversial in the contemporary autism debate, and it seems unlikely that it will find an unambiguous and universally accepted answer in the near future. Nonetheless, the current trend in autism research is directed towards the identification of biomarkers and their application to new forms of diagnostic practice and treatment. My aim in this chapter has been to unsettle some of the assumptions that influence decisions about how research into the causes of autism is carried out. Often the claim that autism is *primarily* a genetic disorder is accepted without reflection on the current state of research or the consequences that such a judgement might have for the lives of autistic subjects. I have suggested that on the basis of existing research we should remain agnostic about the potential for genetic factors to be involved in the aetiology of autism. I have also presented evidence which suggests that the consequences of genetic research are often problematic and open to contestation by certain members of the autism community. Given that the current focus on biological and genetic research has not produced any clinically significant results, and that it is unclear whether or not we would *want* the results that it promises for the future, it is time to reflect on other possible perspectives and priorities. Psychoanalysis offers a different outlook; one which understands autism as a distinct subjective position, and constructs a clinical practice on the basis of the singularity of each subject.

Notes

[1] François Ansermet and Ariane Giacobino, *Autisme: À chacun son genome* (Paris: Navarin/Le Champ freudien, 2012), 13.

[2] Kristin Bumiller, "The Geneticization of Autism: From New Reproductive Technologies to the Conception of Genetic Normalcy," *Signs* 34, no. 4 (2009): 878.

[3] Nikolas Rose, "Normality and pathology in a biomedical age," *Sociological Review* 57, supplement 2 (2009).

[4] Jean-Louis Gault, "La naissance de la science modern," *La Cause du désir* 84 (2013): 63.

[5] Ari Ne'eman, "The Future (and the Past) of Autism Advocacy, Or Why the ASA's Magazine, *The Advocate*, Wouldn't Publish This Piece," *Disability Studies Quarterly* 30, no. 1 (2010): http://dsq-sds.org/article/view/1059/1244.

[6] Jacques Lacan, *The Seminar of Jacques Lacan, Book III: The Psychoses*, ed. Jacques-Alain Miller, trans. Russell Grigg (London: Routledge, 1993), 7.

[7] Jacques-Alain Miller, "L'orientation lacanienne. L'Un tout seul" (course presented to the Department of Psychoanalysis at the University of Paris VIII, March 23, 2011), unpublished.

[8] Éric Laurent, *La Bataille de l'autisme: De la clinique à la politique* (Paris: Navarin/Le Champ freudien, 2012), 25.

[9] Amanda Baggs, "Being an Unperson," YouTube video, 8:47, posted by "silentmiaow," November 3, 2006,
https://www.youtube.com/watch?v=4c5_3wqZ3Lk.

[10] Ne'eman, "Autism Advocacy."

[11] Leo Kanner, "Autistic Disturbances of Affective Contact," *Nervous Child* 2 (1943): 250.

[12] Susan Folstein and Michael Rutter, "Infantile Autism: A Genetic Study of 21 Twin Pairs," *Journal of Child Psychology & Psychiatry* 18, no. 4 (1977); Edward Ritvo et al., "Concordance for the syndrome of autism in 40 pairs of afflicted twins," *American Journal of Psychiatry* 142 (1985); Suzanne Steffenburg et al., "A Twin Study of Autism in Denmark, Finland, Iceland, Norway and Sweden," *Journal of Child Psychology & Psychiatry* 30 (1989); Anthony Bailey et al., "Autism as a strongly genetic disorder: Evidence from a British twin study," *Psychological medicine* 25 (1995).

[13] Dorret Boomsma et al., "Classical Twin Studies and Beyond," *Nature Reviews Genetics* 3 (2002).

[14] Folstein and Rutter, "Infantile Autism."

[15] Anthony Bailey, Wendy Phillips and Michael Rutter, "Autism: towards an integration of clinical, genetic, neuropsychological, and neurobiological perspectives," *Journal of Child Psychology & Psychiatry* 37, no. 1 (1996).

[16] Joachim Hallmayer et al., "Genetic Heritability and Shared Environmental Factors Among Twin Pairs with Autism," *Archives of General Psychiatry* 68, no. 11 (2011).

[17] Jay Joseph, *The Gene Illusion: Genetic Research in Psychiatry and Psychology Under the Microscope* (New York: Algora, 2004), 67.

[18] Joachim Hallmayer et al., "Genetic Heritability," 1095-1096.
[19] Jay Joseph, "Not in Their Genes: A Critical View of the Genetics of Attention-Deficit Hyperactivity Disorder," *Developmental Review* 20 (2000): 543.
[20] Jay Joseph, *The Missing Gene: Psychiatry, Heredity, and the Fruitless Search for Genes* (New York: Algora, 2006), 17.
[21] Angela John Thurman et al., "Psychiatric symptoms in boys with fragile X syndrome: A comparison with nonsyndromic autism spectrum disorder," *Research in Developmental Disabilities* 35 (2014).
[22] Antonio Persico and Valerio Napolioni, "Autism genetics," *Behavioral Brain Research* 251 (2013), 97.
[23] Kristen Lam, Michael Aman and L. Eugen Arnold, "Neurochemical correlates of autistic disorder: A review of the literature," *Research in Developmental Disabilities* 27, no. 3 (2006).
[24] Gabrielle Barnby and Anthony Monaco, "Strategies for autism candidate gene analysis," in *Autism: Neural Basis and Treatment Possibilities, Novartis Foundation Symposium 251*, ed. Gregory Bock and Jamie Goode (Chichester: John Wiley & Sons, 2003), 56.
[25] Richard Anney et al., "A genome-wide association scan for common alleles affecting risk for autism," *Human Molecular Genetics* 19, no. 20 (2010).
[26] Ibid., 7.
[27] Persico and Napolioni, "Autism genetics," 105.
[28] Ansermet and Giacobino, *Autisme*, 13.
[29] Ibid., 73.
[30] Bumiller, "The Geneticization of Autism," 878.
[31] Adam Hedgecoe, "Schizophrenia and the Narrative of Enlightened Geneticization," *Social Studies of Science* 31, no. 6 (2001), 885.
[32] Bumiller, "The Geneticization of Autism," 878.
[33] Anthony Bailey and Jeremy Parr, "Implications of the broader phenotype," in *Autism: Neural Basis and Treatment Possibilities, Novartis Foundation Symposium 251*, ed. Gregory Bock and Jamie Goode (Chichester: John Wiley & Sons, 2003), 30-31.
[34] Hedgecoe, "Schizophrenia," 885.
[35] Jay Joseph, *The Missing Gene*, 225-226.
[36] Daria Grafodatskaya et al., "Autism Spectrum Disorders and Epigenetics," *Journal of the American Academy of Child and Adolescent Psychiatry* 49, no. 8 (2010).
[37] N. Carolyn Schanen, "Epigenetics of autism spectrum disorder," *Human Molecular Genetics* 15, review issue 2 (2006).
[38] Jennifer Singh et al., "Trends in US autism research funding," *Journal of Autism & Developmental Disorders* 39 (2009).
[39] Liz Pellicano, Adam Dinsmore and Tony Charman, *A future made together: Shaping autism research in the UK* (London: Institute of Education, 2013), 21.
[40] Ibid., 22-23.
[41] Ibid., 29.

[42] Dana Lee Baker, *The Politics of Neurodiversity: Why Public Policy Matters* (Boulder: Lynne Rienner, 2011), 9.
[43] Jim Sinclair, "Being Autistic Together," *Disability Studies Quarterly* 30, no. 1 (2010), http://dsq-sds.org/article/view/1075/1248.
[44] Connie Anderson, "Behavioral Therapies: Key Interventions in ASD," last modified June 27, 2012, http://iancommunity.org/cs/simons_simplex_community/behavioral_therapies.
[45] Sue Herera, "Autism research focuses on early intervention: Genetic clues sought in fight against disorder," *CNBC News*, February 23 (2005), http://www.nbcnews.com/id/7013251/#.VMuZc19FD4g.
[46] The timer originally appeared at http://www.ventura33.com/clock but has since been removed.
[47] Jim Sinclair, "Don't Mourn For Us," *Our Voice* 1, no. 3, http://www.autreat.com/dont_mourn.html.
[48] Ibid.
[49] Laurent, *La Bataille de l'autisme*, 25.
[50] Ibid., 89.
[51] Ansermet and Giacobino, 74.
[52] Bruno de Halleux (ed.), "*Quelque chose à dire à l'enfant autiste" Pratique à plusiers à l'Antenne 110* (Paris: Editions Michèle, 2010).
[53] Jean-Claude Maleval, *L'Autiste et sa voix* (Paris: Éditions du Seuil, 2009), 18.
[54] Ne'eman, "Autism Advocacy."
[55] Maleval, *L'Autiste*, 9.
[56] François Ansermet, "Science," in *L'ordre symbolique au XXIème siècle. Il n'est plus ce qu'il était, Quelles consequences pour la cure?*, ed. Jean-Daniel Matet (Paris: Collection rue Huysmans, 2012), 329.
[57] Marco Focchi, "Number and science in psychoanalysis," trans. Laura Tarsi, *Psychoanalytical Notebooks* 27 (2013), 38.
[58] Jacques-Alain Miller, "L'orientation lacanienne. L'Autre qui n'existe pas et ses Comités d'éthique" (course presented with Éric Laurent to the Department of Psychoanalysis at the University of Paris VIII, November 20, 1996), unpublished.
[59] Ibid.
[60] Miquel Bassols, "There is no science of the real," trans. Roger Litten, *Psychoanalytical Notebooks* 27 (2013), 25.
[61] Ibid.,
[62] Jacques-Alain Miller, "Biologie lacanienne et événement de corps," *La Cause freudienne* 44 (2000), 11.
[63] Ibid., 17.
[64] Ibid., 17.
[65] Jacques Lacan, *The Seminar of Jacques Lacan, Book XX: Encore*, ed. Jacques-Alain Miller, trans. Bruce Fink (New York: W. W. Norton, 1999), 22.

References

Anderson, Connie. "Behavioral Therapies: Key Interventions in ASD," last modified June 27, 2012. Accessed January 8, 2015. http://iancommunity.org/cs/simons_simplex_community/behavioral_therapies.

Anney, Richard., Lambertus Klei, Dalila Pinto, Regina Regan, Judith Conroy, Tiago R. Magalhaes, Catarina Correia et al. "A genome-wide association scan for common alleles affecting risk for autism." *Human Molecular Genetics* 19, no. 20 (2010): 4072-4082.

Ansermet, François . "Science." In *L'ordre symbolique au XXIème siècle. Il n'est plus ce qu'il était, Quelles consequences pour la cure?*, edited by Jean-Daniel Matet, 329-3. Paris: Collection rue Huysmans, 2012.

Ansermet, François and Ariane Giacobino. *Autisme: À chacun son genome*. Paris: Navarin/Le Champ freudien, 2012.

Baggs, Amanda. "Being an Unperson," YouTube video, 8:47, posted by "silentmiaow," November 3, 2006. Accessed January 8, 2015. https://www.youtube.com/watch?v=4c5_3wqZ3Lk.

Bailey, Anthony and Jeremy Parr. "Implications of the broader phenotype." In *Autism: Neural Basis and Treatment Possibilities, Novartis Foundation Symposium 251*, edited by Gregory Bock and Jamie Goode, 26-47. Chichester: John Wiley & Sons, 2003.

Bailey, Anthony, Ann Le Couteur, Irving Gottesman, Patrick Bolton, Emily Simonoff, E. Yuzda and Michael Rutter. "Autism as a strongly genetic disorder: Evidence from a British twin study." *Psychological Medicine* 25 (1995): 63-77.

Bailey, Andrew, Wendy Phillips, and Micheal Rutter. "Autism: towards an integration of clinical, genetic, neuropsychological, and neurobiological perspectives." *Journal of Child Psychology & Psychiatry* 37, no. 1 (1996) 89-126.

Baker, Dana Lee. *The Politics of Neurodiversity: Why Public Policy Matters*. Boulder: Lynne Rienner, 2011.

Barnby, Gabrielle, and Anthony Monaco. "Strategies for autism candidate gene analysis." In *Autism: Neural Basis and Treatment Possibilities, Novartis Foundation Symposium 251*, edited by Gregory Bock and Jamie Goode, 48-63. Chichester: John Wiley & Sons, 2003.

Bassols, Miquel. "There is no science of the real." Translated by Roger Litten. *Psychoanalytical Notebooks* 27 (2013), 21-28.

Boomsma, Dorret., Andreas Busjahn and Leena Peltonen. "Classical Twin Studies and Beyond." *Nature Reviews Genetics* 3 (2002): 872-882.

Bumiller, Kristin. "The Geneticization of Autism: From New Reproductive Technologies to the Conception of Genetic Normalcy," *Signs* 34, no. 4 (2009): 875-899.

De Halleux, Bruno (editor). *"Quelque chose à dire à l'enfant autiste" Pratique à plusiers à l'Antenne 110*. Paris: Editions Michèle, 2010.

Marco Focchi. "Number and science in psychoanalysis." Translated by Laura Tarsi. *Psychoanalytical Notebooks* 27 (2013), 37-50.

Folstein, Susan, and Michael Rutter. "Infantile Autism: A Genetic Study of 21 Twin Pairs." *Journal of Child Psychology & Psychiatry* 18, no. 4 (1977): 297-321.

Gault, Jean-Louis. "La naissance de la science modern." *La Cause du désir* 84 (2013): 58-64.

Grafodatskaya, Daria, Brian Chung, Peter Szatmari, Rosanna Weksberg. "Autism Spectrum Disorders and Epigenetics." *Journal of the American Academy of Child & Adolescent Psychiatry* 49, no. 8 (2010): 794-809.

Hallmayer, Joachim., Sue Cleveland, Andrea Torres, Jennifer Phillips, Brianne Cohen, Tiffany Torigoe, Janet Miller. "Genetic Heritability and Shared Environmental Factors Among Twin Pairs with Autism." *Archives of General Psychiatry* 68, no. 11 (2011): 1095-1102.

Hedgecoe, Adam. "Schizophrenia and the Narrative of Enlightened Geneticization." *Social Studies of Science* 31, no. 6 (2001): 875-911.

Herera, Sue. "Autism research focuses on early intervention: Genetic clues sought in fight against disorder." CNBC News, February 23 (2005). Accessed January 8, 2015. http://www.nbcnews.com/id/7013251#.UwYIId2YqdY.

Joseph, Jay. "Not in Their Genes: A Critical View of the Genetics of Attention-Deficit Hyperactivity Disorder." *Developmental Review* 20 (2000): 539-567.

Joseph, Jay. *The Gene Illusion: Genetic Research in Psychiatry and Psychology Under the Microscope*. New York: Algora, 2004.

Joseph, Jay. *The Missing Gene: Psychiatry, Heredity, and the Fruitless Search for Genes*. New York: Algora, 2006.

Kanner, Leo. "Autistic Disturbances of Affective Contact." *Nervous Child* 2 (1943): 217-250.

Lacan, Jacques. *The Seminar of Jacques Lacan, Book XX: Encore*, edited by Jacques-Alain Miller. Translated by Bruce Fink. New York: W. W. Norton, 1999.

Lacan, Jacques. *The Seminar of Jacques Lacan, Book III: The Psychoses*, edited by Jacques-Alain Miller. Translated by Russel Grigg. London: Routledge, 1993.

Lam, Kristen, Michael Aman and L. Eugen Arnold. "Neurochemical correlates of autistic disorder: A review of the literature." *Research in Developmental Disabilities* 27, no. 3 (2006): 254-289.

Laurent, Éric. *La Bataille de l'autisme*. Paris: Navarin/Le Champ freudien, 2012.

Maleval, Jean-Claude. *L'Autiste et sa voix*. Paris: Éditions du Seuil, 2009.

Miller, Jacques-Alain. "L'orientation lacanienne. L'Un tout seul." Course presented to the Department of Psychoanalysis at the University of Paris VIII. March 23, 2011. Unpublished.

Miller, Jacques-Alain. "Biologie lacanienne et événement de corps." *La Cause freudienne* 44 (2000), 7-59.

Miller, Jacques-Alain. "L'orientation lacanienne. L'Autre qui n'existe pas et ses Comités d'éthique." Course presented with Éric Laurent to the Department of Psychoanalysis at the University of Paris VIII. November 20, 1996. Unpublished.

Ne'eman, Ari. "The Future (and the Past) of Autism Advocacy, Or Why the ASA's Magazine, The Advocate, Wouldn't Publish This Piece." *Disability Studies Quarterly* 30, no. 1 (2010). Accessed January 8, 2015. http://dsq-sds.org/article/view/1059/1244.

Pellicano, Liz, Adam Dinsmore and Tony Charman. *A future made together: Shaping autism research in the UK*. London: Institute of Education, 2013.

Persico, Antonio and Valerio Napolioni. "Autism genetics." *Behaviour Brain Research* 251 (2013): 95-112.

Ritvo, E. R., B. J. Freeman, A. Mason-Brothers, A. Mo and A. M. Ritvo. "Concordance for the syndrome of autism in 40 pairs of afflicted twins." *American Journal of Psychiatry* 142, no. 1 (1985): 74-77.

Rose, Nikolas. "Normality and pathology in a biomedical age." *Sociological Review* 57, supplement 2 (2009): 66-83.

Schanen, Carolyn, N. "Epigenetics of autism spectrum disorders." *Human Molecular Genetics* 15, review issue 2 (2006): R138-R150.

Sinclair, Jim. "Don't Mourn for Us," Our Voice 1: 3 (1993). Accessed January 8, 2015. http://www.autreat.com/dont_mourn.html

Sinclair, Jim. "Being Autistic Together." *Disability Studies Quarterly* 30, no. 1 (2010). Accessed January 8, 2015. http://dsq-sds.org/article/view/1075/1248.

Singh, Jennifer., Judy Illes, Laura Lazzeroni, Joachim Hallmayer, "Trends in US autism research funding." *Journal of Autism & Developmental Disorders* 39 (2009): 788-795.

Steffenburg, Suzanne., Christopher Gillberg, Lars Hellgren, Lena Andersson, I. Carina Gillberg, Gun Jakobsson, and Michael Bohman.

"A Twin Study of Autism in Denmark, Finland, Iceland, Norway and Sweden." *Journal of Child Psychology & Psychiatry* 30 (1989): 405-416.

Thurman, Angela John., Andrea McDuffie, Randi Hagerman, Leonard Abbeduto. "Psychiatric symptoms in boys with fragile X syndrome: A comparison with nonsyndromic autism spectrum disorder." *Research in Developmental Disabilities* 35 (2014): 1072-1086.

CONTRIBUTORS

Giacomo Croci graduated in philosophy at the Free University of Berlin. His current researches focus on contemporary philosophy of subjectivity and psychoanalytical theory. giacomocroci@gmail.com

João Gabriel Lima da Silva is doctoral researcher (Ph.D. candidate) in the Psychoanalytic Theory Postgraduate Programme at the Universidade Federal do Rio de Janeiro, Brazil. joaogabriellimadasilva@gmail.com

Carla Ambrósio Garcia completed her PhD in Film Studies (funded by Fundação Ciência e Tecnologia in Portugal) at King's College London in 2013, where she is currently a teaching assistant. She is interested in psychoanalytic approaches to film, the experience of film, and the practice of filmmaking, and her research focuses on the work of Wilfred Bion and Donald Meltzer. Alongside her writing, she develops her artistic practice, working primarily with 16mm film. Her first film (*Film #1*, 2003) was awarded a special mention at L'Alternativa Independent Cinema Festival in Barcelona. Recent publications include the chapter 'Process and Medium in the Practice of Filmmaking: The Work of Jayne Parker' for a book edited by Agnieszka Piotrowska (2015) titled *Embodied Encounters: New Approaches to Psychoanalysis and Cinema*. carla.ambrosio_garcia@kcl.ac.uk

Melissa Greenberg is a doctoral candidate in clinical psychology at the Graduate School of Applied and Professional Psychology, Rutgers University. She received her Master's degree in the History of Art from the Institute of Fine Arts, New York University. She has written and presented on the ways in which children and gender are portrayed in the arts and media. Her doctoral dissertation investigates how the concept of "emotion regulation" is used in contemporary psychotherapy literature and practice. melissa.greenberg@gmail.com

Thomas Harding is a PhD student in the Centre for Critical Theory at the University of Nottingham. His doctoral research focuses on the development of the clinic of autism within Lacanian psychoanalysis. Other research interests include: psychoanalysis and the life sciences, clinical

approaches to intellectual disability, and the application of psychoanalysis in institutional settings. Thomas is the founder of the Critical Autism Forum (CAF), an interdisciplinary network of researchers, practitioners and community members which promotes critical reflection on autism. He is also a support worker for autistic adults in Leicestershire. For more information about CAF please contact ajxtrhar@nottingham.ac.uk.

David Henderson, PhD, is senior lecture in psychoanalysis at the Centre for Psychoanalysis, Middlesex University and a member of the Association of Independent Psychotherapists, London. d.henderson@ mdx.ac.uk

Ben Hooson completed a PhD on Freud and Lacan at London University. He is currently a trainee at the Centre for Freudian Analysis and Research in London. ben.hooson@translatingandediting.co.uk

Naftally Israeli is a PhD student in the Program for Psychoanalysis and Hermeneutics in Bar-Ilan University, Israel. The topic of his doctoral dissertation is "Language, Emotion and Experience: Interrelations", and in it he suggests a new linguistic approach to the connection between language, agency and the unconscious. He is a clinical psychologist in the Psychological Services of the Hebrew University and in a private clinic in Jerusalem. naftally@gmail.com

Amir Klugman is a PhD student in the Program for Psychoanalysis and Hermeneutics, Bar-Ilan University, Israel. His doctoral thesis is concerned with the “speaking body” in the works of David Grossman, from the perspective of Lacanian psychoanalysis. He is a clinical psychologist in a public health clinic and in private practice. amir@klugman.co.il, www.klugman.co.il

Olena Lytovka is a PhD student at the Chair of Anglo-Irish Literature, Maria Curie-Sklodowska University in Lublin, Poland. The title of her thesis is *The Uncanny House in Elizabeth Bowen’s Fiction*. Olena is particularly interested in European modernist literature, time and space representations in fiction, psychoanalysis and feminist literary criticism. chvan.lytovka@gmail.com

Raphael Montague is a musician in Ireland and practices psychoanalysis. raphael.montague@gmail.com

Mauricio Rugeles Schoonewolff is a psychoanalyst, PhD student in philosophy at Université Paris 8. He has three master's degrees, in Psychoanalysis and Philosophy from Université Paris 8 and in Clinical Psychology from Université Rennes 2. mauriciorugeles.s@gmail.com

Akshi Singh is a PhD student at the School of English and Drama, Queen Mary, University of London. akshi.singh@qmul.ac.uk

Chenyang Wang is a PhD student in the Department of Psychosocial Studies, Birkbeck College, London. cwang06@mail.bbk.ac.uk